DEVELOPING F

curriculum — racing chance

ch 10 . p.122

p.88 ch 1 + 2 ✓ ✓

Intro. P.1   ch 3   p26
Intro P.51   ch 4   P.39
                5   P.54
                6   P68

Companion Volumes

The companion volumes in this series are:
Teacher Development: Exploring our own practice
Edited by: Janet Soler, Anna Craft and Hilary Burgess
Understanding Learning: Influences and outcomes
Edited by Janet Collins and Deidre Cook

All of these readers are part of a course: *Developing Practice in Primary Education*, that is itself part of the Open University MA programme.

The Open University MA in Education

The Open University MA in Education is now firmly established as the most popular postgraduate degree for education professionals in Europe, with over 3,000 students registering each year. The MA in Education is designed particularly for those with experience of teaching, the advisory service, educational administration or allied fields.

Structure of the MA

The MA is a modular degree, and students are therefore free to select from a range of options the programme which best fits in with their interests and professional goals. Specialist lines in management, applied linguistics and lifelong learning are also available. Study in the Open University's Advanced Diploma can also be counted towards the MA, and successful study in the MA Programme entitles students to apply for entry into the Open University Doctorate in Education programme.

OU Supported Open Learning

The MA in Education programme provides great flexibility. Students study at their own pace, in their own time, anywhere in the European Union. They receive specially prepared study materials, supported by tutorials, thus offering the chance to work with other students.

The Doctorate in Education

The Doctorate in Education is a part-time doctoral degree, combining taught courses, research methods and a dissertation designed to meet the needs of professionals in education and related areas who are seeking to extend and deepen their knowledge and understanding of contemporary educational issues. The Doctorate in Education builds upon successful study within the Open University MA in Education programme.

How to apply

If you would like to register for this programme, or simply find out more information about available courses, please write for the *Professional Development in Education* prospectus to the Course Reservations Centre, PO Box 724, The Open University, Walton Hall, Milton Keynes, MK7 6ZW, UK (Telephone 0 (0 44) 1908 653231). Details can also be viewed on our web page http://www.open.ac.uk.

DEVELOPING PEDAGOGY

Researching Practice

edited by
Janet Collins, Kim Insley and Janet Soler

P·C·P
Paul Chapman
Publishing Ltd

in association with

The Open
University

Paul Chapman Publishing Ltd
A SAGE Publications Company
6 Bonhill Street
London EC2A 4PU

SAGE Publications Inc.
2455 Teller Road
Thousand Oaks, California 91320

SAGE Publications India Pvt Ltd
32, M-Block Market
Greater Kailash - I
New Delhi 110 048

British Library Cataloguing in Publication Data
A catalogue record for this book is available from the British Library

ISBN 0 7619 6934 9
ISBN 0 7619 6935 7 (pbk)

Library of Congress catalog record available

Typeset by Dorwyn Ltd, Hampshire
Printed in Great Britain by Athenaeum Press, Gateshead

Contents

Acknowledgements

The editors and publishers wish to thank the following for permission to use copyright material:

The Curriculum Journal for material from Michael Bonnett, Angela McFarlane and Jacquetta Williams (1999) 'ICT in subject teaching: an opportunity for curriculum renewal?', *The Curriculum Journal*, 10:3, pp. 345–59;

Education 3–13 for Andrew Pollard (1999) 'Towards a new perspective on children's learning', *Education 3–13*, 27:3 pp. 56–60;

Elsevier Science for material from Pam Pointon and Ruth Kershner (2000) 'Making decisions about organising the primary classroom environment as a context for learning: the views of three experienced teachers and their pupils', *Teaching and Teacher Education*, 16, pp. 117–27;

Lawrence Erlbaum Associates, Inc for material from Mary Phillips Manke (1997) *Classroom Power Relations: Understanding Student–Teacher Interaction* by Mary Phillips Manke, pp. 75–91, 92–105;

Multilingual Matters Ltd for material from Kathy Hall (1998) 'Critical literacy and the case for it in the early years of school', *Language, Culture and Curriculum*, 11:2, pp. 183–92;

Taylor and Francis for material from Janet Moyles (1997) 'Just for fun? The child as active learner and meaning maker' in N Kitson and R Merry, eds, *Teaching in the Primary School: a Learning Relationship*, Routledge, pp. 9–24; Don Rowe (1999) 'Value pluralism, democracy and education for citizenship' in M Leicester and S Modgil, eds, *Education: Culture and Values*, Falmer; Alistair Ross (2000) *Curriculum: Construction and Critique*, Falmer, pp. 8–17; Elizabeth Wood (1999) 'The impact of the National Curriculum: construction and critique', *Educational Research*, 41:1, NFER, pp. 11–22; Mike Davies and Gwyn Edwards (1999) 'Will the curriculum caterpillar ever learn to fly?', *Cambridge Journal of Education*, 29:2, pp.

Introduction to Section 1
Concepts in Primary Education

The three concepts of learning, knowledge and pedagogy are explored in this first section. Learning and teaching are important considerations when looking at primary education, but the focus in recent years has been on the knowledge to be taught or learnt – the curriculum. Bell and Richie (1999) identify aspects of the curriculum – the hidden curriculum (Pollard and Tann, 1987), the intended (planned) curriculum, the actual curriculum and the official curriculum (the National Curriculum), but quote Kerr (1968) in defining the curriculum as 'all the learning which is planned and guided by the school, whether it is carried on in groups or individually, inside or outside the school' (p. 16)

In 1989 the National Curriculum (DES, 1989–92) was introduced over a three-year period. This marked an increase in the pressures of external influences felt by teachers. Parental expectations had always been a consideration, but now there were governmental expectations, linked to public assessment of children at the four key stages. Teachers had always been answerable but now there was a supposed measure of their performance – the standard assessment tasks (SATs). Accountability had become the 'in word'.

The National Curriculum proved not to be the answer to children's learning. It needed 'slimming down' and in 1994 the Dearing version (SCAA, 1994) was welcomed by schools. However, the introduction of the literacy hour caused schools to call for further revision, especially realizing that a numeracy strategy was also planned, and in 1998 the Secretary of State for education lifted the statutory regulations for schools in the foundation (non-core) subjects of design and technology (D&T), history, geography, art, music and physical education (PE) for two years. In the year 2000 Design and Technology schools began to take on the revised National Curriculum (DfEE/QCA, 1999) as well as to establish literacy and numeracy strategies. The focus on curriculum giving one sort of knowledge, therefore, is still prevalent.

This focus has caused many teachers to become concerned that the methods of teaching and learning, the strategies of pedagogy, have 'taken a back seat'. Some heard this message: the numeracy strategy identifies methods as well as knowledge with a focus on encouraging children to explore skills within mathematics as well as to know answers. The structures of both the literacy and numeracy strategies have influenced the teaching of other subject areas, so many teachers recognize the 'whole class, groups, plenary' framework for lessons.

McNamara (1994) argues that teaching and learning should be 'teacher centred' as opposed to the Plowden Report's view of child-centred education (CACE, 1967). Both can be seen as pedagogic processes as can Jeffrey's 'child considered/child embracing' approach (Chapter 12 this volume). However, pedagogy is not a word commonly used in the UK although it is beginning to 'infiltrate' the language. Simon (1981) argues that it is the lack of respect for pedagogy as a subject domain such as English or mathematics that has caused it to be little used (see also Galton, 1989). It has been described as the science (and/or the art) of teaching, but van Manen (1999) is clear about what pedagogy should be considering.

> as an academic discipline, pedagogy problematizes the conditions of appropriateness of educational practices and aims to provide a knowledge base for professionals who must deal with childhood difficulties, traumas and problems of childrearing. Central . . . is the normativity of distinguishing between what is appropriate and what is less appropriate for children and what are appropriate ways of teaching and giving assistance to children . . . (p. 14)

McGilchrist, Myers and Reed (1999) identify three dimensions of teacher effectiveness as being

- the knowledge and understanding about the content of teaching
- knowledge and understanding about how pupils learn
- knowledge and understanding about how to manage the process of learning and teaching. (p. 40)

However, they identify that it is what the school does with this knowledge that is 'all important . . . *how* it uses it to improve its own effectiveness' (p. 110, original emphasis). How the newly revised curriculum will be incorporated into the very full primary school day has yet to be seen, but the 11 years since the National Curriculum was first established has been a time of change and adaptation by teachers, parents and children. The dynamic nature of teachers' professionalism continues.

Given this curriculum context, this section then explores three main themes:

- the value of socio-constructivist models of education;
- active learning as an established process in education;
- children's influences on knowledge and learning.

In Chapter 1 Andrew Pollard argues that recent English education policy has been influenced by external, economic and political factors, rather than founded on a valid understanding of how children's learning actually takes place. He considers a 'performance' model of learning and reviews socio-cultural models. He suggests that in the near future we will need to see a change in the model of learning suggested by national strategies in curriculum development. His argument is that teachers need to prepare for this so that ownership of teaching comes back to them.

Chapter 2 follows on by strengthening the argument for play and active learning. Here Janet Moyles questions the need to prepare children to become a future workforce suggesting that individual learning needs are more important. She does this by exploring beliefs about children's active learning, examining them in terms of how they may be translated into curricular practices in different settings. She recognizes the importance of children's voices using their perceptions of the world and their relationships with it to identify the role of the teacher.

Mary Phillips Manke in Chapter 3 takes up this same theme. By recognizing the importance of childhood as a time in its own right, she acknowledges the power children have in the classroom. She explores how they use it to change and mould the agenda for teachers. This she argues changes the actual knowledge that is taught in the classroom, so further establishing the power children have within the school society.

In Chapter 4 Sonia Nieto takes this even further and establishes how children influence changes in the school. She defines critical pedagogy, identifying the relationship within it between children and their teachers. Part of her argument involves consideration of the value of social action in establishing this pedagogy, so resulting in the empowerment of children and teachers to reflect on the knowledge and contexts of education.

References

Bell, D. and Richie, R. (1999) *Towards Effective Subject Leadership in the Primary School*, Buckingham, Open University Press.

CACE (Central Advisory Council for England) (1967) *Children and their Primary Schools*, London, HMSO.

DES (Department of Education and Science) (1989–92) *Orders for the National Curriculum*, London, HMSO.

DfEE/QCA (Department for Education and Employment/Qualifications and Curriculum Authority) (1999) *The National Curriculum: Handbook for Primary Teachers in England*, London, DfEE/QCA.

Galton, M. (1989) *Teaching in the Primary School*, London, David Fulton.

Kerr, J. F. (ed.) (1968) *Changing the Curriculum*, London, Heinemann.

McGilchrist, B., Myers, K. and Reed, J. (1999) *The Intelligent School*, London, Paul Chapman Publishing.

McNamara, D. (1994) *Classroom Pedagogy and Primary Practice*, London, Routledge.

Pollard, A. and Tann, S. (1987) *Reflective Teaching in the Primary School*, London, Cassell.

SCAA (Schools Curriculum and Assessment Authority) (1994) *The Review of the National Curriculum*, London, SCAA.

Simon, B. (1981) 'Why no pedagogy in England?' in B. Simon and W. Taylor (eds) *Education in the Eighties*, London, Batsford Academic and Educational.

van Manen, M. (1999) 'The language of pedagogy and the primacy of student experience', in J. Loughran (ed.) *Researching Teaching, Methodologies and Practices for Understanding Pedagogy*, London, Falmer.

1

Towards a New Perspective on Children's Learning?

Andrew Pollard

Competition, Performance, Policy and Practice

International economic interdependence increasingly undermines the capacity of national governments to control their particular economies – and at the same time generates severe anxieties about national competitiveness. Thus, in recent years and across the whole of the UK, we have experienced an enormous increase in the political attention paid to education, as successive governments have striven to address the competitiveness agenda. Irrespective of the beliefs, expertise and interests of teachers, education has become an area in which governments can present themselves as 'looking to the future' and as 'acting decisively' in the national interest.

The 'performance model' of education in the UK, which has been developed with remarkable continuity between recent Conservative and Labour governments, has defined educational discourse and focused professional attention in ways that articulate with competitiveness. Thus we have the language of curriculum delivery, attainment, targets, competence, appraisal, inspection, etc. Teachers and schools, we are told, must perform more 'effectively'. For primary education in particular, this must be achieved by raising pupil attainments in the basics of English and mathematics. The pressure of the performance model thus ultimately comes to bear on the expectations that are made of pupils.

Of course, there are echoes of the old elementary school system in relation to this narrow basic curriculum, but teachers certainly do not now characterize pupils as passive recipients of knowledge and instruction. Indeed, the continuing influence of constructivism sustains a commitment to pupils as active learners who 'make sense' of their experiences. A significant professional development therefore, achieved despite years of simplistic derision of 'child-centred' methods, is that the role of the teacher has been reconceptualized as 'assisting performance' through *appropriate* direct instruction. The use of the term 'appropriate' is crucial here, for it denotes the application of professional judgement in the cognitive and motivational matching of children and new tasks.

At the end of the twentieth century, therefore, English primary educators can be seen as managing a tension between two forms of discourse. The public statements of politicians and the media are often assertively categoric and simplistic – and have unfortunately been reinforced regularly by Her Majesty's Chief Inspector for Schools. On the other hand, the educationalist discourse of committed teachers has become defensively organized and reflects practical struggles in the difficult circumstances of classrooms and schools as well as responses to debates and 'moral panics' of the moment. Teachers continue to be creative in responding to new demands while seeking to retain their educational principles, but the introduction of hard-edged, performance systems and structures does appear to be gradually changing concepts, taken-for-granted assumption and ways of thinking. This, of course, can be seen as the product of a sophisticated exercise of power. Thus systems, processes and relationships are created that lead people to conceptualize 'reality' in particular ways. Perception, understanding and even 'common sense' become defined in terms of a new leadership. One element of this is the explicit concern with international economic competitiveness, while a second maintains tacit and unproblematized assumptions about how children are deemed to learn.

Through its systems of curriculum and pedagogy, the discourse of performance assumes that there are sufficient continuities in how children learn on which to base valid prescriptions. Thus it becomes possible to set out the detailed contents and processes of a 'literacy hour' or a 'numeracy hour'. The discourse of performance further asserts legitimacy because of its universal and 'objective' application. Implicitly, it assumes that there is sufficient homogeneity in pupil circumstances and learning potential to make valid assessments and comparisons. Such comparisons, it is assumed, can be built up from the performance of individual pupils, taking the attainment of each child as the basic unit of analysis. The claims of universalism, measurement and individual achievement are thus clear and strong – and even educational researchers can now, it seems, be selectively enlisted to demonstrate 'what works'.

However, what if there are weaknesses in the validity of the underlying conception of learning? What if there has been a consistent oversimplification of educational issues by policy-makers, so that policies do not recognize complexities and dilemmas that are actually endemic? More radically, what happens if we start from somewhere else – from a focus on learning *per se*?

I make no claim at this point to be able to offer a complete or perfectly honed alternative perspective, but I want to highlight some issues that are of undeniable significance and which are certainly underplayed at present. My thinking about this derives from research at the interface of sociology and psychology, and constitutes a socio-cultural approach to learning.

A Socio-cultural Approach to Learning

Socio-cultural psychology has been influenced considerably by Vygotsky (1978), and three core themes can be identified in his work. I will review these, and then draw on Bruner's *The Culture of Education* (1996) to highlight two further themes that are of particular significance for the modern application of the approach. For each of these five themes, I will provide a few illustrative examples of relevant research.

First, there is an emphasis on understanding learning developmentally – in 'genetic' terms. This approach was, of course, shared with Piaget, and draws renewed attention to developmental issues, particularly in relation to the learning of young children (Cole, 1992). Physical development, as established long ago by Tanner (1961), also remains of great significance in relation to the fulfilment, or otherwise, of biological potential. And biological factors are becoming increasingly well understood, both in terms of genetic variations and in terms of the neurological functioning of the brain (Greenfield, 1997; Claxton, 1997).

Second, the approach draws attention to the *social* origins of mental functioning – emphasizing the ways in which intellectual capacity is intimately connected to social activity (Wertsch and Tulviste, 1996; John-Steiner, 1997). Vygotsky analyzed how ways of thinking are modelled in social relations and activities, before becoming internalized and available for more independent thought. Similarly, the concept of the 'zone of proximal development' emphasizes the role of a more knowledgeable other (teacher, parent, peer) in providing instruction to 'scaffold' and extend a learner's understanding beyond the level of which he or she is capable alone. Tharp and Gallimore (1978) and Mercer (1995) have provided excellent studies of such processes within schools. The classic book on young children learning in interaction with their parents by Tizard and Hughes (1984) is being complemented by more work on the importance of family and other relationships (e.g. Dunn, 1993). [. . .]

The third core theme concerns mediation, and the processes by which thought is influenced by 'tools' and 'signs'. Of course, the development of human capabilities has been closely linked to the use of physical tools and technologies. However, socio-cultural theory draws attention to the ways in which the availability and use of the tools of a society actually shapes and forms cognition. A telling modern illustration of this argument concerns the use of computer tools, with both hardware (such as the mouse, joy-stick or microphone) and software (such as word-processors, spreadsheets, databases and simulators) enabling and structuring new practices and thought processes. The importance of the mediation of thought through sign systems is even more marked. Thus the symbolic logics of languages, scripts, numeric and algebraic systems, art, texts, diagrams and other forms of representation shape and make possible our thoughts. Such tools and sign systems are the products of socio-cultural history, and are appropriated and internalized by individuals as they develop within their societies (Rogoff and Lave, 1984; Wertsch, 1991). Some interesting concepts have been developed to describe these processes. For instance, there is the notion of a 'distributed intelligence' that exists within our culture, and is embodied in a range of 'cognitive tools'. Lave and Wenger (1991) argue that 'communities of practice' develop in everyday social relationships in which particular ways of knowing are embedded. New learners engage in 'legitimate, peripheral participation' before they become enculturated and knowledgeable within the social practices. At another level completely, anthropological and comparative studies have demonstrated how different cultures embed and reproduce particular ideas and social practices. Thus detailed intercultural case studies of children's upbringing are becoming available, such as those of Richards and Light (1986) and Whiting and Edwards (1988).

Bruner (1996) has built on this approach in his discussion of the 'culture of education', and our fourth theme is derived from this work. Bruner begins by affirming the Vygotskian position be seeing 'reality' as the 'product of meaning-making shaped by traditions and by a culture's toolkit of ways of thought' (p. 19), but he then highlights education as a key institutional process whereby a society shares existing knowledge and negotiates new forms. As he puts it, educational institutions 'do the culture's serious business' (p. 30). This serious business is not, however, without some risk to individuals, and Bruner highlights an 'unpredictable mix of coercion and voluntarism' within schooling systems. The institutional culture, social processes and micro-politics of each school is also vital here (Hoyle, 1982; Ball, 1987). Indeed, in some of my own longitudinal work with Ann Filer, we have tracked the ways in which the 'strategic biographies' of children are affected by their annual cycles of social experience as they move through school careers (Pollard and Filer, 1999). Their particular mix of success and failure, opportunity and frustration reflects the social construction of 'ability' within the school and is crucial to their self-belief as learners.

Finally, the 'risk' to individuals draws attention to 'the phenomenon of self', which Bruner characterizes as 'perhaps the single most universal thing about human experience' (1996, p. 35). While there is cultural variation in the ways in which self-esteem is experienced, Bruner asserts that 'any system of education that diminishes the school's role in nurturing its pupils' self-esteem fails at one of its primary functions' (1996, p. 38). In summary, he argues that 'education must help those growing up in a culture to find an identity within that culture. Without it, they stumble in 'their effort after meaning' (1996, p. 42). [. . .]

Here then, we have an approach to learning that attempts to envision the links between history, culture, language, symbols, thought, relationships, social organizations, activity, biological development, self, identity and even (if we follow Bruner) the 'meaning of life'!

Dilemmas, and a Task

The socio-cultural model is impressive in its range, depth and vision. It aspires to a holism that will resonate with the tacit understandings and experienced knowledge of everyday life. However, some may say that it is foolhardy to attempt to embrace so many factors, and may feel much more secure with the clear-cut and technical logic of the performance model. I have some sympathy for this view at this stage in the development of the socio-cultural perspective. Research is still at a creative and formative point, with many leads and directions being followed, and it will take time for a more integrated set of tenets to become established and presented in forms that are likely to make a direct impact on education policy. Nevertheless, in my opinion, this is exactly what we will see in future decades as the performance model begins to disappoint and as alternative conceptions become more coherent.

However, it is instructive to consider the particular strengths of the perspectives, and dilemma analysis offers a tidy way of doing this. There appears to be a basic dilemma between the multifaceted attempt at holistic validity offered by the socio-cultural model and the practical construction of a structured and measurable education system that is underpinned by the performance model. There are echoes here of the classic researchers' dilemma between validity and reliability. When validity is prioritized, the complexity of relevant phenomena may become unmanageable, but when reliability is emphasized, research may fail to produce findings of meaningful significance. Among researchers, a constructive tension between the twin priorities of validity and reliability is generally accepted, and this gradually leads to innovation and improvement in quality. Sadly, the recent climate of educational debate has not been so constructive, for the systematic prosecution of the performance model has been linked to a discourse of derision and a confrontational approach towards those with reservations or alternative perspectives. If those who are not 'for' are simply deemed to be 'against', then the powerful may prevail – but tragically, they also deny themselves an opportunity to learn.

Nevertheless, because of the range and basic validity to which the socio-cultural model aspires, policies that are consistent with it do break through from time to time. For instance, during the 'Year of Reading' attempts were made to enlist companies, communities and the media in activities to support literacy activity. While the overall initiative was highly managed, it nevertheless recognized the significance of embedding literacy within social relations and harnessing the efforts of existing social institutions. Even more radical initiatives might have been attempted if the full implications of Barton and Hamilton's mould-breaking book on 'local literacies' (1998) were followed up. Similarly, the recent efforts of the Social Exclusion Unit to develop provision on large estates suffering from multiple disadvantages also shows awareness of the holistic conditions that affect learning and development. In particular, it suggests that, at least somewhere in Whitehall, there is recognition that social development needs more than the naming, blaming, shaming and failing of schools. The Demos publication on 'learning beyond the classroom' (Bentley, 1998) is an encouraging publication in this context. But such initiatives seem haphazard, and do not appear to reflect sustained, strategic awareness of the management of the key dilemmas.

Some apparent dilemmas that are posed by the performance and socio-cultural models are:

- *Goals* that are clear and measurable – or potentially diffuse, long term or even ephemeral;
- *Roles* which are specific and delimited – or interdependent and integrated;
- *Relationships* of authority – or which call for multiple partnerships;
- *Control* that is centralized – or relatively devolved;
- *Curricula* that provide consistent entitlements – or are responsive to particular needs;
- *Practices* that are homogenous – or reflect the complexities of modern cultures and traditions.

The overall position may seem to contrast 'precise' with 'fuzzy', and there is an element of truth in this. However, in my view, the perspectives can also be contrasted in the gross simplification of educational processes that the performance model embodies and the attempt to work from more complex and valid understandings in the case of the socio-cultural approach. Of course the latter is more difficult, and of course politicians cannot wait in the optimistic hope that researchers will arrive (uniquely) with new 'truths' about learning and how best to facilitate it. However, we should not forget that thoughtful and aware parents and teachers have always understood many of these issues, even if they may not have been easy to articulate analytically. In this context, we could all benefit from more recognition of the inherent difficulty of both understanding learning and improving our education system – and it would be good to conceptualize the shared task, and work together.

References

Ball, S. (1987) *The Micropolitics of Schooling*. Routledge: London.
Barton, D. and Hamilton, M. (1998) *Local Literacies: Reading and Writing in One Community*. Routledge: London.
Bentley, T. (1998) *Learning Beyond the Classroom*. Routledge: London.
Bruner, J. S. (1996) *The Culture of Education*. Harvard University Press: Cambridge, MA.
Claxton, G. (1997) *Hare Brain, Tortoise Mind*. Fourth Estate: London.
Cole, M. (1992) 'Culture in development', *Developmental Psychology*, LEA: Hillsdale, NJ.
Dunn, J. (1993) *Young Children's Close Relationships*. Sage: Newbury Park, CA.
Greenfield, S. (1997) *The Human Brain: A Guided Tour*. London: Weidenfeld and Nicholson.
Hoyle, E. (1982) 'The micropolitics of educational organisations', *Education, Management and Administration*, 10, 87–98.

John-Steiner, V. (1997) *Notebooks of the Mind: Explorations of Thinking.* Oxford University Press: New York.

Lave, J. and Wenger, E. (1991) *Situated Learning: Legitimate Peripheral Participation.* Cambridge University Press: New York.

Mercer, N. (1995) *The Guided Construction of Knowledge.* Multilingual Matters: Clevedon.

Pollard, A. and Filer, A. (1999) *The Social World of Pupil Career.* Cassell: London.

Richards, M. and Light, P. (1986) *Children of Social Worlds.* Polity Press: Cambridge.

Rogoff, B. and Lave, J. (1984) *Everyday Cognition: Its Development in Social Context.* Harvard University Press: Cambridge, MA.

Tanner, J. M. (1961) *Education and Physical Growth.* University of London: London.

Tharp, R. and Gallimore, R. (1988) *Rousing Minds to Life.* Cambridge University Press: New York.

Tizard, B. and Hughes, M. (1984) *Young Children Learning.* Fontana: London.

Vygotsky, L. S. (1978) *Mind in Society.* Harvard University Press: Cambridge, MA.

Wertsch, J. V. (1991) *Voices of the Mind.* Harvard University Press: Cambridge, MA.

Wertsch, J. and Tulviste, P. (1996) 'L. S. Vygotsky and contemporary developmental psychology', in H. Daniels (ed.), *An Introduction to Vygotsky.* Routledge: London.

Whiting, B. B. and Edwards, C. P. (1988) *Children of Different Worlds.* Harvard University Press: Cambridge, MA.

2

Just for Fun? The Child as Active Learner and Meaning-Maker

Janet Moyles

Introduction

For the past several decades in many parts of the world, play and active learning have been acknowledged as crucial to the cognitive and other developmental processes of children. That the child learns through making his or her own physical and mental connections with the world, through sensory explorations, personal effort, social experiences and the active seeking of meanings from experiences, has been established in the theories of psychologists and educationalists such as Froebel, Montessori, Isaacs, Steiner, Vygotsky and, later, Piaget and Bruner. Yet it is by no means easy for teachers and other adults in schools and kindergartens to achieve these ideals in practice, where so-called 'child-centred' education and individualized learning are either logistically, pragmatically or culturally considered inappropriate or unrealisable. Similarly, while many educators may see themselves as providing opportunities for children to be actively engaged in their learning, how far this is a reality will depend upon the interpretation and evaluation of these beliefs in practice.

In many countries, curricular debates have focused around the perceived imperative to balance the needs of society for a suitably educated workforce and the needs of children to learn at their own pace and in ways deemed appropriate to their current developmental phase. One view would suggest that we must allow young children to revel in their childhood and childhood experiences before we consider them to be future employees, with an entitlement to have the needs of their particular age group met before they, in turn, must meet the needs of an industrial society (Moyles, 1996). The whole concept of an industrially and economically dominated curriculum militates against a curriculum based upon individual learning needs which is deemed by many to be at the heart of effective primary school practices (Siraj-Blatchford and Siraj-Blatchford, 1995).

This chapter sets out to identify the basis upon which these various beliefs about children's active learning as both part of their intellectual development and of their rights as children are justifiable. It also examines their substance in terms of the teaching and learning relationship and how such beliefs may be translated into curricular practices in different cultural settings.

Primary Children Making Sense of the World

> The children in the kindergarten were told by the adult that it was nearly time to go outside for outdoor play. It was a beautiful, hot, sunny day though Anna, aged 4 years, moved towards the coat-racks and asked the adult to help her put on her coat. The adult laughed, saying, 'You don't need your coat. It's too nice out there. Go and feel how hot it is.' Anna stood on the steps outside the nursery door and was seen to stretch out her arms and then pinch her fingers and thumbs together in a 'feeling' action.

As an example of 'intelligent' behaviour, the reader may wonder what on earth Anna was doing. But looked at from the child's perspective, Anna was doing exactly what she perceived the adult had told her to do: in Donaldson's (1978) words she was attempting to make 'human sense' of what had been said to her. The fact that she so literally interpreted the action behind the adult's words is not uncommon in young children for it takes some time for them to grasp the different interpretations implicit in the words and actions of others.

Children in the primary years learn directly about their immediate environment through exploration using their senses: by attending to the world around them through touching, listening, tasting, smelling and looking, they begin to make generalizations. By generalizing from these experiences, children begin to form the basis of lasting understandings. Without the ability to generalize and put 'chunks' of learning into large wholes, we would all rapidly become overloaded and overwhelmed with information (McShane, 1991). But this very need to generalize means that children will not always be 'right', for, as Edwards and Knight (1994, p. 21) emphasize, 'Young children have less information on which to build new understandings and their strategies for organizing and holding information are less well developed'. [. . .]

Sensory learning combined with existing experience leads children to perceive the world in certain ways which, at different stages in the child's development, leads to different levels of understanding being available to the child. As Merry (1995, p. 84) points out, 'Perception is not a passive taking-in of our surroundings but a highly active process in which the information supplied by our brains is at least as important as the information received by our senses'. [. . .]

Reality from the child's perspective

Children's views of the world are very much human-centred: they perceive and conceive of events and things through the experiences they themselves encounter and in which adults offer support and models. But there are times when perception dominates children's thinking, and if they cannot perceive something they may well doubt its existence. Even when primary-age children do perceive something they frequently misinterpret what the reality is by attending only to those aspects which are immediately recognizable, adopting what Piaget and Inhelder (1969) called 'unscientific causations'.

From much research (see, e.g., Langford, 1987; Willig, 1990; Bonnett, 1994) it is clear that children bring a different kind of 'logic' to situations from which it is possible for the practitioners to learn a great deal with which to inform primary practice. Consider the following: after a short discussion about how they learned to read with a group of 11-year-olds clustered around a computer, the writer was presented with the following text and asked to 'read' it:

ΩηΨ χαν τ ψου ρεαδ τηισ? Ιτ ισ περφεχτλψ σιμ$πλε – προϖιδεδ ψου υνδερστανδ τηε$ λανγυαγε ανδ τηε σψμβολσ ιν τηε$ φιρστ πλαχε!

The children explained that this was how many of them had perceived reading as young children, a series of squiggles on paper which meant very little to them but which they knew that somehow they were intended to read. (The text, in Symbol font, actually says 'Why can't you read this? It is perfectly simple – provided you understand the language and the symbols in the first place!')

Other instances spring to mind. Consider the child who answered '11' to the seemingly simple sequence of numbers 2, 4, 6, 8, _. Although we would immediately perceive the answer from a numerical base as 10, this child's interpretation was equally valid because she was actually perceiving the numbers to relate to a social and personal (egocentric) context: she is one of five children whose ages are 2, 4, 6, 8 and *11* years. The misinterpretation of the context of learning needed to be understood by the adult in order for the child's 'error' to be understood.

Language proves to be no less confusing. Consider the child who has just had a large dish of their favourite food and is asked if they would like to have some 'more'. What will they inevitably get? Well, certainly *less* than they had the first time! Or the child who, when asked which out of two ribbons is the longer, the red or the yellow, confidently responds 'The yellow one – because I like that colour'. As Hughes (1983) points out, whereas adults would recognize that they have insufficient information, children do not always know the appropriate questions to ask and assume that a response is possible because the question has been asked by an older person.

Abstraction and symbolism

As adults, we are in danger of forgetting just how abstract – and symbolic – much of what we present to children really is. What must be recognized is

Can the same be said of dyslexic children's thinking?

that children's thinking is not inferior to adults, but rather that it is different in form and experience. Their thinking is embedded in a context which has some meaning to them, whereas much school activity, such as filling in the blanks in a workbook, is what Donaldson (1993, p. 19) describes as 'disembedded' tasks: tasks divorced from a context in which children can see purpose and meaning and which, therefore, make the processes of learning much more difficult. Sotto (1994, p. 44) suggests that meaning emerges slowly from the learner's active involvement in thinking through and understanding the 'patterns' which underlie understanding, and emphasizes that learning is not the same as remembering. [. . .] As Bruce *et al.* (1995, p. 59–60) suggest,

> Adults seize on the child's developing ability to make and use symbols and often cannot wait to begin to teach directly the symbols of their particular society. In some cultures this begins at a very young age . . . What is it that activates these important symbolic developments in children and . . . what turns them into ever deeper levels of symbolic learning? The key issue in answering this revolves around what kind of symbols children are most at ease with in their early years. This will dictate what symbols they can most readily engage with.

Bruce and her colleagues go on to propose that the development of the use of symbols in children is most likely to take place through 'real experiences' and 'a consideration of the links among play, experience, relationships and creativity', rather than pressure from adults to conform to learning which is outside the children's current potential to understand.

It is acknowledged that, towards the end of primary schooling, children are more able to cope with disembedded tasks as their thinking becomes more abstract. However, as primary practitioners, we need to consider (and observe for) embedded thinking when we set out to teach different kinds of knowledge and understanding, for, whatever the content demands of a curriculum subject, the children need to have tasks presented to them which offer a meaningful context in which they can bring their previous experiences and understandings to bear and which fit in with the new experiences and patterns of understanding they are already acquiring. As Donaldson (1993, p. 20) suggests, 'it is even more important to recognise that the *processes* of coming to know transform us. This is particularly so when these entail sustained, self-directed effort'.

Teaching must acknowledge the learner's role in the essential links between teaching and learning effectiveness. This means particularly recognizing that the ability to think abstractly about things has a starting point in *action*, a feature of the work of Piaget, Bruner and Vygotsky which often manifests itself in the process we call 'play'. [. . .]

Active Learning and Children's Play

The primary classroom is carefully arranged with all materials necessary for the morning's session. The teacher has planned an active lesson for the children aimed at helping them to understand the concept of electricity. Each group of tables is equipped with a collection of bulbs, wires, batteries and switches, a new experience this term for this class of 9-year-olds. The active learning session has arisen because the teacher has recognized that, despite telling the children in a class session yesterday about eletricity, they still do not appear to understand how a circuit is made.

   When the children enter the room from the playground, many of them rush to the tables and, in the teacher's words, start 'messing about' with the materials and arguing over them. It takes some time to bring the class back to order and to gather in the electricity resources. The teacher gives out a worksheet in which the children complete a series of sentences regarding issues to do with electricity.

Children appear to need to play regardless of whether society approves or not. Clearly this teacher did not 'approve' of these children's play, yet indeed that is what it was: play as exploration, in this case, of resources in an effort to understand them. While feeling an empathy with this teacher that his carefully conceived plans were not fulfilled, it is also vital to think of the activity from the learners' point of view. This was the first time in many weeks that the children had been given the opportunity to play with resources which brought electricity to their immediate level of engagement – which gave a direct embedded context for their learning – and they were keen to explore the wires, batteries, bulbs and switches and understand their patterns and purposes. In so doing they were engaging in a form of play – exploratory play – through which they are able to learn about the properties and functions of materials as a preliminary to being able to manipulate them for a given purpose (Hutt *et al.*, 1989; Moyles, 1994).

   In Brunerian terms, in this activity children were still at the *enactive* stage in their learning; they needed to learn by actively doing, whereas the teacher was expecting them to operate at an *iconic* (image or pictorial) or even *symbolic* (abstract) stage by filling in the sentences on a worksheet. What distinguishes 'active learning' from 'play' is to do with the processes in which the children engage and with concepts such as 'ownership' and 'locus of control' which, in play, rest with the player but in active learning situations can be under the direction of another person, e.g. the teacher (see Bruce, 1991; Moyles, 1991).

   [. . .] Vygotsky (1978) suggests that play and play processes *lead* children's development (rather than development leading play). He suggests that play acts as a catalyst for children's learning and ensures that they are able to perform ahead of their current developmental level. Children acquire concepts, skills, knowledge and attitudes towards learning and towards others in their play and, for this reason, play should occupy a central part in children's lives. Play happens in some mode or another even in cultures where there are few apparent play opportunities (Curtis, 1994), and many studies have indicated how effective play is in ensuring motivation in learning and providing the context for lasting understanding. For example, much primary-level learning focuses around developing schema which are the amalgamation of smaller pieces of information which have entered consciousness through children's active engagement in seeking meaning. [. . .]

The more sophisticated the schema, the deeper one's knowledge. Schema, in turn, enable the formation of *concepts* – big ideas, which are capable of being generalized and which enable us to use the knowledge gained in one situation in a new context. Research by Athey (1990), Gura (1991) and Nutbrown (1994) with children under 6 has shown clear evidence of schema development in children's play and in their representations of the world, particularly in pictures and model-making. There is no evidence to suggest that this does not apply equally to older primary children.

One tangible element of play is that it is an *observable behaviour* and, therefore, one could argue that at least one value of play is being able to observe and assess the outcomes of the learning process through what one sees. Schwartzman (1983) supports this view in suggesting that children play what they know and, therefore, through play we can find out about their deeper understandings.

Indeed, there is now a plethora of research showing that play and active learning allow children to understand the meanings behind the symbols they create, whether it is in art, music or pretend play (Matthews, 1994). Socio-dramatic play, in particular, has been shown to be at a level between the concrete and the symbolic where one meets the other in the child's world (Kitson, 1994). Not only is this an important link for primary children's developing skills in the area of number, reading, writing and representation, but it is also believed by some writers (see Smilansky and Shefataya, 1990) to contribute to greater cognitive gains in such areas as verbalization, richer vocabulary, higher language comprehension, better problem-solving strategies, higher intellectual competence, better performance on conservation tasks and greater concentration.

Play and learning theory

Play provides children with an active learning mode in which to:

1. explore;
2. use their developing skills;
3. solve problems;
4. practise skills;
5. rehearse.

These five aspects link closely with established theories of learning, such as that developed by Bennett and his colleagues (1984) from an earlier model by Norman (1978) which suggests that learners need to show evidence of their ability to:

1. acquire new knowledge and skills;
2. use existing knowledge and skills in different contexts;
3. recognize and solve problems;

4. practise what they know;
5. revise and replay what they know in order to retain it in memory.

As well as offering a sound theory, this model also offers a clear relationship to classroom practice, in terms of both children's play and active learning opportunities. It has been found by many writers (see Sylva, Roy and Painter, 1980; Smith and Cowie, 1992; Moyles, 1994) that children's first need in learning about an object or situation is to have opportunities to *explore* the properties, textures, shapes, colours, forms and so on in order to gain basic factual knowledge and handling skills. Having done so, this then enables the child to begin to *use* this knowledge and skill in ways which should eventually result in the *recognition* and *solution* of problems. In returning to a related activity or situation at a later time, the child will be required to *practise* and *revise* as the basis for future learning activities.

It now becomes clear that the children in the electricity cameo were attempting to acquire new knowledge about, and skills in handling, the various materials which, in turn, would have given them a sound basis on which to use that knowledge to develop a circuit. In completing the circuit, they will have needed both to recognize and attempt to solve particular problems in ensuring that a light appeared. A later return to a similar electricity experiment would afford the children opportunity to practise and revise what they have previously learned and commit it to memory. Memorizing of 'facts' alone would be difficult without the developing concept of electricity which has, in turn, been refined through further additions to developing schema.

Trial-and-error learning

One of the things which seems to be important in relation to play and active learning situations is that, because having real, firsthand experiences is in itself motivating to children, the processes of play provide a valuable means of allowing children to learn through their own efforts and their own mistakes. Play also increases children's powers of concentration which, in itself, has been found to be a good indicator of children's potential (Keough, 1982). As well as knowledge, skills and opportunities to practise, children need to believe that they *can* achieve in school: they need confidence and a good image of themselves as 'learners'. This is much more capable of being achieved in situations where success is not judged only in terms of recognizable outcomes, but where making mistakes is itself valued as part of a successful learning process.

In the process of 'coming to know' something it is likely that most of us will not achieve success every time (Holt, 1991). Unfortunately, many learning situations in school accept only 'right' answers: mistakes are not something to be learned from but seen as a sign of 'failure'. Yet, as we have seen, many psychological theories over the past few decades have suggested strongly that children's learning occurs more effectively in the context of trial-and-error opportunities where fear of failure is replaced with open-ended challenges which are under the control and direction of the child and, furthermore, do not undermine children's self-esteem. Yet practitioners insist on emphasizing right answers, particularly in countries with a heavily dominated paper-and-pencil-based curriculum where children either can or cannot do the tasks presented to them and are, therefore, either right or, if they do not perform correctly, wrong. The question must be raised as to whether children should be penalized for not understanding or whether practitioners need to rethink their practice in terms of allowing children opportunities to learn through exploring their own understandings without fear of failure. [. . .]

The Practitioner's Role in Active Learning Approaches

The teacher sits down beside a group of four 10-year-old children who are attempting to design and make a pulley system from a range of different materials. The children have been having some difficulty in making their pulleys work and concentration has begun to wane. The teacher, without speaking, manipulates the various pieces of wood, pulley wheels and string under the watchful eye of the children. One child approaches and asks her what she is doing. The teacher replies that she has a problem in trying to make her pulley work and wonders if the child can think of a way of doing so. The rest of the children gather round and make various suggestions, all of which the teacher tries until one achieves the desired result and the pulley is made to work. The children analyse with the teacher how success has been achieved and evaluate the outcome, then they quickly return to their own efforts and consult with each other on producing the desired outcome. The teacher leaves the technology table, returning around ten minutes later to find a series of different pulleys being eagerly discussed and experimented with by the children.

In the 1960s there was a view which still prevails today among some people in Western societies, that children's active learning and play should not be 'interfered' with by adults: that it is somehow sacrosanct to the child and that adults cannot have a role in it other than as providers. This is now seriously in question, since studies (like those of Bruner, 1980; Smilansky, 1968; Hutt *et al.*, 1989; Smilansky and Shefataya, 1990) have shown clearly that children's play and active learning can be significantly enhanced educationally and academically by adult involvement [. . .].

[. . .] In the previous cameo the case for children's active engagement in their own play and learning has been argued in relation to children creating meaning and making sense of the world.

Through the actions of the teacher, the children were enabled to be successful in their learning outcomes *and* to retain the ownership and control of their own play and active learning. This is surely at the heart of good teaching when applied to the model of learning which has been previously outlined. For children to achieve learning goals set by others and to add to their existing schema, they need adults who can 'scaffold' their attempts (Bruner, 1973) and allow them to use firsthand experiences within what Vygotsky terms 'the zone of proximal development': i.e. the gap between what the child can currently do alone and what he or she could do with support.

The teacher could have approached the children with a range of questions about what they were doing or, indeed, have given directions as to what they should do to achieve the desired outcome. This would, however, have meant that the teacher needed to understand exactly what level each child was capable of achieving with her support – no mean feat! This approach could also have left the children with the feeling that only someone outside of themselves could provide the answer to their problem, rather than the answer coming from within the children's own intellect and experiences.

Children's independence and adult models

With the adult operating both as model and as facilitator of the children's own thinking and questioning, the children were challenged to provide their own solutions rather than generating a dependency upon the teacher. The latter has been shown by researchers to create impossible situations in classes of 30 and more children, who are then all potentially dependent upon the teacher for their learning actions (see Barrett, 1986; King, 1978; Bennett and Kell, 1989). This in itself creates environments in which, according to Galton (1995, p. 18), there are often queues of children waiting for the teacher, which decreases the time that children are able to devote to their learning tasks. Darling (1994, p. 4–5), in discussing learner-centred education, proffers the Dewey view that

> Once children see education as something that other people do to them . . . they lose the ability to take any initiative or responsibility for their own learning . . . In particular the kinds of enquiry that children naturally pursue are not reflected in the way traditional schooling categorises knowledge into different 'subjects'. It is this lack of correspondence which accounts for children's low motivation . . . child-centred educational theory suggests that we could and should have classrooms where learning is largely self-motivated and the atmosphere is fairly relaxed.

A model that perceives children as having a central role in their own learning also has to acknowledge teachers as *learners* themselves, rather than as general purveyors of existing knowledge (see Pollard and Tann, 1992). This means a fundamental shift in some teachers' thinking and in the strategies they apply to children's learning. Dweck and Legett (1988) [. . .] emphasize, like Bruner and Vygotsky, children's need for support as they struggle to understand and make sense. One might also add the children's need to be *trusted* to negotiate, discuss and understand their own learning needs and be responsible for some of the outcomes. This requires practitioners who have a clear view of their own role.

Table 2.1   *Teaching strategies for active learning*

1. *Entering strategy*
   What will be your starting point(s)? Introduction?
2. *Exploration mode*
   What exploration will the children undertake? What materials/resources need to be available? How/by whom would they be set up?
3. *Contents*
   What do you intend the children should learn? Subject and/or processes and/or skills?
4. *Ownership and responsibility*
   How/at what point will it be possible for the practitioner to withdraw and allow the children ownership? How will the children know what they are supposed to learn through their active involvement?
5. *Adult value strategies*
   What will the practitioner role be? How will you interact/intervene in the learning and sustain/extend it? What level of support will the children require?
6. *Evaluation and analysis*
   How/when will you observe to see what children were learning in relation to concepts covered?
7. *Reflection*
   What opportunities will you provide for children to reflect on their learning and be part of the evaluation/analysis of processes and outcomes?
8. *Justification*
   What kind of outcomes will you expect? How will the value of these be communicated to others?

Based upon the kind of learning model explored earlier, teachers should consider several factors shown in Table 2.1, which will lead to the active learner retaining some control over the learning activities and having opportunities to reflect on their own cognitive processes. The order can be adjusted according to the task.

This model is readily applied to a range of teaching and learning situations and links with the kind of teacher action shown in the cameo at the start of this section. The teacher's entering strategy was to model the kind of actions undertaken by the children in order to enable them to understand not only the processes of their own learning but the content of the technological activity. The children could see from the teacher's actions what they were intended to learn and had opportunities to reflect on her outcomes and evaluate them in terms of their own potential achievement. The adult valued and trusted the children, giving them the responsibility and ownership of their task by leaving them to complete it, having scaffolded their attempts. She valued and evaluated the active processes of their learning equally with the outcomes. This is what could be termed 'the learning relationship'.

Ownership, control and the sensitive teacher

[. . .] Even in exploratory play children do not necessarily have a sense of ownership: it is when they take things on board intrinsically that ownership is established. Teachers can support this by the way they present tasks to children within the curriculum. It can be the teacher's idea or learning objective, but then the children need to be persuaded to make it part of their learning. Much of the research already discussed has shown the long-term value of programmes which are characterized by the latter type of learning involvement and of children taking ownership and responsibility: e.g., the outcomes of the longitudinal High/Scope study in the United States (see Royal Society of Arts, 1994; Sylva, 1994).

It is worth noting from the research that what children choose to do (even if by adults' perceptions it is work) is still deemed 'play' by children and is often characterized by greater motivation, persistence and concentration (Karrby, 1989; Moyles, 1989; Robson, 1993). Edwards and Knight (1994, p. 21) note that 'Teaching is above all led by sensitivity to the state of the learner. A learner's state will include motivations, confidence and existing understandings'.

Teachers do have several dilemmas when engaging in making this kind of learning provision for children: large class sizes, the dictates of imposed curricula, pressures from others (including parents) to provide paper evidence of children's learning, to mention but a few. Practitioners should consider, however, the outcomes of *not* providing appropriate experiential learning; the result is often demotivated children, who can 'perform' and conform to adult requirements but who often have little understanding of learning intentions and little responsibility for themselves as learners (Bennett and Kell, 1989). An example would be the young child who can readily count to ten and beyond but has no concept of the 'fiveness' of five, or what constitutes 5 + 1. Hughes (1986) has shown clearly that, when adults allow children to manipulate the numbers in concrete terms through having the objects to handle and move, they are capable of much greater levels of understanding, not only of numbers but of their own metacognitive processes.

The practitioner's sensitivity to/empathy with the way children make sense of learning opportunities is vital, for, as Willig (1990, p. 184) shows,

> Teaching is about negotiation of meanings between teachers and pupils . . . skilled teachers encourage pupils' contributions and look for links between the knowledge children bring to the situation and the new experiences to which they are being introduced. The act of learning then becomes an exchange of viewpoints where the learner works hard on the new material, grafts it on to existing learning and comes out of the experience with fresh insights.

– a true learning relationship. [. . .]

[. . .]

Providing for an Active, Play-based Curriculum

A teacher, new to the Infants School, was presented with a series of headings under which each term's curriculum was to be presented to the children in different year groups. The first-year children were to undertake some of their

Figure 2.1   *Environmental geography*

work based on the subject of 'Environmental Geography'. The teacher had some
concerns as to how she could develop this into an appropriate scheme of activities for these 5-year-olds. She decided to ask the children at discussion time
what they understood of 'environmental geography' and, despite great keenness
on the children's part to explore all kinds of things to do with their homes, toys,
families and so on, her own concerns were confirmed when children appeared
unable to offer any explanation of the subject. However, some time later, Leigh
came to her with a drawing which the child explained showed 'environmental
geography'. When asked to describe what she had drawn, Leigh said 'This is the
whole wide world, with some people in the grass, some flowers and some trees.'
(See Figure 2.1.)

As teachers, we are often set seemingly impossible tasks in trying to teach
children about issues which are not directly within their experience but
which 'society' in its broadest sense, through a designated curriculum, feels
it appropriate for children to learn. It is vital that those directly responsible
for the curriculum in action in classrooms are sensitive not only to what
they must teach but to the children's starting points in setting out to learn
about different aspects (Blenkin and Kelly, 1994). As Doyle affirms, 'tasks
communicate what the curriculum is to students' and 'meaning is seldom at
the heart of the academic tasks they work on' (Doyle, 1986, pp. 366, 374).

In discussing with the children the concepts behind 'environmental geography', this practitioner was able to draw from at least one child what her
perception of the subject involved, and was, therefore, able to evolve activities within the curriculum which would operate from the basis of the
children's existing knowledge and understanding.

In fact, learning experiences were planned which involved considering
the earth beneath the children's feet and the things which grew upon it and
lived underneath. The activities were within the children's understanding,
with scaffolding from the teacher. While the child's interpretation of environmental geography may, by adult standards, be very incomplete and
rather naive, as we have seen earlier in this chapter practitioners need to
relate to children's ways of thinking and to acknowledge that these are not
somehow 'faulty' but represent the world as the child perceives and
conceives it. This must be the starting point for any active learning curriculum, for how can any child actively engage with something about which
they have no schema, or, as Sotto (1994) suggests, no 'model inside the
head'? Sotto goes on to state:

[I]f I do not have such a working model, I find I may understand the individual words said to me, but I do not really understand their full *meaning*. The result is that I begin to lose track of what is being said to me . . . until I am actively engaged [in developing this model] I do not really learn. (Sotto, 1994, p. 33)

In observing and evaluating children's approaches to activities, practitioners gain a clear understanding of how to match curriculum intentions to children's learning. [. . .] The curriculum, as it is imposed upon the children from outside, needs also to be considered in terms of what is developed through the kinds of learning experiences which match with children's capacity to understand and make sense of the world at any given time. Broadly it could be said that the curriculum is everything the child experiences in the context of schooling which is intended to foster learning. The curriculum must acknowledge the central role of the learner and have a relationship to the child's life, otherwise the learning will be sterile and will not create opportunities for the child to make sense. Curriculum activities should ensure that children are motivated and want to try and to succeed. Above all, what children can do alone and with support, evidenced in their attempts to make sense of the world and gain meaning from their experiences, must be the starting point, rather than what they cannot yet do alone. The curriculum has its own processes which can be seen to link effectively with learning processes if one conceives of it in this way. The curriculum is the medium through which children should be enabled to think, feel, do, acquire knowledge and skills, solve problems, investigate, apply knowledge, practise, revise, co-operate and communicate.

What practitioners will be attempting to do is to ensure that all of these processes are engaged in by children during most of the school day. The interaction between the teacher, the child – the learning relationship – and the curriculum is crucial. McAuley (1990, p. 89) rightly emphasizes that

[I]t is the teacher–child interaction that is at the heart of the educational process and it must always be *about* something. That 'something' is the task which, if it is routinely conceived as an exercise for skills and competences rather than a problem, will devalue the teacher–child interaction. The latter will become demonstrational, instructional, transmissional rather than the exploration of making sense and figuring out.

[. . .] Only if we offer children the opportunities to create their own meaning and understand their own learning through play and active engagement at a developmentally appropriate time in their lives are we likely to ensure our future citizens have the necessary adaptability, flexibility and clarity of understanding to be the source of technological innovation so necessary for economic survival.

References

Athey, C. (1990) *Extending Thought in Young Children*, London: Paul Chapman.
Barrett, G. (1986) *Starting School: An Evaluation of the Experience*, Final Report to AMMA. CARE. Norwich: University of East Anglia.

Bennett, N., Desforges, C., Cockburn, A. and Wilkinson, B. (1984) *The Quality of Pupils' Learning Experiences*, London: Lawrence Erlbaum.
Bennett, N. and Kell, J. (1989) *A Good Start? Four Year Olds in Infant Schools*, Oxford: Blackwell.
Blenkin, G. and Kelly, A. (1994) *The National Curriculum and Early Learning: An Evaluation*, London: Paul Chapman.
Bonnett, M. (1994) *Children's Thinking: Promoting Understanding in the Primary School*, London: Cassell.
Bruce, T. (1991) *Time to Play in Early Childhood*, London: Hodder and Stoughton.
Bruce, T., Findlay, A., Read, J. and Scarborough, M. (1995) *Recurring Themes in Education*, London: Paul Chapman.
Bruner, J. (1973) *Beyond the Information Given*, London: Allen and Unwin.
Bruner, J. (1980) *Under Five in Britain*, London: Grant McIntyre.
Curtis, A. (1994) 'Play in different cultures and different childhoods', in J. R. Moyles (ed.), *The Excellence of Play*, Buckingham: Open University Press.
Darling, J. (1994) *Child-Centred Education and its Critics*, London: Paul Chapman.
Donaldson, M. (1978) *Children's Minds*, Glasgow: Fontana.
Donaldson, M. (1993) *Human Minds: An Exploration*, London: Penguin.
Doyle, W. (1986) 'Classroom organisation and management', in M. Wittrock (ed.), *Handbook of Research on Teaching* (3rd edn), New York: Macmillan.
Dweck, C. and Leggett, E. (1988) 'A social-cognitive approach to motivation and personality', *Psychological Review*, 95(2), April, pp. 956–73.
Edwards, A. and Knight, P. (1994) *Effective Early Years Education: Teaching Young Children*, Buckingham: Open University Press.
Galton, M. (1995) 'Do you really want to cope with thirty lively children and become an effective primary teacher?', in J. R. Moyles (ed.), *Beginning Teaching: Beginning Learning*, Buckingham: Open University Press.
Gura, P. (1991) *Exploring Learning: Young Children and Blockplay*, London: Paul Chapman.
Holt, J. (1991) *Never Too Late*, Ticknell: Education Now.
Hughes, M. (1983) 'On asking children bizarre questions', in M. Donaldson, R. Grieve and C. Pratt (eds), *Early Childhood Development and Education: Readings in Psychology*, Oxford: Basil Blackwell.
Hughes, M. (1986) *Children and Number*, Oxford: Basil Blackwell.
Hutt, S. J., Tyler, S., Hutt, C. and Christopherson, H. (1989) *Play, Exploration and Learning: A Natural History of the Pre-School*, London: Routledge.
Karrby, G. (1989) 'Children's perceptions of their own play', *International Journal of Early Childhood*, 21(2), pp. 49–54.
Keough, B. K. (1982) 'Children's temperament and teachers' decisions', in R. Porter and G. Collins (eds), *Temperamental Differences in Infants and Young Children*, London: Pitman.
King, R. (1978) *All Things Bright and Beautiful?* London: John Wiley.
Kitson, N. (1994) 'Please Miss Alexander: will you be the robber? Fantasy play: a case for adult intervention', in J. R. Moyles (ed.), *The Excellence of Play*, Buckingham: Open University Press.
Langford, P. (1987) *Concept Development in the Primary School*, London: Croom Helm.
McAuley, H. (1990) 'Learning structures for the young child: a review of the literature', *Early Child Development and Care*, 59, pp. 87–124.
McShane, J. (1991) *Cognitive Development: An Information-processing Approach*, Oxford: Basil Blackwell.
Matthews, J. (1994) *Helping Children to Draw and Paint in Early Childhood: Children and Visual Representation*, London: Hodder and Stoughton.
Merry, R. (1995) 'Take some notice of me! Primary children and their learning potential', in J. R. Moyles (ed.) *Beginning Teaching: Beginning Learning*, Buckingham: Open University Press.

Moyles, J. R. (1989) *Just Playing? The Role and Status of Play in Early Education*, Milton Keynes: Open University Press.

Moyles, J. R. (1991) *Play as a Learning Process in your Classroom*, London: Collins.

Moyles, J. R. (ed.) (1994) *The Excellence of Play*, Buckingham: Open University Press.

Moyles, J. R. (1996) 'Nationally prescribed curricula and early childhood education: the English experience and Australian comparisons–identifying the rhetoric and the reality', *Australian Journal of Early Childhood*, 21(1), pp. 27–31.

Norman, D. A. (1978) 'Notes towards a complex theory of learning', in A. M. Lesgold (ed.), *Cognitive Psychology and Instruction*, New York: Plenum.

Nutbrown, C. (1994) *Threads of Thinking*, London: Paul Chapman.

Piaget, J. and Inhelder, B. (1969) *The Psychology of the Child*, London: Routledge and Kegan Paul.

Pollard, A. and Tann, S. (1992) *Reflective Teaching in the Primary School: A Handbook for the Classroom* (2nd edn), London: Cassell.

Robson, S. (1993) 'Best of all I like choosing time. Talking with children about play and work', *Early Child Development and Care*, 92, pp. 37–51.

Royal Society of Arts (1994) *Start Right* (The Ball Report), London: RSA.

Schwartzman, H. (1983) 'Play as a mode', *Behavioural and Brain Sciences*, 5, pp. 168–9.

Siraj-Blatchford, J. and Siraj-Blatchford, I. (eds) (1995) *Educating the Whole Child*, Buckingham: Open University Press.

Smilansky, S. (1968) *The Effects of Socio-Dramatic Play on Disadvantaged Pre-school Children*, London: Academic Press.

Smilansky, S. and Shefataya, S. (1990) *Facilitating Play: A Medium for Promoting Cognitive, Socio-Emotional and Academic Development in Young Children*, Gaithersberg: Psychosocial and Educational Publications.

Smith, P. and Cowie, H. (1992) *Understanding Children's Development* (2nd edn), Oxford: Basil Blackwell.

Sotto, E. (1994) *When Teaching Becomes Learning*, London: Cassell.

Sylva, K. (1994) 'The impact of early learning on children's later development', in Royal Society of Arts, *Start Right* (The Ball Report), London: RSA, pp. 84–96.

Sylva, K., Roy, C. and Painter, M. (1980) *Childwatching at Playgroup and Nursery*, London: Grant McIntyre.

Vygotsky, L. (1978) 'Mind in society: the development of higher psychological processes', in M. Cole, V. John-Steiner, S. Scribner and G. Souberman (eds), *Mind in Society*, Cambridge, MA: Harvard University Press.

Willig, C. J. (1990) *Children's Concepts and the Primary Curriculum*, London: Paul Chapman.

3

Defining Classroom Knowledge: the Part That Children Play

Mary Phillips Manke

Because schools are intended to be places where learning occurs, the question of what will count as knowledge is especially important. What counts as knowledge is a determining factor in what students actually learn. That is why this aspect of classroom power relationships – how students contribute to the process of determining what will count as classroom knowledge – is the focus of this chapter.

In traditional sociological and political analysis, the power to define what will count as knowledge is assigned to the teacher. The larger society – defined as the structure of the school, the expectations of administrators, parents and community members, and all kinds of curriculum materials – is thought to influence the teacher's use of this defining power.

Although the actions of students described in this chapter are surely affected by the same larger society that influences teachers' actions, the analysis I present here focuses on student actions exerting influence on what will be learned in a given classroom. I stress this point because so many writers in education have focused on the influence of the teacher, or of society through the teacher. Some view this influence as a primary instrument for the oppression or control of students, particularly those who are culturally different from the majority; others see it as a necessary part of the transmission of the desirable aspects of an historic culture. Without denying that one of the ways teachers contribute to constructing classroom power relationships is to influence the definition of classroom knowledge, I look in this chapter at how students also influence this definition. In doing so I am opening up the possibility of looking at how the influence of the surrounding society works through the students, rather than only through the teacher.

Yet, I am not trying to answer questions about why, or under the influence of what outside forces, students promote certain knowledge and demote other knowledge. A primarily observational study like this one cannot seek out the reasons, affective or cognitive, for actions observed. Instead, I offer instances of teachers' and students' actions that appear to promote contrasting or co-operative agendas with respect to classroomknowledge – I have avoided speculating on the reasons for their choices.

Some researchers have observed students sharing in the process of defining classroom knowledge. For example, Alison Jones (1981), a researcher in New Zealand, described and named an instance of student control over what counts as classroom knowledge. She studied a classroom in which teachers tried to focus instruction on higher-level thinking about their subject; they knew that such thinking would be necessary if the students were to pass school-leaving examinations. Students in the classroom resisted including in the curriculum anything other than facts that could be memorized; thus they effectively defined what would count for them as classroom knowledge.

A student Jones (1981) observed said, 'Well, that's what we're really doing here, isn't it, the notes . . . to get the notes' (p. 23). One girl said of the teacher, 'She asks me to ask questions. I never ask questions. I just keep quiet and I always say, "What?" when she asks me questions so she has to ask them twice' (p. 24). Another said, 'We never talk if she, you know, wants us to say things . . . talk about something. Everyone shuts up . . . What's the point? It's a waste of time' (p. 24). Jones could only speculate about the roots of the student beliefs leading to this particular (and, as it happened, destructive to the students' chances of academic success) definition of classroom knowledge, but she showed clearly that these older students were well aware that they shaped what the teacher did.

[. . .]

In a related vein, Michelle Fine (1991), who studied the politics of dropouts in New York City, gave a vignette of a high school student constructing her own definition of classroom knowledge. She told how a social studies teacher set up an in-class debate on Bernard Goetz, the so-called 'subway vigilante'. The teacher told those who agreed with Goetz to go to one side of the room and those who disagreed to go to the other. This command defined the question of violence and responses to it as having only two possible answers. A number of students stayed in the middle of the room, and the teacher scolded them: 'Don't be lazy. You have to make a decision. Like at work. You can't be passive . . . Those of you who have no opinions, who haven't even thought about the issue, you won't get a chance to talk unless we have time' (p. 42). According to Fine:

> Deidre, a Black senior, bright and always quick to raise contradictions otherwise obscured, advocated the legitimacy of the middle group. 'It's not that I have no opinion. I don't like Goetz shooting up people who look like my brother, but I don't like feeling unsafe in the projects or in my neighborhood either. I got lots of opinions. I ain't bein' quiet 'cause I can't decide if he's right or wrong. I'm talkin'. (pp. 42–3)

Deidre actively expanded the teacher's dichotomous notion of 'having an opinion' to one that took account of shading and context. She influenced, at least for herself and perhaps for others in the class, what would count as classroom knowledge.

The students in Jones's and Fine's studies are older than the ones I observed; they are more explicit about their part in defining classroom knowledge than were the first and fifth graders in my study. Yet, I frequently observed these young students engaged in the same process.

Ms Corvo's Room: Defining the Range of Knowledge

One way of defining what will count as knowledge is to decide what range of knowledge will be open for consideration at any one time. This question underlies the distinction between holistic and fragmented educational methods. For example, in teaching students to read, the teacher can focus broadly on the entire text, with all the meaning and aids to comprehension it offers, or on the details of the correspondence between spelling and sound. For the teacher, making this kind of decision about what will count as knowledge is like focusing a microscope lens. A wider and less precisely defined field can be chosen, or the focus can be tightened so that only a narrow segment of the field is in view. In the classroom I studied, I saw teachers who had chosen a particular focus, but who found that focus modified by student actions.

Aileen Corvo's fifth-grade classroom, where the teachers generally tried to control all areas of student action, proved to be a rich source of such examples of student refocusing of the lens defining what would count as classroom knowledge. During one spelling test, I saw LaToya widen the teacher's focus for herself two times. This class had a weekly spelling pre-test on Wednesday and the test on Friday, conducted according to rigid patterns of expected behavior. There seemed to be little room for student influence on what was occurring, and LaToya's actions were subtle though revealing:

> *It is so quiet. All the students are writing, focused on their papers. Ms Bridgestone pronounces word number 5, period. There is a giggle from LaToya, who appears to be entering puberty.*

> Ms Bridgestone pronounces the next word, *poet*. La Toya turns in her seat and looks at the text of 'Stopping by the Woods on a Snowy Evening', which is posted on the wall.

In both these instances, LaToya's action did something that let the observer know, or at least make a strong guess, about what was in her mind as she heard the words on the spelling list. The words were part of a context of knowledge for LaToya; the teacher, through the spelling test activity, defined them only as collections of letters to be placed in the correct order. In this class, spelling lists were sharply marked as worthwhile knowledge, and because they came from books prepared outside the class, they had only the most tenuous connection with the students' actual use of words in reading, speaking and writing. LaToya refused to leave the spelling words in this disconnected state; she redefined what would count as knowledge for her in that moment.

In contrast to this detached treatment of spelling and vocabulary, at another time Ms Bridgestone (the student teacher) taught two lessons that were meant to build students' confidence in their ability to understand unfamiliar words with the help of context. She gave students a list of words from the novel they were reading. First, she asked them to guess what the words meant, using the context only; then she asked someone to look up the meaning of each word in a dictionary to confirm that the students' guesses were correct.

Here too, however, students were in conflict with her over what was to count as knowledge. She repeatedly affirmed that the students' sense of what the word meant, derived from the context, was valid knowledge. That was, in fact, the point of the lesson.

Keiyon and Donald, however, were both seen surreptitiously looking up the word meanings in their dictionaries and offering the dictionary definitions as meanings they had derived from context. They seemed to interpret the activity as a contest between the students and the dictionary, which they could win by cheating; they did not accept their guesses as valid knowledge. So they did not learn what Ms Bridgestone intended to teach them: confidence in their own ability to use context as they read.

Another group of observations of Aileen Corvo's class contrasted the teachers' understanding with the students' understanding of what knowledge was supposed to be acquired through the writing workshop. The teachers thought of this as a time to learn to write well. If students followed the steps in the writing process (the teachers believed and told both students and interviewer), good writing would be produced, and the students would internalize a process that produced good writing. The steps in the process were permanently displayed on wall posters around the room, and were often reviewed with the students, either briefly in the course of giving directions or in a full-scale lesson. Everything that happened during writers' workshop, from the teachers' viewpoints, was in the service of 'learning to write well'.

[. . .]

An essential element of this model of the writing process was that students were free to write on topics of their choice and to write pieces of the length they felt was appropriate for their topic. Teachers could not, if they wished to obtain the results promised by the process, exercise control over the content of student writing.

It appeared that from the students' point of view, the writers' workshop was nothing more than an opportunity to write and talk about topics that interested them, and to conduct social interchange on those and other topics with their friends; they did not seem to define learning to write well as knowledge in this context. Possibly, this was a result of the emphasis on the steps of the writing process – rather than on understanding what good writing actually is – that characterized writing process instruction in this classroom.

[. . .]

Most of the time, students chose to conference with their friends, and as I walked around the room at this time I could hear them using their 'conferences' to discuss a variety of topics, especially television shows, movies and comic books. There was little or no evidence that they perceived the workshop as an opportunity to improve their writing. Marie, in fact, almost explicitly denied that goal in this interchange:

> *Marie*: I finished my piece.
> *Ms Corvo*: Have you conferenced on it?
> *Marie*: Yeah, I made it shorter so I wouldn't have to type so much.

The question of what topics students should write about in the writing workshop was also a matter of conflict between student and teacher wishes. Most students had a strong preference for themes of horror, gang warfare, and violence:

> Ms Bridgestone is at the chalkboard, and students are calling out their ideas for pieces they might write.
> *Voices call*: Gangs! Vampires! Murders! Gangs in Los Angeles!

The teachers told both the class and the interviewer that they were uncomfortable when these fifth graders wrote about these topics, but were unsure how to respond. The writers' workshop principle that students should write about what interests them was in conflict with the teachers' sense of what constituted appropriate subjects to address in school. Students continued to choose the questionable topics most frequently. Their concerns and interests prevailed over what the teachers thought was suitable.

For example, the students wrote 'modern fairy tales', that were to be displayed for parents and then sent to the principal of the school, who was ill. Many of them chose tales like Little Red Riding Hood and Three Billy Goats Gruff, stories that already contained elements of violence. They multiplied as well as modernized the level of violence in the tales. Many of them seemed more proud of and pleased with this work than with any other piece of school work I saw them do. Perhaps this was because they had succeeded in controlling what would count as classroom knowledge.

Ms Kaminski's Room: Conflict Over What Counts as Classroom Knowledge

In Ms Kaminski's first-grade classroom, what Ms Kaminski named as knowledge was most often accepted as such. She planned and prepared for her class rigorously, and the definition of knowledge that came out of this planning – an instance of her 'invisible' contribution to building the classroom power structure – was usually the one that prevailed. Compared to traditional first-grade teachers, Ms Kaminski used a broad focus in defining what would count as classroom knowledge, accepting much that would not everywhere be defined as proper first-grade knowledge.

For example, in this incident, Ms Kaminski named an activity as part of the knowledge area 'music', an official part of first-grade curriculum. This incident has to be understood against the possibility of her defining what the students did as 'not music', or as some kind of inappropriate behaviour:

The children are gathered on the rug and are singing with a tape which is playing on the stereo. Two of the boys go over to the table where the stereo is, pick up rhythm instruments, and join in with the song. When the song ends, Ms Kaminski praises 'the musicians'.

Student: They're not musicians.
Ms Kaminski: Musicians are people who make music. Weren't they making music with the bells and the tambourine? Then they're musicians.

During a maths activity time, Ms Kaminski shaped the students' work to match her definition of school knowledge. 'Sorting' was considered, in this classroom, a proper part of school mathematics knowledge. Simply making judgements of 'pretty' and 'not pretty' was not. Ms Kaminski introduced the word 'sorting' into what the students were, in fact already doing:

Juana, Sara, and Jennifer were seated at one of the tables with a box of buttons. Each one had taken a handful of buttons and was looking at them, stopping to exclaim over and show to the others the particularly 'pretty' ones. Ms Kaminski came over and sat down with them. She picked up on their saying that they were finding the pretty ones and encouraged them to sort all the buttons into categories of 'pretty' and 'not-pretty'.

Again, during readers' workshops, children were supposed to be involved with books. Reading, looking at a book, pretending to read, telling the story of a book while looking through it, listening to a tape while looking at the book it records, and reading with a friend or listening to a friend read were all defined as appropriate. Many other activities, such as painting, playing with blocks, or making patterns with Unifix cubes, were not to be done at this time. (At other times, they could be a source of classroom knowledge. Ms Kaminski used the terms 'working with blocks' and 'working with Unifix cubes' to indicate that these activities were within the realm of classroom knowledge.)

During the first weeks of the year, however, the class was heavily involved in a study of insects, and Ms Kaminski was willing to stretch the definitions for reading time to include this topic.

On the fifth day of school, most of the children were involved with books during readers' workshops. Nathaniel, however, was wandering around the room with the raccoon puppet, making it squeak. (This was an activity which clearly was not defined as relating to reading.) Ms Kaminski suggested that he look at the monarch caterpillars. He did, and two other students joined him.

In this way, Ms Kaminski defined 'looking at caterpillars' as a source of school knowledge, and placed it on a par with 'reading' as an appropriate activity during readers' workshop. In an interview, she said that as the year went on, students would be expected to read or write about animals and the like that they might be observing during readers' and writers' workshops, but that at this point, observing was enough.

All these instances illustrate how Ms Kaminski worked to establish a definition of what would count as school knowledge in her classroom. Yet, at other times, even these young children were either welcomed by Ms Kaminski to participate in defining what would count as knowledge in their classroom or created their own definitions of what knowledge would be brought into the classroom. For example:

> Thomas had used his free choice time to make a 'map book', which he shared. He had put several cities in the United States on his maps. Ms Kaminski pulled down a map of the United States, which hung next to her seat, and they pointed out various places on the large map. Someone asked where Africa is. Ms Kaminski pulled down a world map. They looked at it and located places around the world for a few minutes.

Geography, as this might be called, may not be part of the planned first-grade curriculum, but it counted as school knowledge here, and Ms Kaminski was ready to accept it.

> At other times, children were clearly creating these definitions against Ms Kaminski's resistance. Certain children were highly successful in doing this; Andra, who was an African-American girl from a family living in poverty, was such a child. The children had Lincoln Logs to use during free choice time because it was before Thanksgiving and they were doing a unit on early Americans and because building with Lincoln Logs was defined by Ms Kaminski as a math activity. (The logs are designed proportionally, so that notions of half, double and the like can be derived from working with them.) By this time in the year, 'a math activity' was the one thing students must do during some part of free choice time. Andra had been asked to build a house with Lincoln Logs, but she had chosen instead to draw a house on paper, using Lincoln Logs as rulers to get straight lines. When she displayed the picture at sharing time, Ms Kaminski told the children how Andra had made the drawing, but pointed out that tomorrow Andra *would* really use Lincoln Logs to build.

Andra's most powerful and successful effort to set up her own definition of classroom knowledge took place over many months. I first became aware of it when, at sharing time, Andra wanted to show a book into which she had copied words from *The Very Hungry Caterpillar* (Carle, 1989):

> One of the children said that you were not supposed to copy words from books; you were supposed to write your own words. Ms Kaminski said that was the rule during writers' workshops, but that Andra did this activity at free choice time, and it was OK if she used part of her free choice time to do that.

This interchange reflected Ms Kaminski's belief that children learn to write by generating their own words through invented spelling, rather than by copying the words of others. Some children enjoyed copying from books or from others' writing, and she wanted to limit the time they spent on that, pushing them to what she saw as the more challenging task of 'writing their own words'.

Andra, however, persisted in copying words throughout the year when she was supposed to be reading or writing. It was one of her preferred activities, and she spent much time on this forbidden or marginally acceptable activity. By March, she had a large vocabulary of words that she could read and write, which she apparently had learned by copying. Along the way she had learned to sound out many words and to create invented spellings, but she preferred to learn words by copying them. She succeeded in at least partially substituting her own way of learning to read, her own definition of what constituted learning to read, for the one specified by Ms Kaminski.

A somewhat related incident took place when Carlton chose to work at a table at which children were to write and draw pictures about the class guinea pigs, one of whom had given birth on the previous day. The aide was there to help them write about the guinea pigs. I had the impression that providing this rather defined activity was intended to help the children shift the focus of their interest in the guinea pigs because the mother and babies could not be safely touched soon after the birth. Yet, Carlton wanted to work with a book about monsters that he had brought from home:

Aide: No, this activity is about guinea pigs.

Carlton went to his cubby and got his book.

Aide: Put it back, Carlton.

Carlton complied, but stood looking carefully at the cover of the book before putting it in the cubby. Then he came back to the table and wrote MONST on his paper. He got up, went back to his cubby, pulled out the book and looked at it again. He returned to the table and wrote ERSW. Then he wrote KNEPK (an invented spelling of the words 'guinea pig').

Carlton: It says, 'Monster Guinea Pig'.

Then Carlton settled down to draw an elaborate picture of the cage with a guinea pig in it. There was nothing monstrous about the guinea pig he drew.

The last instance of conflict over what would count as classroom knowledge in Ms Kaminski's classroom could be described as ideological. It took place during the study of insects, when there were monarch butterflies, their caterpillars and cocoons, and praying mantises in various terrariums in the room.

One morning, I happened to sit down next to a terrarium containing praying mantises. I noticed that two of them were mating. When Ms Kaminski walked by, I pointed this out to her, as she was usually eager to share with the children anything new about the insects. She said that she and the aide had noticed what was happening, but were telling the children that the two mantises were very good friends and were playing together. Later, in an interview, I asked her about this event. She confirmed that she had decided not to include sexual reproduction in the study of insect life; she considered the topic inappropriate for first graders.

In connection with their insect study, the class had read Eric Carle's book *The Very Hungry Caterpillar*, and they were preparing a play based on it for parent night. Ms Kaminski was choosing volunteers for the various parts in the play, as they paged through the book from the beginning. Students had been chosen to play the caterpillar, the moon, and the various edibles that come into the story. There were several volunteers to be the butterfly, the last part to appear in the book. Ms Kaminski chose James. Philip, Carlton and another boy called out, 'Who is the mate?' At first, Ms Kaminski didn't understand what they were saying. They repeated their question and at last she did understand.

> *Ms Kaminski*: The story doesn't call for a mate. Does that answer your question?

The children's question seemed to represent exactly the kind of extension of ideas that Ms Kaminski usually encouraged, but her response to it, like the first incident, put sexual knowledge firmly outside the category of classroom knowledge. Yet, even though she rejected it as part of the curriculum, the fact that several children raised it together indicates that it had in fact been part of the study for them. This incident is parallel to LaToya's giggle at the spelling word *period*. Teachers may strive to exclude sexuality from the definition of classroom knowledge; children may insist on including it.

Sue Anderson's Room: Inviting Students' Lives into the Curriculum

Of the three teachers, Sue Anderson was the one who most actively sought to engage children in defining classroom knowledge by bringing their own experiences and memories into their learning experiences. This was particularly true during language arts and social studies classes, when she often asked so-called 'high-level questions' that called for connecting the subject at hand with other knowledge. Because her students were quite diverse, with about one-fifth of the students she saw each day coming from families who had emigrated from at least five different countries, and close to the same number from American minorities, this shifting of the definition of classroom knowledge was often in a multicultural direction. Oyler (1996) made a distinction between cases when the students actually set the topic of discussion and those when the topic the teacher raises allows students to shape the content of the discussion out of their personal experience. Although the former is certainly a stronger instance of students contributing to classroom power relations, the latter exemplifies the sometimes collaborative nature of the development of those relations.

Ms Anderson's willingness to allow students' home lives and interests to be defined as classroom knowledge was so great that she held a weekly 'sharing time', at which children brought in objects they owned or had found or told stories about their lives outside of school. Because of this effort on her part, there was rarely an occasion when children redefined classroom knowledge against her will. Yet, it was their individual choices about what to share, what to bring, and what to say that contributed to defining what would be classroom knowledge.

In late autumn, for example, the class was reading a popular children's novel called *Maniac Magee* (Spinelli, 1990). This novel deals with themes of interracial conflict and connection as it tells the story of the adventures of a homeless boy. Ms Anderson had focused on the word *color-blind*, used in the book. She asked whether it was right to say that Maniac was '*color-blind*'.

This turned out to be a hard question, because some students took it to refer literally to colour-blindness, and they thought a colour-blind person would see only black and white, like an old movie. And because the point in the book was supposed to be that Maniac did not notice any difference between Black and White people, the discussion got quite confusing. But it was an important idea in understanding the book. Maniac is strange in a number of ways, but his failure to understand this basic fact of American life, as the book presents it, is certainly part of the reason for his nickname.

Yuri, an Israeli boy whose family was temporarily living in the USA, offered a story to clarify the problem. He gave an example from Israeli history, of *sabras*, native-born Israelis, mistreating new immigrants. He pointed out that this was much the same thing that happened between Whites and Blacks in the United States, but Maniac didn't understand this, and that was why he was called *colour-blind*. Yuri, with his broader frame of reference, had shifted the focus of the discussion – and the definition of this bit of classroom knowledge – from racism in one small town, or in the USA, to conflict between groups in other places and for other reasons.

Some days later, while the class was still discussing *Maniac Magee*, Ms Anderson brought up the matter of Maniac's homelessness and loneliness. 'What could you do if someone you know seems lonely?' she asked. As at many other times, this question led several students to share information about their home situations with others in the class. Vincent, a member of a family that had immigrated from Vietnam, talked about his enjoyment of opportunities to be alone. At home, he said, he often had to take care of his younger siblings and got in trouble if they broke the rules. So he appreciated it when he could be on his own. In fact, that was why he would rather work alone in school, rather than in groups. Later in the year, when they were reading *My Brother Sam Is Dead* (Collier and Collier, 1994), Denny talked about how the tensions and disagreements in that family reminded him of feelings in his own home.

Another occasion of students' bringing in their home situations as school knowledge took place when they were reading *Sign of the Beaver*, a novel in which a White boy is asked to teach English to an American-Indian boy. Ms Anderson was leading a discussion of how students would teach English to a speaker of another language, how the students who took French or Spanish before school were being taught, and how they thought they themselves would learn a new language best.

In this case, she directly solicited information from three of the students who were from immigrant families. Dara, from Iran, said that her family spoke Persian and that she sometimes did her homework in Persian and translated it into English. Avram, from Russia, said, 'We speak Hebrew at home'. Vincent said, 'We speak Vietnamese. I mean, they speak it to me. I can understand it but I would never ever be able to say anything back to them'. The three students opened up for the class a new sense of what knowing or learning a language could mean.

Later in the year, students made American Indian craft items as part of their study of Indian nations. Joshua was Oneida, and he used this opportunity to share with the class what he had learned from his mother, information about where you go to get clay and dyes to use in craft work. The authentic and elegant dream catcher he made also broadened the group's sense of what these crafts could be like – it was quite different from the crude pieces most of them produced.

One of the few instances I saw in Ms Anderson's class in which a student shifted the definition of classroom knowledge away from the expected one without her participation and consent took place during a maths class. The students were in groups working on a problem-solving book; I observed a group that had settled on the floor next to the chalkboard. One of the problems was about going to a restaurant; it had several steps of making menu choices based on a budget and then figuring the bill. The directions said to calculate a 15 per cent tip. Esteban suggested that more than 15 per cent was better, that they could pretend they were rich enough to give a bigger tip, and that waiters need bigger tips than that. They talked intensively about why and how much you tip until Kelly stood up, copied the method in the book on to the chalkboard, and said they should tip as much as the book said.

Clearly, the intention of the activity was to teach about solving maths problems, not about restaurant behaviour, but the group had redefined what would count as classroom knowledge and focused on an interpersonal rather than a mathematical issue.

[. . .]

An instance of actual conflict in this area between Ms Anderson and one of the students took place when Mark was working on his research paper. From Ms Anderson's point of view, the classroom knowledge at issue was how to locate research materials in the library, how to take notes, how to combine material from different sources, how to plan a structure for the paper and how to prepare a bibliography. The students had freely chosen their topics, and Mark had picked a favourite, Robin Hood. After several opportunities to take notes, Mark had two note cards, one listing the names of characters in the Robin Hood stories and one listing major incidents in the stories. It was becoming clear that his plan for the research paper was to tell the Robin Hood story from memory. This exchange took place:

Ms Anderson: I think you need a better topic. A real research topic.
Mark: Naah. I like Robin Hood. I want to do it on Robin Hood.

Ms Anderson: I think you're fighting me on this, Mark.
Mark: I just know a lot about Robin Hood in my head.
Ms Anderson: That's not the point. This is a research paper.

Mark was trying to shift the activity to one focused on 'writing what you know about a topic'. Ms Anderson insisted that it was about 'doing research'. This was clearly not something that Mark felt the need to learn. Ms Anderson had to call Mark's parents and enlist their help before he agreed to produce an actual research paper.

I drew several conclusions from these observations of students and teachers defining what counts as classroom knowledge. First, the construction of a definition of what counts as classroom knowledge is an essential part of classroom power relations. It can be thought of as a substructure of the larger structure of permitted actions for teachers and students being built in the classroom. The name of this substructure is 'What Students Can Learn Here'. Students in each of the three classes could be seen engaging in this process, with or without the support of the teacher. As in other aspects of the development of power relations, teachers most often created a basic framework; students built areas – central or off to the side – in which they could operate independently. Sometimes they built them in ways that interfered with the framework the teacher had established.

Second, a number of the events that teachers saw as interfering with the framework they were constructing were connected with sexuality. Teachers seemed to prefer defining sexual knowledge as not suitable for the classroom. The culture of schools seeks to exclude students' sexuality, even making their denial of it a criterion for students' school success. Meanwhile, students seek to define this important part of their being as appropriate classroom knowledge. Such activity was observed by Grahame and Jardine (1990) who told how a teacher's question to a group of high-school boys about the uses of fleece fabrics quickly led to a set of highly sexual and fanciful responses. The teacher ignored their comments completely, and said, 'I'm just going to put linings (as a use for the fleece fabric)' (p. 295).

Third, the validity of the notion that schools, through teachers, reproduce culture and transmit culturally sanctioned knowledge depends on the premise that it is teachers who decide what will count as knowledge. This premise needs to be rethought in light of evidence that students are important contributors to such definition. An alternative explanation is that such reproduction and transmission are part of students' entire lives and are funnelled *through the students*, as well as through the teacher, from the outside world into the classroom.

Last, teachers need to be aware of how students try to widen the focus of classroom knowledge from fragmented bits of curriculum to a more holistic vision of their world. They are constantly occupied with connecting and extending knowledge (Hynds, 1994). Consistently, students in the three classrooms (with or without their teachers' encouragement) were seen making connections between what was presented as classroom knowledge and what they knew from other experiences. Following Sue Anderson's lead by taking advantage of, rather than resisting, this process seems likely to result in stronger learning experiences for students.

References

Carle, E. (1989) *The Very Hungry Caterpillar*, New York: Scholastic.

Collier, J. and Collier, C. (1994) *My Brother Sam Is Dead*, New York: Scholastic.

Fine, M. (1991) *Framing Dropouts: Notes on the Politics of an Urban Public High School*, Albany, University of New York Press.

Grahame, P. and Jardine, D. (1990) Deviance, resistance and play: a study in the communicative organization of trouble in the classroom. *Curriculum Inquiry*, 20, pp. 283–304.

Hynds, S. (1994). *Making Connections*, Norwood, MA: Christopher-Gordon.

Jones, A. (1981). The cultural production of classroom practice, *British Journal of Sociology*, 10, pp. 19–31.

Oyler, C. (1996) *Making Room for Students: Sharing Teacher Authority in Room 106*, New York: Teachers College Press.

Speare, E. G. (1983) *Sign of the Beaver*, Boston: Houghton Mifflin.

Spinelli, J. (1990) *Maniac Magee*, New York: HarperCollins.

4

Critical Pedagogy, Empowerment and Learning

Sonia Nieto

[. . .] Critical pedagogy and empowerment are at the very heart of learning. To understand the link between learning and empowerment, I will begin by exploring the links between critical pedagogy and multicultural education. [. . .] The personal transformation of students will also be the subject of this chapter, and it will conclude with an exploration of how students can help transform schools to become sites of democratic and liberating learning. A number of teachers' reflections are included as well.

Defining Critical Pedagogy and Empowerment

Critical pedagogy is an approach through which students and teachers engage in learning as a mutual encounter with the world. Critical pedagogy also implies *praxis*, that is, developing the important social action predispositions and attitudes that are the backbone of a democratic society, and learning to use them to help alter patterns of domination and oppression. But critical pedagogy does not imply a linear process from *knowledge* to *reflection* to *action*. It is not a mechanistic strategy or a technical process, but a way of thinking more openly and critically about learning. Critical pedagogy is not a standard set of practices, but rather a particular stance *vis-à-vis* knowledge, the process of learning and teaching, and the educational environment in which these take place (Leistyna, Woodrum and Sherblom, 1996; Walsh, 1991).

According to Paulo Freire (1970), the opposite of a critical or empowering approach is 'banking education' or 'domestic education', where students learn to regurgitate and passively accept the knowledge they are handed. A critical education, on the other hand, expects students to engage in learning with others, to be curious, to question, and to become problem-solvers. Because a critical pedagogy is founded on the belief that problems and issues can be viewed from a variety of perspectives, there is rarely just

39

our curricu[...]
again – time   is linear
ie Aug P[...]   Jup–[...]

one right answer to most problems. When students have the opportunity to
view situations and events from a number of viewpoints, and when they
begin to analyse and question what they are learning, critical thinking,
reflection and action are promoted.

Most students usually do not have access to a wide range of viewpoints,
but this is essential if they are to develop the important critical judgment
and decision-making skills they will need to become productive members
of a democratic society. Critical pedagogy begins where students are at; it is
based on using students' present reality as a foundation for further learning
rather than doing away with or belittling what they know and who they are.
Critical pedagogy acknowledges cultural, linguistic, social class and other
forms of knowledge based on student diversity. It encourages students to
use their experiences to extend their learning, and it insists on student
voice as a primary element in curriculum and classroom pedagogy. At the
same time, critical pedagogy does not simply privilege individual and personal experience as the source of all knowledge; experience becomes another way, but by no means the only one, in which to confront and analyse
knowledge.

Ira Shor's (1992) analysis of critical pedagogy begins with the assumption
that because no curriculum can be truly neutral, it is the responsibility of
schools to present students with a broad range of information they will
need to learn not only to read and write, but to read and write *critically* and
in the service of social change. Moreover, critical pedagogy does not operate on the principle of substituting one canon for another; instead, students
and teachers are invited to reflect on multiple and contradictory perspectives to understand reality more fully. Without a critical perspective, reality
frequently is presented to students as a given, and underlying conflicts and
problems are barely mentioned.

[. . .]

Where does *empowerment* fit into critical pedagogy? Empowerment is
both the *purpose* and the *outcome* of critical pedagogy, and empowerment
is the other side of the coin of domination. That is, while *power* is implicated in both, in domination it is used to control, and in empowerment it is
used to liberate. As described by Seth Kreisberg (1992), domination is
characterized by *power over* and implicated with violence, selfishness, hierarchy and victimization. On the other hand, empowerment is characterized
by *power with*, and it challenges those patterns of domination. According
to Kriesberg, empowerment is manifest in *relationships of co-agency*. That
is, it is not simply the development of individual consciousness, but a
social engagement. In education, empowerment suggests a redefinition of
relationships between and among teachers and students, parents and
administrators.

Given this more complex understanding of empowerment, a number of
questions arise. Can empowerment ever be just individual advancement, or
is it always a social and collective act? Richard Ruiz (1991) has asked the
penetrating question, 'Would empowered students become critical, or

*Determining that for each
individual – problematic*

✳

*which alternate
groups.*

merely successful?' (p. 222). Although becoming successful is certainly a marked improvement over being unsuccessful, Ruiz poses an intriguing question. Banks and Banks (1995) express the dilemma rightly when they challenge pedagogies that prepare students merely to fit into an unjust society rather than to challenge the injustices that undergird that society. The question then becomes, is empowerment simply a replication of business as usual, or does it propose a different paradigm by challenging the model of success as just individual advancement? Paulo Freire (Shor and Freire, 1987) insisted that liberation is a *social act*; nevertheless, although he rejected the idea of empowerment as self-liberation, he also wrote, 'While individual empowerment or the empowerment of some students, the feeling of being changed, is not enough concerning the transformation of the whole society, it is *absolutely necessary* for the process of social transformation' (p. 110).

[. . .] While it is safe to say that empowerment is a collective and social process, being academically successful as individuals and developing a critical stance towards the world are not necessarily in conflict. In truth, being successful and critical can go hand in hand. Lilia Bartolomé (1994) suggested as much when she proposed that teachers can support positive social change through their pedagogical strategies, including heterogeneous groups and democratic learning environments. How can strategies such as these lead to empowerment rather than simply to individual achievement? She explained that students, 'once accustomed to the rights and responsibilities of full citizenship in the classroom, will come to expect respectful treatment and authentic estimation in other contexts' (p. 179).

Multicultural education as practised in many schools has little to do with critical pedagogy and empowerment; in many cases, it is reduced to only a celebratory approach. But if it is to make a real difference in student learning, multicultural education needs to be situated within a more critical perspective.

[. . .]

Building on Students' Strengths

The first and most important lesson I learned as a novice teacher was this: *build on what your students know*. In spite of its very simplicity and exquisite common sense, this idea is radical because it is based on the judgement that intelligence is not the sole province of students from specific groups but of all students regardless of their identity and status. Unfortunately, however, bicultural students very often are thought not to have *any* strengths upon which to build. Even speaking another language – a condition that in most parts of the world would classify as an asset – is a liability for bicultural students in the USA.

The oft-repeated phrase, 'All students can learn', is a worthy ideal, but it has become more a slogan than a belief. [. . .] But teachers who are successful with bicultural students regularly begin with the premise that students have valuable insights and skills that can be used in the service of learning. This was certainly the case with the effective teachers of students of diverse backgrounds in California identified in research by Laurie Olsen and Nina Mullen (1990). The curriculum approach used by the teachers they profiled usually shared a number of features: it was based on the specific experiences of students; it was developed in a climate of high expectations and positive affirmation of students' intellectual abilities; it validated and built on students' cultures while also broadening their perspectives; it reflected excitement about diversity; and it emphasized students learning from one another as well as from the teacher.

Building on students' strengths means, first, acknowledging that students have significant experiences, insights, and talents to bring to their learning and, second, finding ways to use them in the classroom. If teachers begin with the supposition that students bring nothing, they interpret their role as simply needing to fill students with knowledge. On the other hand, if teachers begin with an awareness that all students have useful experiences that can become the foundation of their learning, their role becomes a radically different one: to research what their students' strengths might be, and then to co-construct learning experiences to build on those strengths. In his comprehensive review of the characteristics of effective teachers of linguistically and culturally diverse students, Eugene García (1994) concluded that these teachers incorporated into the curriculum attributes of the local cultures, used instructional strategies that were student-centred and collaborative, and, most significantly, cared deeply about their students.

[. . .]

In the following section, I will explore how teachers can go about accommodating the perspectives and experiences of their students and their students' families in curriculum and pedagogy.

Bridging Cultures, Bridging Lives

[. .]

An example of teacher as bridge can be found in a classroom ethnographic study reported by Martha Montero-Sieburth and Marla Pérez (1987). The teacher, Marla, used her intimate knowledge of the community, culture, and lives of her students as a bridge to help them become critical learners. Rather than the general impression that many bicultural students get that school and home can never be connected, the students in this classroom found that school was a place where their daily lives could be connected with their academic learning. For example, the teacher's role became a highly varied one, and she came to see herself as a 'teacher, friend, mentor, social worker, translator, counselor, advocate, prosecutor, group therapist, hygienist, and monitor' (p. 183). She made it clear that she cared about and for her students, and she made her classroom a place where students could reflect and talk about their lives and experiences in a way that was not allowed in other classrooms. In the process, she turned her classroom into 'problem-posing forums' in which the issues that were important to students became the focus of the curriculum. At the same time, she consciously taught the students the norms of mainstream school and society to facilitate their identity as successful students (Montero-Sieburth and Pérez, 1987).

[. . .]

[. . .] However, negative attitudes about language and culture may find their way into schools and teachers' thinking. Turning this situation around is not a matter of instituting a particular strategy, but rather a matter of incorporating students' and families' perspectives and experiences into schools. An ethnographic study by Concha Delgado-Gaitán and Henry Trueba (1991) of first-generation Latino children found that the children's home environments often provided rich linguistic and cultural resources. The researchers concluded that, from an educational point of view, the children were ready to learn when they reached school. Unfortunately, however, the schools were not ready to take advantage of what the children brought with them. Delgado-Gaitán and Trueba concluded that 'children's language and opportunities for development of higher cognitive skills were much richer in their homes and communities than in the classroom' (p. 140).

In another example of how negative views of language and culture can negatively influence student engagement with school, Margaret Gibson (1995) investigated the factors that promoted or impeded success among Mexican-descent students in a California high school. She found that students and their parents generally viewed acculturation in an additive way, that is, as adding another culture and language instead of eliminating their native ones. Nevertheless, the school environment consistently reinforced a subtractive acculturation. Moreover, although parents perceived language maintenance for their children as absolutely essential, almost half of the teachers believed that *monolingualism was the best avenue for success*. As incredible as this belief may seem to be, it had a decided impact on teachers' behaviours and attitudes concerning their students who spoke Spanish. Gibson found that the negative attitudes teachers had about the Spanish language influenced how students felt about school, about their teachers, and even about their own identity and culture. Specifically, she found that those students who expressed the greatest unease with the devaluation of their language and culture were also those at the greatest risk of dropping out; these students felt the pressure to either reject their identities and become successful students, or accept their identities and reject academic success.

In order to make genuine cultural learning a part of the classroom environment, Frederick Erickson (1997) has suggested that students and teachers be used as primary resources in the curriculum. Specifically,

Erickson recommends using *critical autobiography* both as curriculum and as the basis for action research. This strategy entails making particular student and family cultures the object of study by all students. What makes this approach *critical* is that culture is approached not as a fixed or static state of being, but rather as socially constructed and changing; the goal is not to encase cultures in protective wrappings but instead to deconstruct the meanings behind them. In this way, students and teachers can develop a critical stance about their own and other people's cultures and histories. This process also relieves students of having to be 'cultural experts', a prime danger in classrooms where teachers assume that students' cultural membership automatically makes them capable of teaching others about their culture, a questionable assumption at best.

Empowerment and Learning

When a critical perspective is used, students can become instruments of their own learning and use what they learn in productive and critical ways; their knowledge can be used to explore the reasons for certain conditions in their lives and to design strategies for changing them. Moreover, critical pedagogy helps to expand teachers' perspectives regarding their students' knowledge and intellectual capabilities. A critical, empowering pedagogy can have a powerful influence on learning because when students approach their education as active agents, they begin to understand that they have a role to play in the world.

Students frequently have been overlooked as central players in school restructuring and reform efforts. If included at all, it is most often as recipients of particular policies and practices. Yet just as the redefinition of the role of teachers is crucial in developing a critical pedagogy (Cummins, 1996), so too is the redefinition of students' roles. According to Dick Corbett and Bruce Wilson (1995), this role redefinition is a 'linchpin between adult reform behavior and student success' (p. 12). Some examples of the positive influence that critical pedagogy can have on student learning follow.

Embracing 'dangerous discourses'

In their case study of teachers' responses to multicultural texts, Ellen Bigler and James Collins (1995) found that merely opening up the possibility of using a multicultural approach in schools and classrooms can pose a threat because it has the potential to unearth the deep 'silences' (Fine, 1991) that exist in schools concerning issues such as race and class. While they found that teachers in the school they studied were by and large happy to 'celebrate diversity' if it did not go too far, most of them became uneasy when the talk turned to racism or inequality. In their research, they defined 'dangerous discourses' as any discussion that challenged the accepted literary canon or that questioned underlying social ideologies. These discussions were avoided studiously by most teachers.

Paradoxically, it is precisely these 'dangerous discourses' that appeal to many students, particularly those who live daily with the realities that such discourses uncover. Encouraging these kinds of conversations is a message to students that the classrooms belong to them also because they are places where meaningful dialogue can occur around issues that are central to students' lives. And when students feel that the classrooms belong to them as well as to their teachers, they are free to learn. If teachers and students are prohibited from challenging the canon, we might well ask what education is for. As Benjamin Barber (1992) has stated cogently, 'A canon that cannot be reinvented, reformulated, and thus reacquired by a learning community fails the test of truth as well as of pertinence, and is of no use to that community' (p. 214).

[. . .]

Students transforming schools

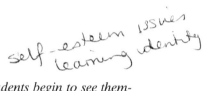

We need to remember that *learning begins when students begin to see themselves as competent, capable and worthy of learning.* One way that students begin to see themselves in this way is when their voices and perspectives are included in the transformation of schools. Including students in school transformation is especially significant in multicultural education because of the inherent student-centredness of the field. Moreover, attending to what students have to say about their experiences and listening to their suggestions can result in a more critical conception of multicultural education.

Although students have a lot to say about schools and learning, their perspectives frequently are not sought. Listening to students can reveal whether they perceive schools as responsive or unresponsive to them and why. Students' views have important implications for educational reform because their insights can prove to be important for developing meaningful, liberating and engaging educational experiences. Through this process, students can become energized and motivated about schooling. The very act of speaking about their ideas can act as a catalyst for more critical thinking about their education in general. Young people often feel encouraged by the mere fact that somebody wants to listen to them and take their views seriously. Listening seriously to students is especially important for young people whose cultures and languages are invisible in the school setting and who may feel aliented due to their cultural, racial, social, class, linguistic or other differences. Giving voice to the challenges they face in school and at home, and to the frustration of accommodating to an environment that may be hostile to their differences, can indeed be empowering for them.

In essence, educators lose a powerful opportunity to learn how schools could be better if they do not encourage the critical involvement of their students. Attending to students' questions and ideas for improving schools can reap important benefits for transforming schools. For example, how do students feel about the curriculum they must learn? What do they think about the books they read? Do they think of school as an engaging and exciting place? Are their own cultural, racial, gender and other identities important considerations for them? Although these are key questions that affect their schooling, few students have an opportunity to discuss them. Even more important, students' views are often consistent with current thinking in education: Patricia Phelan, Ann Locke Davidson and Hanh Thanh Cao (1992), in a two-year research project designed to identify students' thoughts about school, discovered that their views on teaching and learning were notably consistent with learning theory, cognitive science and the sociology of work.

Students can provide a great deal of food for thought for critical multicultural educators interested in transforming schools and classrooms. But in spite of the profound changes that can take place in the lives of students when their viewpoints are actively sought by educators, listening is not enough if it is not accompanied by profound changes in expectations of student learning and achievement. Listening to students should not be treated as a 'touchy-feely' exercise or as therapy, nor should students' views be treated as if they were always correct. Instead, their opinions and views need to be used in tandem with those of teachers and families to help make their schooling more meaningful and positive.

[. . .]

Curriculum that draws on students' experiences can energize them because it focuses precisely on those things that are most important to them. In this way, curriculum can provide what María Torres Guzmán (1992) has referred to as *cognitive empowerment*, encouraging students to become confident, active and critical thinkers who learn to think about their background experiences as important tools for further learning. [. . .]

An example of critical pedagogy in action with young children is provided by Patty Bode. Patty, an art teacher who worked with children from grades 1 through 6 when she wrote the following, reflected on her experience with a first-grade child who was concerned about unfair representation in some of the books she was reading.

A LETTER FROM KAELI

By Patty Bode

A few weeks ago, I found this letter in my message box from one of my first-grade students:

Dear !!!!!! mis Boudie

  Ples! halp. my moom was spcing to me abut wite piple leving bran and blak piple out of books.

Love Kaeli

[Please help! My mom was speaking to me about White people leaving Brown and Black people out of books.]

My response:

> *Dear Kaeli,*
>
> *Today I found your note in my message box. I was very interested to hear that you were speaking to your mom about White people leaving Brown and Black people out of books. I am glad you asked for help.*
>
> *This is a problem that we need to help each other with. We need to ask our friends and teachers and families for help so we can work together.*
>
> *I think we should work on this problem in art class. Maybe our class could design our own books which include all kinds of people of all colors, races, and all families. Maybe we could write some letters to book publishers and send them our artwork to give them some good ideas for improving their books.*
>
> *See you in art class!*
>
> *Love,*
Ms Bode

[. . .]

When Kaeli's class came to the art room, she read her letter aloud, and she showed her classmates the book that she had been reading at home which had attracted her attention to the inequalities of racial representation. It was a fairly new book, published in 1993 by a prominent publishing house, about the human body. Out of the hundreds and hundreds of pictures in the book, Kaeli counted only 22 pictures of Brown and Black people.

The students discussed why this was a problem. In their first-grade voices and 6-year-old vocabulary, they discussed 'fair' and 'unfair', 'discrimination', 'stereotypes' and more. Through their dialogue, they decided – without any prompting – that it was OK for some books to exclusively depict Black people or Brown people or White people or others if it was a story about a specific family or event. But books that claimed to be about the 'human body' or about 'people of the world' needed to be much more balanced to pass the scrupulous eye of this first-grade class.

[. . .]

Patti Bode's experience with her first-grade class reinforces that critical multicultural education need not be reserved for the college classroom, or just for classes in history or English. Even an art class for 6-year-olds is fertile ground for planting the seeds of critical thinking and social justice. Many other illustrations of critical pedagogy in action written by classroom teachers are included in publications by Rethinking Schools (Bigelow *et al.*, 1994) and the Network of Educators on the Americas (Lee, Menkart and Okazawa-Rey, 1998). In these powerful accounts, critical multicultural pedagogy is the force behind student learning, and specific curricular and pedagogical innovations that promote learning are discussed.

Summary

Critical pedagogy, empowerment and multicultural education are firmly interrelated concepts and approaches. As we have seen, multicultural education defined simply as the transmission of content is inconsistent with an approach that values critique and transformation, even if the content differs substantially from the traditional curriculum. Although changing the content of the curriculum may be a momentous shift because it represents a genuine challenge to a monolithic canon, if the new content is presented uncritically and unquestioningly, little change will occur in how students think and learn. Learning inevitably is enhanced when students are actively engaged, immersed in both the content and the context of their education.

References

Banks, C. A. M. and Banks, J. A. (1995) Equity pedagogy: an essential component of multicultural education, *Theory into Practice*, 34(3), 152-8.

Barber, B. R. (1992) *An Aristocracy of Everyone: The Politics of Education and the Future of America*, New York: Oxford University Press.

Bartolomé, L. I. (1994) Beyond the methods fetish: towards a humanizing pedagogy. *Harvard Educational Review*, 64, 173–94.

Bigelow, B., Christensen, L., Karp, S., Miner, B. and Peterson, B. (eds) (1994) *Rethinking our Classrooms: Teaching for Equity and Justice*, Milwaukee: Rethinking Schools.

Bigler, E. and Collins, J. (1995) *Dangerous Discourses: The Politics of Multicultural Literature in Community and Classroom* (Report Series 7.4), Albany: State University of New York at Albany, National Research Center on Literature Teaching and Learning.

Corbett, D. and Wilson, B. (1995) Make a difference *with*, not *for*, students: a plea to researchers and reformers, *Educational Resercher*, 24(5), 12–17.

Cummins, J. (1996) *Negotiating Identities: Education for Empowerment in a Diverse Society*, Ontario, CA: California Association for Bilingual Education.

Delgado-Gaitán, C. and Trueba, H. (1991) *Crossing Cultural Borders: Education for Immigrant Families in America*, London: Falmer Press.

Erickson, F. (1997) Culture in society and in educational practices, in J. A. Banks and C. A. M. Banks (eds), *Multicultural Education: Issues and Perspectives* (3rd edn; pp. 32–60). Boston: Allyn and Bacon.

Fine, M. (1991) *Framing Dropouts: Notes on the Politics of an Urban High School*, Albany: State University of New York Press.

Freire, P. (1970) *Pedagogy of the Oppressed*, New York: Seabury Press.

García, E. E. (1994) *Understanding and Meeting the Challenge of Student Cultural Diversity*, Boston: Houghton Mifflin.

Gibson, M. A. (1995) Perspectives on acculturation and school performance, *Focus on Diversity* (newsletter of the National Center for Research on Cultural Diversity and Second Language Learning), 5(3), 8–10.

Kreisberg, S. (1992) *Transforming Power: Domination, Empowerment, and Education*, Albany: State University of New York Press.

Lee, E., Menkart, D. and Okazawa-Rey, M. (1998) *Beyond Heroes and Holidays: A Practical Guide to K-12 Anti-racist, Multicultural Education and Staff Development*, Washington, D.C.: Network of Educators on the Americas.

Leistyna, P., Woodrum, A. and Sherblom, S. A. (eds) (1996) *Breaking Free: The Transformative Power of Critical Pedagogy* (Reprint Series No. 27), Cambridge, MA: Harvard Educational Review.

Montero-Sieburth, M. and Pérez, M. (1987) Echar palante, moving onward: the dilemmas and strategies of a bilingual teacher, *Anthropology and Education Quarterly*, 18(3), 180–9.

Olsen, L. and Mullen, N. A. (1990). *Embracing Diversity: Teachers' Voices from California's Classrooms*. San Francisco: California Tomorrow.

Phelan, P., Davidson, A. L. and Cao, H. T. (1992) Speaking up: student's perspectives on school, *Phi Delta Kappan*, 73(9), 695–704.

Ruiz, R. (1991) The empowerment of language-minority students, in C. E. Sleeter (ed.) *Empowerment through Multicultural Education* (pp. 217–27), Albany: State University of New York Press.

Shor, I. (1992) *Empowering Education: Critical Teaching for Social Change*, Chicago: University of Chicago Press.

Shor, I. and Freire, P. (1987) *A Pedagogy for Liberation: Dialogues on Transforming Education*, New York: Bergin and Garvey.

Torres-Gutzmán, M. E. (1992) Stories of hope in the midst of despair: culturally responsive education for Latino students in an alternative high school in New York City, in M. Saravia-Shore and S. F. Arvizu (eds) *Cross-cultural Literacy: Ethnographies of Communication in Multiethnic Classrooms*, 477–90, New York, Garland.

Walsh, C. E. (ed.) (1991) *Literacy as Praxis: Culture, Language, and Pedagogy*, Norwood, NJ: Ablex.

Introduction to Section 2
Pedagogic Issues

Andrew Pollard identifies and describes five themes within a socio-cultural approach to learning. Drawing on the work of Vygotsky, Piaget, Bruner and others, Pollard summarises this approach to learning as one which, 'attempts to envision the links between history, culture, language, symbols, thought, relationships, social organizations, activity, biological development, self-identity and even (if we follow Bruner) the "meaning of life"!' (Pollard, Chapter 1 this volume, p. 7). Thus a socio-cultural view of learning highlights, amongst other things, the social origin of mental functioning and the importance of self-esteem for learning. Section Two of this book attempts to develop and expand a socio-cultural view of learning by examining these issues as they are experienced in practice in primary classrooms. Throughout this section, the emphasis is on hearing and valuing the voices of practitioners and pupils as presented in a series of case studies.

Krechevsky and Seidel (forthcoming) argue that every aspect of classroom life is, in some way, constructed around what is to be learned and how teachers think children are most likely to learn. Consequently, whether teachers are able to articulate it or not, their view of learning is likely to be implicit in the way they choose to organize their classroom. Each choice a teacher makes – about the physical layout; curriculum content; the structure of assignments; the availability and use of resources; the nature of classroom interactions and relationships – reflects, to some degree, that teacher's view of learning.

Within a socio-cultural view of learning the importance of classroom interactions as an important medium of instruction and assessment is now well established (e.g. Galton, Simon and Croll, 1980; Mercer, 1995). Interaction between teachers and their pupils is seen as fundamental to both the activity of teaching and to the organization and management of the classroom. By talking to pupils and listening to what they have to say, teachers assess and support pupils' learning. Moreover, there is an implied assumption that, for pupils to be successful and make the most of the learning opportunities offered, it is important that they become active participants in the discourse of the classroom (e.g. Barnes and Todd, 1977; Kutnick and Rogers, 1994).

However, teachers wishing to develop and promote a socio-cultural view of learning face a number of tensions and dilemmas. In the context of this section of the book we will conceptualize these tensions and dilemmas as being threefold. First, recent English education policy has been founded on what Pollard (Chapter 1 this volume) has called a 'performance' model of learning which runs counter to a socio-cultural understanding of learning. Second, there are tensions inherent in applying a socio-cultural view of learning to situations in which teachers have to simultaneously meet the individual needs of large numbers of children as well as develop and foster learning in a social context. Finally, hearing and responding to the opinions of children requires a commitment to egalitarian or democratic approaches to education as well as the time and expertise to listen. This is particularly difficult in the current educational climate and when children are reluctant to speak in class (Collins, 1996).

The issues raised by the chapters in this section include:

- issues of classroom organization;
- dilemmas of balancing individual and group teaching;
- the teacher's role in classroom interactions;
- the importance of listening to pupil perceptions;
- the practicalities of working with quiet pupils.

In Chapter 5, Pam Pointon and Ruth Kershner present the views of three experienced teachers about their management of the classroom learning environment. Drawing on evidence collected as part of a larger research study, this chapter refers to teacher interviews and rating scales completed by their 9–11-year-old pupils. The findings are discussed in terms of general educational principles like pupils' involvement in decision-making, as well as in terms of the importance of specific environmental factors (notably seating arrangements and classroom wall displays). This chapter concludes by highlighting the distinct differences in the teachers' and pupils' identi-fication of significant elements of the classroom environment and the im-plications of these differences in terms of teachers' thinking and practice.

In Chapter 6, Margery D. Osborne argues that there is an inherent dilemma in constructivist teaching between serving the needs of the indi-vidual child and that of the class. In her opinion it is the tensions between individual and group needs and desires, and the tensions between domains of the child, the subject matter and the context, that makes the classroom explorations and conversations progressive and creative. She argues that such dilemmas must remain unresolved in the class. Through a story about the contributions of one particular child she examines ways in which cer-tain disruptive behaviour can be both creative and destructive. She also highlights how a child's behaviour cannot be divorced from subject matter concerns. Her aim in telling this story is to raise the issue of the connection between children's behaviour and the curriculum.

In Chapter 7, Mary Phillips Manke draws on an understanding of dis-course strategies to explore why teachers use politeness formulas and indi-rect speech acts in their communications in the classroom. She goes on to examine how these strategies relate to the structure of power relationships that teachers and students build in classrooms, and to the agenda pursued by teachers and students.

In Chapter 8, Roger Hancock and Melian Mansfield begin with the assertion that teachers should show respect for children as individuals and have regard for their ideas and opinions in the learning process. Given the possible impact of a centralized curriculum package such as the National Literacy Strategy, their rationale for teachers consulting with, and listening to children is extremely timely. Evidence drawn from a series of interviews with a group of primary age children is used to study the pupils' experiences and perceptions of the literacy hour. The children's comments are then used to demonstrate how talking with children can, and should, inform the thinking and practice of teachers.

In Chapter 9, Karen Gallas writes about silence and power in her classroom. It draws on two years of observations of, and conversations with, a 6-year-old girl called Rachel. The chapter begins with a description of the barriers that Rachel's silence placed in the way of her teacher, and her teacher's efforts to penetrate that silence. By the end of the chapter, however, Gallas argues that Rachel's silence should also be fiercely guarded. In comparison with her other work with boys she describes as 'bad', Gallas's work with Rachel provides important insights into issues of gender in the classroom. She provides an interesting view of how a position of power may be constructed and maintained.

References

Barnes, D. and Todd, F. (1977) *Communication and Learning in Small Groups*, London: Routledge and Kegan Paul.

Collins, J. (1996) *The Quiet Child*, London: Cassell.

Galton, M., Simon, B. and Croll, P. (1980) *Inside the Primary Classroom* (the ORACLE Project), London: Routledge and Kegan Paul.

Krechevsky, M. and Seidel, S. (forthcoming) 'Minds at work: applying multiple intelligences in the classroom', in J. Collins and D. Cook (eds), *Understanding Learning: Influences and Outcomes*, London: Sage.

Kutnick, P. and Rogers, C. (eds) (1994) *Groups in Schools*, London: Cassell Education.

Mercer, N. (1995) *The Guided Construction of Knowledge*, London: Multilingual Matters.

5

Organizing the Primary Classroom Environment as a Context for Learning

Pam Pointon, Ruth Kershner

This study is intended to show how three experienced teachers in three different schools undertake the process of managing the classroom learning environment, how their own views and perceptions relate to those of their pupils, and how they involve the pupils in decision-making. In broader terms it is hoped that this small study will provide insight into the way distinctive cultures develop at classroom level, and the degree to which pupils are included in this process. The focus is on teachers working with 9–11-year-old children in English primary schools.

Primary school classrooms tend to have similar characteristics: many more children than adults; child-size tables and chairs; displays on the walls; trays of pencils and rulers; paints, models and books. There are recognizable 'primary school' sounds, colours, lights and atmosphere, which allow visiting children and adults with experience of other classrooms to understand what is likely to happen and what behaviour is expected of them. This familiarity can mean that the classroom comes to be taken for granted as a context for learning and teaching. Yet every classroom is a complex and changing environment that requires creative and decisive day-to-day management by teachers.

New initiatives in education frequently have direct implications for the organization of the classroom environment and it is important to seek evidence about environmental factors that may support or impede children's learning in order to evaluate the initiative convincingly. For example, the 'Literacy Hour' introduced in English schools in September 1998 requires rapid shifts between whole-class teaching and groupwork, with associated implications for seating arrangements in the classroom (DfEE, 1998). The strategy of whole-class teaching itself has implications at school level for the organization of pupils into class groups if, as has been argued, the use of whole-class teaching methods depends for its effectiveness on a low degree of variability between the attainment levels of pupils in the class group (Prais, 1997). Further, in looking at the currently fast-moving development of learning resources, it can be seen that the increasing use of information and communications technology in school involves the physical management of hardware in the classroom as well as the use of software which can help children to find information, develop ideas and express themselves in ways which differ from the traditional uses of books and paper in school. Indeed, Crook (1994) argues that it is essential for the imagery and content of computer programs to be represented in the wider public forum and physical surroundings of classroom life (e.g. wall displays) if the use of information and communications technology is to support children's learning the way that is intended.

These three examples draw attention to the potential significance of factors like seating arrangements, pupil grouping and use of resources for effective learning and teaching, and it should be noted that within the mass of research on classrooms, there have been particular efforts to examine these specific factors, along with others like noise level (Rivlin and Weinstein, 1995) and patterns of activity (Gump, 1987). Some studies focus mainly on sensory or physical features of the classroom environment, and others on social, cognitive and emotional aspects, including the way power and autonomy are represented in the classroom rules, routines and social processes.

However, there is a difficulty of identifying conclusive research findings about the environmental factors that would promote effective learning in school, for a number of reasons:

- lack of agreement about the nature of 'effective learning' and how this may relate to the appearance of 'hard work' and concentration;
- lack of agreement about relevant factors or processes in the 'learning environment', and difficulty in understanding how they interact (for example, the factors included in different studies of classroom environments range from physical conditions and resources to social groups and relationships, curricular aims and activities, timetabling, teaching strategies, values, images, rules and routines);
- difficulty in measuring learning processes and outcomes (leading to a tendency to focus on pupils' observable behaviour, like 'time on task');
- variability in the physical aspects of school environments;
- diversity in students – their preferences and educational needs as well as personal characteristics like age and gender;
- diversity in teachers – their preferences, personal characteristics and teaching styles.

Further, at a perceptual level, it has to be recognized that it is hard to understand another person's experience of the environment, even if one can measure certain objective features. As Howe (1984) remarks,

> each person's experiences of an environment are unique and constantly subject to variation, largely because people learn from their own experiences. Many factors connected with individual development and learning, including perceptual sensitivity, personality and temperament, combine together to ensure that however uniform an environment might appear to be, people's actual experiences differ very considerably. (p. 96)

For these reasons, it is essential to find a way of carrying out research in which the perceptions, beliefs and feelings of teachers and students can be articulated and related to their perceived working preferences and their educational needs. In this way an understanding of the 'architecture' of teachers' and students' minds may be understood more clearly, especially in relation to the multiuse of classroom settings (Nelson and Sundt, 1993). This approach to research is likely to involve teachers and students in investigating their own classroom environments, and in discussing their perceptions and feelings in their own language (Tobin, 1997). It will lead to increasing understanding between teachers and students about their individual preferences and needs, but it need not lead to increasing similarity of opinion, given that learning environments should not be too 'comfortable' for students, and therefore unstimulating (Joyce and Weil, 1996).

In investigating the organization and management of the classroom environment, one of the key factors to recognize about teachers' decision-making is the immediacy and apparent intuitiveness of this process for experienced teachers. As Hargreaves (1994) argues, teachers at primary school level work in a culture 'with high sensitivity to unpredictabilities and particularities of context, to the importance of interpersonal relationships, and to the successful completion of the tasks-in-hand' (p. 104). The balance and order of classroom life needs constant maintenance, and many primary teachers have to develop explicit priorities and strategies for making the best of the classroom space as a context for teaching and learning, given the internal and external limitations of buildings, resources, social expectations and curriculum demands. Our study is intended to contribute towards developing a perspective of how experienced primary school teachers undertake this task.

Research

This study was carried out with a total of 70 9–11-year-olds and their three class teachers in two junior schools (7–11-year-olds; UK Years 3–6) and one primary school (4–11-year-olds; UK Years R–6). This age group was chosen because in the later years of the primary school, children could be expected to be more aware of and more involved in decision-making. The children have also had experience of several classrooms and class teachers by this point, and further, we wanted to keep open the possibility of following up some of the Year 6 pupils to reinterview them at the end of their first year in the new secondary school environment. The schools involved in the study are located in the centre of a small city in the south-east of England. They have similar pupil populations. The three class teachers are all experienced (i.e. teaching for over five years) and two have senior management responsibilities as deputy headteachers. The study was initiated by the authors, who work in a local higher education institution which focuses on initial teacher education. There had already been contact with the schools and teachers through the joint involvement in mentoring for student teacher placements. The teachers all had a personal interest in research and welcomed the opportunity to collaborate in this way. The planning of the project was shared with the teachers in the school year before it began.

The study took place at the end of the summer term 1997, shortly before the Year 6 children were due to move to secondary school. The teachers were interviewed at the end of a small project aimed at the investigation of their pupils' perceptions of the classroom environment. The teachers had therefore already been involved in thinking about the research topic before their own interviews. In the pupils' project we used several different research methods with the intention of providing the children with a variety of opportunities to express their views, individually and in groups. [. . .]

In this chapter, the teachers' views are the main focus although some of the children's views are included to show potentially significant points of comparison and contrast.

Common themes and issues about the decisions the teachers make in organizing the classroom environment emerged from a process of coding and grouping together statements in the teachers' interview transcripts. No attempt was made to quantify this data beyond a recognition of the expression and presence of particular views.

Findings

The findings are presented as three case studies with the common focus of all three being seating and display.

Case Study: School A

School A is a junior school and the teacher Liz has a Year 6 class of 24 pupils. The classroom was originally enclosed, with windows along one wall and a door from the corridor. It had recently been changed to include an opening in the connecting wall (about one-third of the wall size) to the neighbouring classroom. [. . .]

When it comes to making practical decisions about the classroom environment, Liz recognizes the need to take into account a number of interacting factors in arranging the classroom and grouping the children, including for example, friendship, ability levels and gender. She is conscious of the importance of flexible arrangements: 'of course you move the children around according to the activity that you are doing'.

In explaining her decisions about seating arrangements, Liz mentions behaviour management as a major aspect. She feels that the children cannot be allowed to face in any direction. Rather:

> They have to have a focal point, which just happens by the nature of my class-room to be the blackboard area. Whereas if I had a portable board I could probably move away from that.

The board emerges as a key element for her pupils too; in the written questionnaires, when children from the three schools are asked what factors in the classroom help or hinder their learning, all mentions (8) of 'the board' are positive, and all of these come from children in Liz's class. Seven other children in her class refer to the need to see the board as one of the reasons why Liz arranged the classroom like she did. One child both sees the board as a key feature in her teacher's thinking and also comments that it is a help for their learning. A total of 15 children out of Liz's class of 24 mention the board for some reason.

Yet this is not just a matter for Liz of wishing to exert control over the children:

> They have got to face in one direction, so there is a control. But you have to allow flexibility and freedom. You have got to show they can control themselves. It's not just me controlling the whole class, but 'you as an individual controlling yourself'.

The flexibility of the classroom extends to recognizing the need to take the activity into account, rather than adhering all the time to a predetermined layout. Liz says that in her classroom the tables are generally in groups but angled towards the board as a focal point. It is interesting to see that the children's preferences for seating patterns seem to match the way Liz has decided to organize the seating in the classroom. In response to the rating scale item 'It's better to have the tables in rows than in groups', a large majority (17) disagree (including seven who disagree strongly).

Liz also arranges seating with a view to capitalizing on the children's relationships with each other:

> I wanted particular grouping so they can turn inwards to themselves and gain support from each other.

She is aware that friends may distract each other, and the written questionnaires showed that the children know this too, but she points out that:

> On the sheet where I asked them to put the areas of comfort and so on (on a map of the classroom), they immediately identified their seat and the children who sat next to them as being a comfort area.

The implication may be that Liz is prepared sometimes to risk distraction for the sake of maintaining the children's positive feelings about working close to their friends. Yet from the children's interviews, we see that Liz also on occasions creates groups without regard to friendships, and this can be significant for the children's understanding of the working process, even if it is uncomfortable initially:

> Well it doesn't help sometimes when you've got different people, and you're not used to it to start with. But you soon get used to it. (Joanna, Class A)

For some children gender is particularly significant when thinking about seating arrangements and working together. In the written questionnaire, when Liz's pupils are asked what suggestions they would make to change the classroom, four out of the seven comments about changes to seating related to gender. In spite of the issues of gender and wishing to sit with friends, there is some recognition from the children that the effort to work in unfamiliar and less preferred groups can be worthwhile:

> When you're in a group you have different opinions. Rather than finding out what a couple of people think, you can find out what everyone thinks. (Laura, Class A)

> Most girls like to have a group of girls and boys like to have a group of boys. But sometimes in music maybe, some boys are good at music, and some girls are too. If you mix them together you make a good piece of music. (Emma, Class A)

In School A choice of seating is seen as very important. This might be because they are seated in groups with fewer opportunities to sit alone.

Liz has strong views about the importance of display as a key aspect of the learning environment in primary schools, as shown by her comments on what she thinks can be missing in secondary school education:

> They still need to have their work valued. They need to have their work celebrated. They still need to have information. And displays meet these various purposes. So I think the learning environment is just as important at secondary school.

She tries to help the children to understand and use displays effectively, by talking to them about the purposes, just as in developing the school policy she had talked with the teachers in order to develop a common view. In this way she is hoping that her practical decision-making in this area is open to the children and inclusive of them, based on understanding and agreement about its value. One of her pupils confirms her understanding of her teacher's approach to involving the children in decision-making about display:

> Ms B. decided what to put up, but then she'll ask us 'Do you think I should put this here, and this here?' And we'll vote sometimes, and she'll change it to what everyone likes best. (Sarah, Class A)

Liz remarks that her pupils who went to visit the local secondary school 'came back and said "The have got their work pinned up with drawing pins". They were horrified!' In this report the pupils were clearly demonstrating their awareness of their teacher's interests and preferences, which would be shared by many primary teachers in Britain.

Liz would welcome the opportunity to involve the children more fully in decisions about the classroom environment and she has seen the effectiveness of this approach in practice.

> When I was doing some advisory work I encouraged another teacher to plan her classroom with the children. She was very brave in doing this. She got the children in pairs and they designed the classroom and rearranged it, and they had to

live in it for a whole week. She found it frustrating at times, especially with the trays in the wet area . . . Then they assessed it and worked out which was the best way. The pressures of the National Curriculum wouldn't allow you to do that any more, but I think it would be a wonderful way of involving the children. I would if I had time to do it.

However, involving children in decision-making is not unproblematic. Part of the problem can be that the children need strategies to formulate and express their views effectively. [. . .]

Case Study: School B

School B is also a junior school and there are 24 pupils in David's Year 5/6 class. The 'classroom' is in an L-shaped area in an open plan school. As in the rest of the main school, people move through it to get to the next classroom area on one side or the library on the other.

David offers detailed analysis of why the seating is arranged as it is in his classroom area, making use of the unusual shape:

> Because we have got the flexibility, we have got a lot of them seated facing outwards. The L-shape of the room is quite interesting. There was a time when we had the children in fours, and it has just evolved that two are enough. There is enough furniture and enough space for them to be sensitively positioned in pairs facing outwards.

In David's view, this pattern of seating 'raises expectations of on-task performance at a stroke, and the children take it for granted'.

From the children's point of view, as expressed in the interviews, we can see that some of their beliefs about the effects of seating on their behaviour match those that David holds about expectations for concentrated individual work in that classroom layout:

> If you had four to a table, everyone would be chatting to each and everything. And if you had two to a table against the wall they wouldn't be talking to each other. (Simon, Class B)

> You work harder if you face the wall, so then other people cannot look at what we're doing. (Ben, Class B)

The rating scale confirms these views. From the item 'Sitting on your own helps you concentrate' we find that the majority of children at School B agree with this statement, though the boys seem to have stronger views than the girls about this issue. The majority of children in School A also agree with the statement 'It's better to have the tables in rows than in groups'. The six children who completed the written questionnaire all agree that David has arranged the classroom so that he could see them all. There is clearly a shared understanding between teacher and these pupils about this significant organizational decision.

David agrees that display can be very important, but mainly as a representation of the teachers and pupils involved in processes of teaching and learning in school:

> It is rather like how you dress, isn't it? It tells you something about how you are, while you are professionally engaged during the day.

He makes a point of displaying photographs involving the children in class activities, and this serves the purpose of both capturing the children's attention and helping them to see beyond the decorative aspects of displays by using intrinsically interesting and meaningful photographs and objects which make a strong impact. David emphasizes his views about the social meaning of classroom display in suggesting that the older children in a primary school welcome the contrast of a more spartan secondary school learning environment and what it represents to them about maturing:

> I think the children are a bit blase about display. They know the school is going to look nice and I have noticed when they go to visit the local secondary school they quite look forward to these bits of paper being stuck on or pinned up on a notice board, with a drawing pin saying 'Room 7 for meeting about . . . whatever', because I think that is a way of them saying 'Well all that junior stuff is gone now, we are old and grown up'. Inevitably there is a proportion who quite miss that kind of thing but neat double-mounted beautiful pictures are associated with primary schools and not secondary schools.

David's perception doesn't always match the children's perceived needs. David remarks on the children's resistance to noise during the school day:

> There is quite a lot of traffic. We are quite close to the library, so if there's a class going on in there, there is inevitably a little bit of distraction. With an open plan school there is nobody saying 'excuse me, can I come in?' I don't know whether that's a good point or a bad point. They may well go home and say 'My god, it's noisy', but to tell the truth it doesn't seen to affect them for most of the school day. So I think they build up a kind of resistance to any noise.

David believes that the children's personal characteristics can also affect not only their abilities to express themselves but also their expressed opinions:

> The thing that struck me from the questionnaires was that they are very conscious of noise. But you know, looking at who was saying that . . . some of the noisy children were very conscious of noise. So I'm not cynical about it, but I don't get very many complaints from quiet, on-task children about the same level of noise in the classroom as I get from the people who are a bit noisy.

David also notes that the physical environment of the classroom is not the most important influence on learning:

> It seems to be that the activity they are doing, or the value they perceive in doing the activity, is more important than the geography or who is sitting round the corner. I think that seems to be the crucial thing. Thus in secondary school if they are in a room which looks a bit spartan compared to the average primary school classroom, they will go ahead and do the activity if they perceive it to be of value, worthwhile or interesting.

However, David expresses concern about the introduction of self-contained mobile classrooms for some classes, and his views highlight his beliefs about the social value of the open plan environment:

> We might be in one, one day, but we don't like to keep children in there too long, and we don't like to teach in there too long. The reason is they miss out on all the good points of the team approach. You like to see people driving down the same road at the same time and you are more likely to see that if you are in the open plan, rather than disappearing into a mobile classroom, or any box classroom where you disappear at 1.15, you may not be seen again until 4 o'clock.

Case Study: School C

School C is a primary school and the teacher Diane has 22 pupils in Year 5 and 6. The classroom is enclosed, with two doors, and windows on two sides.

Groupings are central to Diane's way of thinking about the classroom, and she emphasizes the children's opportunities to choose where they sit. However, she recognizes the tensions between taking account of children's preferences in seating and arranging the classroom in a way that she thinks will facilitate appropriate learning and the social interaction that she feels they need. Diane allows the children to sample different types of seating arrangement, but in her classroom groups are intrinsic to her preferred teaching style:

> We have tried rows because they said they'd quite like it, but it's always gone back again into the group situation because of the way the work is done.

The ten children from Diane's class who were interviewed about their classroom don't hold to a common opinion about how the classroom seating should be arranged. Half of them express a desire to sit alone, while the others prefer to sit with friends. Their views about sitting with other children are mixed:

> Sometimes they help you because you can confer with them. (Helen, Class C)

> I find it better because I am not sitting next to my friends so I can concentrate more. I never believed that before. I thought you would concentrate more when you are sitting next to your friends but I didn't. (Adam, Class C)

> I would like to be in a group sometimes, but if you wanted to be alone because you were getting a headache from so much talking, then you could go and just be alone, and if you get lonely then you could just go back to the group. (John, Class C)

In seeking to resolve the tensions in classroom organization, given the varying demands of the curriculum, Diane observes that it is important also to take account of the children's individual needs:

> The children come from such different environments. They have got to make their mark on the school environment, and that may be the pictures on the walls or it may be something they've written under the table. I had one child who put

drawing pins into his chair so he knew that was his chair. He couldn't see the drawing pins, they were underneath, but if he did not have that chair he got into a terrible state, and he went round and looked at all the chairs until he got his one back. It's like that when they put their labels on their drawers. That makes it theirs. That sort of mark I think is much more important than anything else.

Just as Liz accepts the children's 'comfort areas', Diane appreciates the emotional aspects of classroom life. Some children need to establish their own place in the classroom and she observes this process without interfering.

Diane also sees display as a focus for the social/emotional aspects of learning. However, Diane thinks that a teacher has to focus the children's attention in the right direction in order for them to use the information in displays as part of their learning:

I'm still not sure how much children notice things. You actually have to often direct the children's attention to the displays, otherwise they don't see them. They may when they come in one morning and see a new display say 'Oh, there's my picture', but that's about it.

She also notices differences in the children's levels of tidiness and appreciation of its importance:

Yet there were certain children who thought that tidiness was of vital importance and their desk trays would be tidy and immaculate. Whereas other ones, and quite often the more creative and able, thought differently.

Diane also notes that the physical environment of the classroom is not the most important influence on learning, as long as the children feel basically secure and comfortable:

I think if it's an environment where the children are happy to come into then that's the important thing . . . It is how the children are encouraged to learn that is more important than what is actually in the room.

There are mixed messages here. Diane says that she was prompted to discuss 'tidiness' with the children after she read their comments on the written questionnaires. She is interested that the children express the dilemmas and conflicting priorities that she recognizes in her own mixed feelings about the management of resources in the classroom.

Diane also believes that although:

The majority of the children are still not able to make very sensible decisions . . . I hope they feel that we respect them, and if we respect them then we will listen to anything they have to say that they think is important.

Yet she also now sees the possibility of involving the children more explicitly from the start of a new year:

Having done this project I will talk a bit more with them at the beginning of the year than I would have done before, and actually ask them how they want things changed – let's try it out.

All three teachers refer to the constant changing nature of primary classrooms as environments for learning with the associated implications for organization. The three teachers also make a number of observations about their pupils' individual needs and preferences, sometimes with apparent surprise but always with acceptance of their diversity. The teachers think carefully about certain aspects of the sensory and physical environment; and there are some non-physical aspects of classroom experience which teachers also see as important (relating to learning purposes/objectives, for example). There are some (usually hidden) assumptions about power and autonomy in both the teachers' and pupils' responses which affect their participation in decision-making.

Discussion

There are some differences in the teachers' decision-making about the classroom environment which seem to relate to pedagogic style. In explaining his decisions about seating arrangements David focuses on behaviour management as a major aspect. Liz also identifies behaviour management as important but also highlights social factors whilst Diane emphasises security and comfort. Whilst all three teachers think displays important as a focus for the social/emotional aspects of learning, Liz in particular emphasizes their importance for cognitive learning.

Regarding the children's involvement in classroom organization, although all three teachers feel that they want to – and do – involve the pupils in different ways, the extent to which the pupils can become involved is limited to certain factors. Whilst the teachers do not usually consult the pupils about noise levels, for example, they do involve the children much more in decisions about the decorative environment. The teachers involve the children in making decisions about the classroom environment in different ways. David says that in his experience 'the children are happy for you to take decisions about the classroom'. However, his expectation is that the children can rearrange things 'on the hoof' as necessary. Diane questions the children's ability to make sensible decisions, though she emphasizes the importance of listening to their views. Liz directly involves the children in decisions about displays and would welcome the opportunity to involve the children more in decisions about the physical environment, but feels constrained by time factors.

Evidence of the match and mismatch between teachers and children regarding certain aspects of the classroom environment raises interesting points which may reflect the teachers' ability to draw on their educational principles and take a broader long-term view, while the children tend to be more concerned with managing their learning in the 'here and now'. There are certain areas of match and mismatch about specific aspects of the classroom environment. In School B teacher and children match in relation to the management of resources and seating arrangements but they mismatch over sensory elements of the learning environment (e.g. noise).

In contrast to what many of the children are saying David would not want to 'add walls' to the teaching area. He values the easy contact with staff colleagues which is facilitated by the open-plan setting, and he has developed his own strategies for coping with the disadvantages which are identified by the children. In School A teacher and children have similar opinions about the visual and seating organizational elements but in this classroom the 'gap' in the wall is differently perceived by them. Again Liz has developed her strategies for tuning out the intrusive noise, and she is looking forward to further developing staff collaboration when the wall is removed to create one large classroom (though this is a response to financial constraints on class groupings).

We can see, therefore, that both teachers differ from their pupils in their use of certain coping strategies and in their broader view of professional roles as members of the whole school staff team. One of the most interesting points arising from our study, however, is the evidence from the teachers that the research process itself helped them understand more about children's views and consider issues which had not been explicitly examined before.

Does a match between teacher and pupils always result in more effective teaching and learning? Does mismatch inevitably lead to tension? There may be important differences between a teacher's assessment of a good classroom for teaching in, and a pupil's view of what is a good classroom to learn in. Our study did not explore these issues in detail but further research would usefully focus on a more elaborated account of teachers' and children's views about the best type of environment for teaching and learning.

This research also raises questions about the relationship between perceived needs and individual preferences for teaching and learning environments. The desire for a tidier classroom, for example, may indicate an emotional preference or recognition of an important influence on an individual's learning. It is not entirely clear how these are related. However, always accommodating children's preferences may not be beneficial; it may be desirable to encourage children to learn in a different way and go against preferences and familiar habits (Joyce and Weil, 1996). The key issue here is one of negotiation between teacher and children. Teachers need to be more explicit about decisions made and they need to extend children's strategies for expressing their own opinions. For informed decision-making, children need to explore 'how they learn best'. Children don't all learn in the same way, there are differences in respect to age, gender, culture and learning style. The vast amount of current literature on 'differentiation' reflects this at a professional level (e.g. see Bearne, 1996).

The process of negotiation itself warrants further investigation. Delamont (1983) analyses classroom processes using the framework of symbolic interactionism and discusses the ways in which the participants negotiate a shared world and act towards it. She argues that the classroom processes can only be understood in their context, i.e. studying their location in time and space and comprehending the organizational and educational background in which they are embedded. Woods (1990) further explores the concept of negotiation and dynamic power relations which exist between teachers and pupils and he notes that often the parties to negotiation have different interests. Although an earlier study (Nash, 1976) observes that many of the expectations pupils have implicitly recognize a passive conception of their role, more recent investigations (Pollard *et al.*, 1994) indicate pupils would like more control in classrooms, though they don't really expect to get it. Their awareness of teacher control and power was considerable: 'pupils recognised constraints but preferred autonomy; recognised teachers' rights to impose requirements but preferred negotiation' (p. 192).

Conclusion

We found some common themes in the small study of teachers' thinking and decision-making about the classroom environment. To a large extent there was apparent agreement about educational principles: the importance of organizing the classroom in a way which develops children's autonomy; the influence of social and behaviour management concerns on decision-making about seating; the ways in which children are allowed choice about certain elements of the classroom environment but not others. However, we have found differences with respect to the teachers' strategies for putting principles into practice, and the particular role and value they and the children place on certain elements in the classroom environment, e.g. display.

For some aspects there appears to be a distinctive class response which echoes the philosophy of their teacher, in others there are important areas of difference. There are also significant individual differences between pupils within each class (Kershner and Pointon, 1999).

This study of three teachers' views is an example of exploratory qualitative research into classroom processes which examines the participants' beliefs and perceptions in detail. The advantage of this approach is that the views expressed are contextualized in classroom settings rather than presented as generalized abstract principles. This type of research, together with other case examples, can extend the body of knowledge about classroom environments in a way that reflects the real significance of the views of different teachers and pupils working in specific classroom contexts. There is also a suggestion from the study that involvement in school-based research projects of this type may in itself help teachers to gain additional insight into their own principles and their pupils' varying perceptions and beliefs. There is a need for further research into the ways in which teachers create classroom environments which help children to learn most effectively (taking account of individual difference). This could usefully focus not only on specific factors like displays, seating arrangements, and access to resources, but also on the dynamic processes by which a classroom culture may develop and the implications of this process for children's learning and social development.

References

Bearne, E. (1996) *Differentiation and Diversity in the Primary School*, London: Routledge.

Crook, C. (1994) *Computers and the Collaborative Experience of Learning*, London: Routledge.

DfEE. (1998) *The National Literacy Strategy: Framework for Teaching*, London: Department for Education and Employment.

Delamont, S. (1983) *Interaction in the Classroom*, London: Methuen.

Gump, P. V. (1987) School and classroom environments, in D. Stokols and I. Altman (eds), *Handbook of Environmental Psychology*, Vol. 1, New York: Wiley (ch. 18).

Hargreaves, A. (1994) *Changing Teachers, Changing Times: Teachers' Work and Culture in the Postmodern Age*, London: Cassell.

Howe, M. J. A. (1984) *A Teachers' Guide to the Psychology of Learning*, Oxford: Blackwell.

Joyce, B. and Weil, M. (1996) *Models of Teaching* (5th edn), Boston: Allyn and Bacon (ch. 24).

Kershner, R. and Pointon, P. (1999) Children's views on the primary classroom as an environment for working and learning (submitted for publication).

Nash, R. (1976) *Teacher Expectation and Pupil*, London: Routledge and Kegan Paul.

Nelson, D. and Sundt, J. (1993) Changing the architecture of teachers' minds, *Children's Environments*, 10(2), 159–69.

Pollard, A., Broadfoot, P., Croll, P., Osborn, M. and Abbott, D. (1994) *Changing English Primary Schools? The Impact of the Educational Reform Act at Key Stage One*, London: Cassell.

Prais, S. J. (1997) Whole-class teaching, school-readiness and pupils' mathematical attainments, *Oxford Review of Education*, 23(3), 275–90.

Rivlin, L. G. and Weinstein, C. S. (1995) Educational issues, school settings and environmental psychology, in C. Spencer (ed.), *Readings in Environmental Psychology: The Child's Environment*, London: Academic Press.

Tobin, K. (1997) Alternative perspectives on authentic learning environments in elementary science, *International Journal of Educational Research* (Special Edition: C. J. McRobbie and C. D. Ellett (eds), *Advances in Research on Educational Learning Environments* (ch. 4), 27(4), 303–10.

Woods, P. (1990) *The Happiest Days. How Pupils Cope with School*, London: Falmer Press.

6

Balancing Individual and the Group: a Dilemma for the Constructivist Teacher

Margery D. Osborne

In this chapter I will argue that there is an inherent dilemma in constructivist teaching between serving the needs of the individual child and that of the class. As a teacher I am fundamentally concerned with the learning of each child. But by being committed to social constructivist learning processes in my classroom (Prawat, 1989; Driver *et al.*, 1994) I am equally concerned with the actions of the group. These two concerns are mutually dependent upon one another. The things that a group does, their new ideas and directions, are determined by the contributions of individuals. Enabling individuals to contribute to their fullest implies that I must balance controlling children's actions and the outcomes of those actions while enabling free, open-ended exploration and expression.

There is an increasing body of literature in educational studies in which practising teachers examine issues in teaching using stories told from their own experience (Paley, 1979, 1981, 1992; Lampert, 1985; Lensmire, 1994; Ball, 1993a, 1993b, 1993c). This approach has the advantage of telling tales of teaching which capture the complexity of teaching. Teaching involves acting within multiple domains concerning the child, the subject matter and the context simultaneously (Kerr, 1981; Shulman, 1986). Often acting within one domain causes conflicts with others (Ball, 1993b; Lensmire, 1993). In the story that follows I explore such a conflict.

I present an argument in this chapter for why such dilemmas must remain unresolved in the class. It is the tensions between individual and group needs and desires, and the tensions between domains of the child, the subject matter and the context, that makes the classroom explorations and subsequent conversations about the science progressive and creative. I will present the body of this argument through an examination of a story of the classroom, a story which illustrates the role of the individual in a group in the constructivist classroom and the role of the teacher in balancing this dilemma.

This is a story about how the contributions of a particular child affect the entire class. The story concerns behaviour: how certain disruptive

68

behaviour can be both creative and destructive, how a child's behaviour cannot be divorced from subject matter concerns. In choosing in this story to tolerate or punish a child's behaviour, I, as teacher, affect both the one child, the whole group and what we are doing in the subject matter.

This story is also about my thinking about this child, his behaviour and about my goals for the classroom as a whole. My goal in telling this story is to raise the issue of the connection between children's behaviour and the curriculum. I wish to argue from the perspective of the teacher that issues of classroom 'management' are tied to those of curriculum and that to 'manage' a classroom so that behavioural problems disappear might have unwanted repercussions for curriculum. Such an observation is not new. McNeil (1988) and others (Waller, 1932; Cusick, 1973) have noted that teachers can sacrifice controversial content in order to maintain classroom control. What I am arguing is that in choosing to teach in ways that engage the children imaginatively and emotionally, one *invites* behavioural 'problems'. In doing so I create an unresolvable dilemma – there are some behaviours I cannot tolerate.

Recent writing on the dilemmas of teaching have emphasized that these are inherent, unresolvable and endemic (Lampert, 1985; Ball, 1993a). They arise from the competing demands and uncertainties within which a teacher works (Dewey, 1902; Lortie, 1975; Jackson, 1986; Shulman, 1987). Teachers are responsible to multiple masters arising from the domains – learner, subject matter, context – of which Shulman and Dewey speak. Often these demands are at odds. As Lampert and Ball point out, the teacher 'brings many contradictory aims to each instance of her work, and the resolution of their dissonance cannot be neat or simple' (Lampert, 1985, p. 181). Rather, Lampert argues, the teacher ends up 'juggling' these multiple demands, never permanently resolving dilemmas in one direction or another. Thus, instead of advocating a solution to the dilemma I raise between imposing disciplined social behaviour and permitting freedom of behaviour (and hence ideas) in the science we are learning, I wish to use this story to muse on the creative potential in maintaining the tension inherent in such a dilemma.

The Context

This story is constructed from data I gathered during the course of a three-year study (1990–93). During this time, I taught science in a public elementary school which serves primarily the children of married students at Michigan State University. (In this chapter, I have given all the children pseudonyms which preserve as much as possible an indication of their culture.) The classes in which I worked were a first grade, a first- and second-grade combination and a third grade. These classes each had approximately 20 children. Classes took place three times a week and ran from an hour to an hour and a half in length. Usually half an hour was given to whole class discussion of ideas and findings. The data I used to write this story are from transcripts of audio-tapes – (I audio-taped each class and transcribed the tapes myself. I also kept copies of most of the children's written work. The children were always aware of the audio-taping going on and quite interested in what I was doing. The children periodically requested that they listen to the tapes and would comment upon them. The children also knew that I was writing about my teaching in the classes and using the classroom discussions in these writings.)

These classroom discussions were usually teacher centred – I determined who would talk and usually what about. To do this I required the children to raise their hands and be recognized by me before they could speak. Often a child gave a semi-formal presentation of an idea or of some item and then the procedure was that they controlled the conversation, again semi-formally – children who wanted to ask questions or make comments raised their hands and were recognized by the speaker. Classroom discussions in the first and first–second grade combination usually occurred in a 'learning circle' – the children and I would sit in a circle at the front of the room. These discussions almost always, though, became conversations in which the children directly addressed each other rather than waiting for my recognition to talk. These free conversations were punctuated by my taking the control back and choosing who would talk. So discussions would usually start with me posing a question or asking for a description, calling on a number of children until this pattern broke down into a freer discussion. I would allow this discussion to go on for a few minutes and then I would stop conversation and return to my initial pattern of calling on people.

Cory

I had a child in my second-grade science class I had also had in first grade so he and I knew each other pretty well. I'm going to call him Cory. Cory was a bit of a problem. He was a very active and energetic 8-year-old boy. He was fun and funny, emotionally sensitive and selfish, creative and destructive. He was fearless physically, and in his interactions with others. He was a leader – others loved to be around him (including me). He was easily bored, but when his attention was caught, he would work at something for hours and his enthusiasm for what he was doing was contagious. He could handle more than one occupation at a time, including, but not limited to, carrying on a science discussion with me and the whole class, different private conversations with children sitting next to him, kicking the person across from him and playing with something (anything) in his desk. Turning your back on him could be quite dangerous: at one moment, he would be carefully and precisely measuring the height of the plants that his science group was growing and conversing about growth differences with other children; at the next moment, he was demonstrating karate kicks at the back of the room.

Let me give an example. During the year that he and I were in first grade, I taught a unit on scientific theory-making, focusing on dinosaurs. As part of this unit, the class examined various sources of information about dinosaurs and prehistoric life. These included trade books presenting 'factual material' about dinosaurs and fictional material in which scientific ideas were interwoven with fantasy. I wanted the class to think about and discuss what they thought might be real in these books and what was not. Most particularly, I wanted the class to think hard about why they thought these things might be real.

We started by talking about the movie, *The Land Before Time* (Spielberg *et al.*, 1988), which the children had just viewed. I asked the children what they thought were real or stretched truths about dinosaurs in that movie. The children said things like, 'Dinosaurs are real', and 'They did lay eggs'. But Claire, a little girl in the class, disagreed with this generalization. 'Only some laid eggs', she claimed. Each time they said these things I challenged their statements: 'How do you know that, though?' Finally, Tatyana responded to one of my questions: 'Um, in *The Land Before Time*, fairy tales were real'. Many in the class vigorously disagree.

> *Teacher*: Fairy tales were real in *The Land Before Time* . . . Is that what you just said?
> *Maria Theresa*: But magic wasn't real.
> *Teacher*: You don't think magic was real?
> *Bulli*: Magic was real.
> *Teacher*: Magic was real? [Lots of talking and debating starts up.] What do people think about what Tatyana just said? I think that was an interesting comment and Maria Theresa doesn't agree with her. Tatyana said that in *The Land Before Time*, fairy tales were real and Maria Theresa says that even in *The Land Before Time* magic wasn't real. What do people think about that?

Kyong Min says that she doesn't while others continue to agree with Maria Theresa. Finally Cory says that he thinks that some magic was real. I press him, asking what magic he thought was real.

> *Cory*: People coming alive! There are, um, if we weren't there, then who would be? We were magic because . . . there was nobody in the world and there's nobody in the world if no people were there and it's got [to be] . . . it was magic 'cause some people came alive?
> *Teacher*: Ahhh, you mean because there became people . . . there weren't people in the old days and then there were people so therefore there had to be magic?
> *Cory*: Yeah . . . yeah . . .

Cory is speculating on the origins of man; how can there be people when there weren't people to begin with? His comment is insightful and imaginative. It indicates the degree to which Cory engages in the spirit of the science we are exploring. It is really interesting and exciting to me when children talk about their awareness, their contemplations, and their attempts at sense-making of mysterious things. This perception and appreciation of the mysterious is part of what causes people to become scientists, writers, poets.

Missing from the narrative, though, is that just before this exchange I had disciplined Cory twice for disrupting the conversation by imitating the fierceness of Tyrannosaurus Rex. When Tatyana made her comment about magic, Cory was one of the loudest in disagreeing with her. This was especially problematic because it had personal overtones and edged on disrespect of a person's (Tatyana's) genuinely expressed ideas – something that I won't tolerate. I had to specifically ask Cory to stop yelling at this point in the class. Fifteen minutes after this excerpt, I sent Cory to the principal's office, again for disrupting the class.

We had started discussing whether or not dinosaurs take care of their young. The children seemed inclined to think that they did but I challenged this assumption, reminding them that some other animals did not. Quite a lively debate started up concerning crocodiles, turtles and various birds, all of whom lay eggs but not all of whom care for their young. At the mention of crocodiles Cory and Chen began to giggle and imitate scenes from the movie *Crocodile Dundee* (1985). In general, I am willing to tolerate quite a lot of side conversations as long as they are not disruptive because I find that often important ideas come out of them. I asked the two children to stop when Cory stood and shot Chen across the room with his finger. Not only did this seem disruptive to me but I also find this sort of play personally repellent. Cory, though, continued an undercurrent of his conversation with Chen throughout the following discussion.

I introduced a theory to the class:

> I'll tell you a theory that I heard. And this is complicated so you have to listen close. What I heard is that different dinosaurs are different. Some dinosaurs take care of their babies and some dinosaurs don't. And what I heard, which I think is very interesting, I have heard that the big dinosaurs like brontosaurus or tyrannosaurus . . . [Kojo interrupts to correct me, 'Tyrannosaurus *Rex*!'] . . . Tyrannosaurus Rex, those guys, the great big dinosaurs, they were the ones that took care of their babies.

This statement catches everybody's attention.

> I'll tell you why . . . oh, and the little dinosaurs didn't take care of their babies . . . and I'll tell you why. This is the theory that I've heard. I'm not saying that it is true or not. I'm just telling you what I've heard. I heard that all dinosaurs, *all dinosaurs*, whether they were great big dinosaurs as big as buildings or just little tiny dinosaurs, *all dinosaurs*, had about the same size babies. So even if it was a brontosaurus baby, it was this big. [I hold my hands up about eight inches apart.] And even if it was just a little tiny dinosaur it was still about this big. The babies were about the same size. And so because great big dinosaurs, they were born this size, they had to grow up to be great big dinosaurs, the parents took care of them a lot longer. That's what I've heard. What do you think of that?

I turn and make a face at Cory who is once again talking to Chen. The children start debating my idea.

Tatyana says that it should be the other way around. That little dinosaurs should take care of their babies because they'll be more likely to die and big dinosaurs don't need to worry about it.

> *Cory*: Uh, I disagree! The little dinosaurs can just take care of their selves. But the big dinosaurs, they take care of their babies. But I know why the little dinosaurs don't . . . because the big dinosaurs, if they find them, they'll eat them. So that's why they go and hide and leave their babies there.
> *Teacher*: Oh, because it's more dangerous for them because they might be eaten? Huh, that's pretty interesting.

Cory has just made another very interesting new extension to the logic of our argument. Tatyana, though, argues back,

> The big dinosaur doesn't, the big dinosaur really cares about their babies 'cause the big dinosaur hides them in the cave not to be dead and the medium ones don't care about the babies they are really kind of big but they think that they are small, that's why they don't care about their babies until they grow.

Kojo also disagrees with Cory. 'Um, I wanted to say that one of you guys are wrong, one of you are wrong. I think Cory's all wrong. Quite a few dinosaurs don't take very good care of their babies.' I asked him why he thought that. Kojo replied, 'Because they leave their babies to look for food, then something might happen. They might be in danger, tyrannosaurus might kill everything!' Then Chen speaks, agreeing that dinosaurs might have to leave their babies to fend for themselves in order to avoid predators. This might be temporary though – they might still return at times to care for their young.

> *Chen*: They take care of the babies. They have to run away from the other dinosaurs that will kill them.
> *Tatyana*: I disagree!
> *Cory*: I disagree!

Well, now Chen and Cory were arguing in the class discussion as well as carrying on their other discussion about *Crocodile Dundee*. I asked the two boys to quiet down, to sit down, and when I saw Cory shooting Chen with his finger again, I finally sent him to the office to call his parents (an arrangement that the school had made at the last parent-teacher conference). 'Cory, go to the office and call your dad, that's one too many times that you've done that, go,' I started to summarize the various arguments because I wanted other children in the class to be able to respond. [. . .] But without Cory to respond and participate, adding his innovative ideas which so often stimulated others' thoughts, the discussion felt empty and petered out.

A Teacher Comments

Cory is very insightful, observant and knowledgeable about the way things work. He is curious and enthusiastic. He is happy to talk and I love and need for him to talk in my class – he says really helpful and stimulating things that the others hear and we use to challenge ideas and move our discussions along to new things. But in order for that to happen he has to speak when it's appropriate: when other children are ready to hear. He is speaking not just for himself but also for the sake of others. To get him to do this I have to walk a fine line allowing him to misbehave so that I don't squash him and disciplining him into talking and acting only when I want him to. This is very hard and very obvious to me with Cory because he is so ebullient but I think that the same tension between being an individual and being a member of a group is true for every person in the class. For example, the quiet children – are they really participating in their heads or are they someplace else? In this sort of environment in teaching, where I am dependent upon children taking a chance and thinking out loud, I can't force participation for when a child does speak, they are speaking as an individual and they have gone public with their individuality. This requires a lot of trust. I have to wait for that trust to develop because it's a trust in self as well as a trust in others.

In thinking, writing, teaching in this manner, I am developing my own critical consciousness; becoming aware of some of my own moral and ethical choices because they are confronted by instances of this paradox of the individual and the group in my teaching. What I tolerate from Cory and what I don't allow become conscious choices because reacting to his bad behaviour can have such negative effects on the curriculum, the teaching and the learning of that class. But, conversely, I need to suppress some of Cory's behaviour so that he can participate in a group, hear and understand the things that others contribute. This is not an argument to resolve that paradox of the individual in the group. Asking Cory to leave the classroom did momentarily resolve the paradox but that meant the end of a very good discussion. We all lost when I did this.

Restraining Cory, containing him, giving him free rein – these are all continuous tensions in my class. Cory is an extremely important part of my science instruction. The insights that he gives me and his peers in science are invaluable as is his contagious participation in various tasks. Teaching him to 'act correctly' in class is a paradox. Do I mean for him to be 'on task', doing things I tell him to, do his work as a part of a group, or be his ebullient, individualistic self? Both components are important both for him, individually, and for the whole of the class.

Discussion

My goal in teaching is constructivist in nature – that the children explore the science together and construct meaning through conversation with each other and with the teacher (Hawkins, 1974a; Osborne and Wittrock, 1985; Duckworth, 1987). In my ideal *we*, as a class, construct a community focused by our study of science. At the core of such a community are people talking together about shared questions, profiting from differences and similarities (Schwab, 1976). This is the essence of a community –

people interacting with each other for a purpose, out of a need for the unique contributions that only other members can make (Sartre 1963, Bellah *et al.*, 1985). Such a community is vital: it can grow, change, shift focus and direction. It is bound together by members' similarities and differences. The individuals' uniqueness and their capacity to work within a group are both necessary to the workings of this type of class.

In teaching science in a socially constructed manner I am dependent upon the ideas and the creativity of each child. New thoughts and directions come from the children, as well as from me. Each child must feel comfortable and free to pursue their ideas and to express them to the group. Maintaining both facets of the classroom environment – where children can act as individuals but also as part of a group is at times contradictory and always filled with tension for the teacher. It is the differences in perspective which constitute individuality *shared* that drive the development of a community – the children share their ideas about the science, both learning from each other and from the process of sharing. This depends upon the children acting as individuals in formulating their concepts and in speaking them. It is also dependent upon the individual's ability to act as a member of a group. The individuals *need* the group for the development of their ideas.

In such a classroom the roles children take on – how they act and interact – must be self-generated. Likewise the science that we do, the questions and the form those questions take, are also emergent. The applicant of predefined roles and the careful structuring of tasks for effective group practice (Cohen, 1986; Noddings, 1989) do not fit. The comfort (for the teacher) of the discipline imposed by such arrangements is unavailable. Rather the teacher is left with the nebulous desire to impose certain ways of behaving and trying to guide the content of interactions in more powerful directions.

I argue that the classroom community is shaped both by the ways that I encourage the children to interact with each other (respect for each other and each other's ideas) and by the children's engagement with the science. Both are intertwined and interdependent. There is an idealistic way of thinking that tends to emphasize the latter – that it is the sense of shared purpose in the subject matter that enables the construction of ways of interacting. This is not entirely true; the community of the clsssroom is dynamic, its purposes and focuses shift and reshape themselves as our explorations evolve. The constant is the way I wish the children would interact with each other. Because I ask the children to act in a certain way (and they usually comply), the focus of the community can change without the community dissolving. The children value each other and so they value expressions of new ideas. These ideas become new purposes for both individuals and the group as more and more children explore them. But this goes in the other direction also – because the community reflects differences as well as similarities it is beset by centripetal as well as centrifugal forces. The teacher must act to balance the two.

Joseph Schwab has commented upon the centripetal and centrifugal forces which shape the classroom. In his paper 'Education and the state: learning community' (1976) he talks about the role of the home and of the school in moral education. The role of the home is to represent differences in ideas, beliefs and moral choices. The role of the school is to represent the choices of the larger community. The latter is what allows the individuals within a community to live together. The former enables the collective to grow and change, and not stagnate within one world-view. As he (Schwab, 1976, p. 243) writes:

> The two together, however – centripetal school, centrifugal homes – should give us neither a dangerous homogeneity nor the divisiveness and faction threatened by exclusive hegemony of differing homes. Home balanced by school would yield diversity of perspectives and propensities toward action. School balanced by home would yield appreciation of the uses and advantages of diversity and would confer communication and collaboration among the diverse. A communicating, collaborative diversity of perspectives and propensities would yield satisfactions in the very acts of communication and collaboration, as well as material advantages perceptible to those involved. Such satisfactions and advantages are the essential nutrients of community.

These two forces and their analogous sources are present within a classroom. The beliefs of each individual are different from another's and act centrifugally. The consensual behaviour and beliefs of the classroom as a group, whether imposed by me or achieved organically, bind the individuals together. The two forces enable the children to live together – there is some set of agreed upon foundations for action and communication – and enable both the individual and the group to change ideas, directions and even norms of behaviour. The classroom becomes a community because the centripetal qualities of the individual and the centrifugal qualities of a group are respected and allowed to bear fruit.

There is a central role in this for conflict between class members. New ideas and explanations are not automatically accepted and celebrated. Rather the group must be convinced of their superiority. Children make statements of their beliefs and ideas. These can be accepted as they are, accepted for consideration, or immediately argued against by others who hold different views with equal certainty. The community in this class is, I think, characterized by children entering imaginatively, intellectually, empathetically into one another's conceptions of the world. This is done in order to understand each other. This thinking becomes critical and then creative (Belenky *et al.*, 1986). The progression of such thinking becomes increasingly revisionary.

For children to consider ideas other than their own, for them to change their ideas – modify them with the ideas of others – their own sense of certainty must be affected by our conversations. Because each child has to try to recognize and maybe understand the other's argument in order to argue against it, certainty is recast as uncertainty (Dewey, 1939; Wittgenstein, 1969; Vygotsky, 1978; Billig, 1987). This is an important quality of my community. It is an illustration of how I try to use conflict to strengthen the community, strengthen the need that people with different ideas and opinions feel for each other. When certainty can be recast as uncertainty, the children can value their differences. This is a community based upon differences between people as much as on likeness. But this conflict is difficult to control. It must be expressed in ways which still communicate respect. It must be done in ways that don't violate our valuing for each other. Although my desire is that conflict shall result in a strengthened community it can still potentially divide the community and possibly destroy it.

The teacher as well as the children are members of a community. A community contains people who share some goals, purposes, values, ways of acting and communicating, but not others. I participate in the development of the science both as a member of the class and as a person standing apart, looking from the outside. I share in some of the children's pursuits but I also have other goals which they do not share, that they are the subject of, not participants in developing. The basis of a community is similarity on one or more dimensions – without similarity a community would not exist, could not function. The children and I must share some interests for my claim to be a member of the community to be valid. On some level the science we are doing is new to me. The connections we make are different from ones I have made before. The driving force, however, the life force behind a community is difference – we need each other because we are different from each other. I wouldn't have these new connections without the stimulus of the children. They wouldn't have them without my active shaping of our tasks and approaches to those tasks.

When we act in a community, we act on an assumption of similarity but often our actions expose our differences. For example when the children talk they bring to the surface each other's different ideas and goals in the science. When they talk I often become aware of my more fundamental values which I haven't explicitly shared with the children around their discourse and behaviour. This exposure motivates change, in ourselves as we learn from this and in the community as its members evolve. I personally come to question many of my values around the children's interactions. The children question their scientific ideas. This process is fundamental to my classroom. All of this depends on expressions of conflict – our recognitions that many of our ideas and values are in conflict, are not shared.

Communities are defined by the relationships between people and these are constructed through a medium. Through this medium these relationships develop a reason for being (Sartre, 1963; Hawkins, 1974b). In my classroom, this medium is the pursuit of the science. A community is composed of people who are different and the same simultaneously. Similarities are recognized and/or constructed by developing a common language and ways of doing things framed by the medium, the science. This process is driven by a shared purpose. The essence of community is people interacting with each other because each can contribute something different and unique towards a common purpose, towards fulfilling a mutual need.

I have up to now been talking about a conflict in my classroom between children over their ideas about the science. A second and equally fundamental conflict is between myself and the children. My value choices around how the children should act and interact as well as about the science arise from my own history and background both conscious and unconscious. The children are not blank slates either, lacking values or scientific knowledge and understanding.

There is a conflict between how I think people should act and how the children assume they should act. This is conditioned by the fact that we are both in the setting of the school. We inherit roles and relationship expectations that we didn't create, a conflict not of our making. This is heightened, I would argue, because during our classes it is hard for me to interrupt conversations or the children's activities to make explicit the qualities of their behaviour that I think are acceptable or not. To make such interruptions would be in a sense a violation of the community, a statement about myself as a non-member. I am often unwilling to do this because I do view myself as a member of the community and I believe that my authority to shape both science and behaviour comes from this membership as well as my memberships in other outside communities.

We often have conversations, divorced and temporally disconnected from our actual engagement in science, about 'proper' behaviour. These conversations are different from those about behaviour when we actually have become immersed in the science or our conversations. I think that in the heat of our activities and interchanges it is all too easy for the children and myself to act on our unstated assumptions and desires about how we might like to behave and because these assumptions are unstated the conflict doesn't become articulated, talked about. It remains a struggle beneath the surface. This is how learning and change occur on both sides (myself and the children's).

As I have said, it is because of this discordance between what different individuals want or between what an individual wants and a group demands that I, and others, come to re-examine our values as we become aware of them. Part of this process of evaluation is to measure the worth of our values within a new context generated by this subterranean conflict between people who are, as yet, not abstracted from that context (Heidegger, 1962; Habermas, 1991). If the struggle was explicit, on the surface and divorced from context, sooner or later an apparent resolution would be reached and the problem would appear to disappear, but the point is that if the community is to remain alive and vital, it can't and shouldn't be allowed to reach a resolution.

The role of the teacher is in fact to maintain the tension of this struggle in such a way that it doesn't become resolved. One force cannot be permitted to dominate over another. The teacher should do this in such a manner that the struggle between forces, the conflicts within a class, remain both a progressive force and a creative one in learning. This role presents a number of ethical dilemmas for the teacher – how to construct experiences so that all children can participate and contribute, how to reward both individual and group actions, how to maintain control in a classroom where freedom is also of great importance.

The argument I present in this chapter recasts the goal of classroom management. Rather than thinking of the goal of management as avoiding conflicts between children and between children and teacher, it becomes one of managing those conflicts, even fostering them at times. I am asking that the tensions inherent in such conflict be embraced for their creative potential. The source of new and interesting ideas and ways of behaving in the subject matter are within the conflicts between individual beliefs and desires and behavioural norms of the class as a whole. [. . .]

I would argue, pre-service teachers should be taught the creative potential of conflict and how to work with such conflict to help students develop critical thinking skills as well as imagination and originality. All three of these classroom goals – critical thinking, imagination and originality – arise as an interplay between individuals thinking on their own and individuals participating in a group with consensual ideas about the way things ought to be.

All of this places teachers at the centre of an unresolvable dilemma – balancing both the needs of the individual and of the group. Serving one side or the other causes both sides to lose. In my story of Cory, both Cory and the group are dependent upon one another. Cory's individualism could not be allowed to run rampant, however, but neither could the norms of the group with their rules for 'proper behaviour' be allowed to suppress him. Rather, ideally his individualism should be allowed to enhance the thinking of the group and the group should help him to discipline his thinking in such a way that he becomes more thoughtful both about the science and about himself. Trying to balance these two competing demands when working with children is not easy. In a social constructivist classroom it proves an inherent dilemma.

References

Ball, D. L. (1993a) With an eye on the mathematical horizon: dilemmas of teaching elementary school mathematics, *Elementary School Journal*, 93(4), 373–97.

Ball, D. L. (1993b) Moral and intellectual, personal and professional: restitching practice, in M. Buchmann and R. E. Floden (eds), *Detachment and Concern: Topics in the Philosophy of Teaching and Teacher Education* (New York: Teachers College Press), 193–204.

Ball, D. L. (1993c) Halves pieces and twoths: constructing representational contexts in teaching fractions, in T. P. Carpenter (ed.), *Rational Numbers* (New York: Erlbaum), 157–95.

Belenky, M. F., Clinchy, B. M., Goldberger, N. R. and Tarule, J. M. (1986) *Women's Ways of Knowing: The Development of Self, Voice, and Mind* (New York: Basic Books).

Bellah, R. N., Madsen, R., Sullivan, W. M., Swidler, A. and Tipton, S. M. (1985) *Habits of The Heart: Individualism and Commitment in American Life* (New York: Harper and Row).

Billig, M. (1987) *Arguing and Thinking: A Rhetorical Approach to Social Psychology* (Cambridge: Cambridge University Press).

Cohen, E. (1986) *Designing Groupwork: Strategies for the Heterogeneous Classroom* (New York: Teachers College Press).

Cusick, P. (1973) *Inside High School: The Student's World* (New York: Holt, Rinehart and Winston).

Dewey, J. (1902) *The Child and the Curriculum* (Chicago: University of Chicago Press).

Dewey, J. (1939) *Democracy and Education* (New York: Free Press).

Driver, R., Asoko, H., Leach, J., Mortimer, E. and Scott, P. (1994) Constructing scientific knowledge in the classroom, *Educational Researcher*, 23(7), 5–12.

Duckworth, E. (1987) *The Having of Wonderful Ideas and Other Essays on Teaching and Learning* (New York: Teachers College Press).

Habermas, J. (1991) *Moral Consciousness and Communicative Action* (Cambridge, MA: MIT Press).

Hawkins, D. (1974a) Messing around with science, in D. A. Hawkins, *The Informed Vision: Essays on Learning and Human Nature* (New York: Agathon Press), 63–75.

Hawkins, D. (1974b) I, thou and it, in D. A. Hawkins, *The Informed Vision: Essays on Learning and Human Nature* (New York: Agathon Press), 48–62.

Heidegger, M. (1962) *Being and Time* (New York: Harper).

Jackson, P. W. (1986) *The Practice of Teaching* (New York: Teachers College Press).

Kerr, D. H. (1981) The structure of quality in teaching, in J. Soltis (ed.), *Philosophy and Education*, 80th Yearbook, Part 1, of the National Society for the Study of Education (Chicago: University of Chicago Press), 61–93.

Lampert, M. (1985) How do teachers manage to teach? Perspectives on problems in practice, *Harvard Educational Review*, 55(2), 178–94.

Lensmire, T. J. (1993) Following the child, socioanalysis, and threats to community: teacher response to children's texts, *Curriculum Inquiry*, 23(3), 265–99.

Lensmire, T. (1994) *When Children Write* (New York: Teachers College Press).

Lortie, D. (1975) *Schoolteacher: A Sociological Study* (Chicago: University of Chicago Press).

McNeil, L. (1988) *Contradictions of Control: School Structure and School Knowledge* (New York: Routledge).

Noddings, N. (1989) Theoretical and practical concerns about small groups in mathematics, *Elementary School Journal*, 89(5), 607–23.

Osborne, R. and Wittrock, M. (1985) The generative model and its implications for science education, *Studies in Science Education*, 12(1), 59–87.

Paley, V. G. (1979) *White Teacher* (Cambridge, MA: Harvard University Press).

Paley, V. G. (1981) *Wally's Stories* (Cambridge, MA: Harvard University Press).

Paley, V. G. (1992) *You Can't Say You Can't Play* (Cambridge, MA: Harvard University Press).

Prawat, R. S. (1989) Promoting access to knowledge, strategy, and disposition in students: a research synthesis, *Review of Educational Research*, 59(1), 1–41.

Sartre, J. P. (1963) *In Search of a Method* (New York: Vintage Books).

Schwab, J. J. (1976) Education and the state: learning community, in *Great Ideas Today 1976* (Chicago: Encyclopaedia Britannica), 234–71.

Shulman, L. S. (1986) Those who understand: knowledge growth in teaching, *Educational Researcher*, 15(2), 4–14.

Shulman, L. S. (1987) Knowledge and teaching: foundations of the new reform, *Harvard Educational Review*, 57(1), 1–22.

Spielberg, S., Lucas, G., Kennedy, K. and Marshall, F. (1988) *The Land Before Time*, Universal Pictures.

Vygotsky, L. (1978) *Mind in Society: The Development of Higher Psychological Processes* (Cambridge, MA: Harvard University Press).

Waller, W. W. (1932) *The Sociology of Teaching* (New York: Wiley).

Wittgenstein, L. (1969) *On Certainty* (New York: Harper and Row).

7

'Sally, Would You Like to Sit Down?' How Teachers Use Politeness and Indirect Discourse

Mary Phillips Manke

'Sally, would you like to sit down?' If Sally is a visitor in my home or office, I might ask this as a genuine question, or at least a suggestion. Sally might answer that she'd rather stand and admire the view from the window, or that she'd been sitting for hours in the car and would prefer to stay on her feet for a while.

But suppose that Sally is a student, and I am a teacher, and I say 'Sally, would you like to sit down?' The most likely interpretation of what I have said is a direct command, 'Sit down, Sally'. The most likely result is that Sally will take a seat.

White (1989) pointed out that 'unrelenting politeness' is an 'institutionalized presence' in American public schools. Yet, as he said, everyone recognizes what lies behind the politeness – the institutionalized authority of teachers. Rare is the classroom where teachers and students have built power relationships in which a student need not attend to a command or request from a teacher (see Swidler, 1979, for descriptions of free schools where such rare classrooms existed). So what is going on when teachers who mean 'Sit down', say 'Would you like to sit down?' or 'Please, will you sit down', or even, 'I would like to get started' – yet children respond to what seem to be polite requests or neutral statements as though they were in fact commands? Why do my observations from three elementary classrooms in three different schools contain so many instances of teachers' contributing to the construction of power relations, not in overt or obviously authoritarian ways, but in ways that seem to soften the edges of their claims to control student actions? Why do teachers make such heavy use of politeness formulas and indirect discourse strategies as they further the colluded-on agenda of co-operation in learning?

The question of when, how, and why speakers use language in ways that do not convey lexical meaning has been a focus of sociolinguistic study. Its examination has taken place in the following sequence: Searle (1966) developed the concept of *indirect speech acts*, which may have an apparent meaning quite different from their actual force in the conversation; Grice (1975) suggested that when someone makes a statement whose real meaning is different from its surface meaning, there is a reason, an intention, behind the discrepancy; and Brown and Levinson (1978) hypothesized that the principal reason for using politeness formulas is to avoid threatening the 'face', or personal dignity, of other participants, and that they are used more often by weaker participants than by stronger.

In this chapter, I ask why teachers use these discourse strategies, and how they are related to the structure of power relationships that teachers and students build in classrooms, and to the agendas pursued by teachers and students.

Indirect Discourse Strategies

The term *discourse strategies* as used here is derived from Mishler's (1972) discussion of the effects on classroom relationships and learning of teachers' decisions about how to speak to students. He used the term to refer to a variety of choices a teacher might make about what to say and how to say it, and to the patterns of such choices that become apparent. He spoke of both direct and indirect discourse strategies chosen by teachers; interestingly, his analysis indicated that indirect strategies were a mark of superior teaching.

Delpit (1988) and others have suggested that this is a culturally based assumption that leads to miscommunication, adopting the widespread belief that use of such formulas and strategies is a characteristic of White American culture, and that students of colour do not understand that they are being told what to do when a teacher uses them. These writers suggest that in the homes of children from various minority groups, adults address children very directly, and that nonminority teachers confuse them when they use indirect discourse to express their wishes.

McDermott and Roth (1978), however, held that people placed in cross-cultural groups quickly learn to understand what others are communicating, or to comprehend the expectations of others, as they jointly construct a context for interaction. When 'communication problems' persist, they have another source besides misunderstanding. Specifically, they described an incident in which a classroom power relationship was being constructed. They found a child violating three established norms of his classroom (he touched the teacher on the buttock, called her by her last name without a prefix, and interrupted her as she worked with a small group), norms that, at other times, the child revealed he knew. As a result of these actions, he succeeded in getting the teacher to scold another student with whom he had been arguing. It is in the detailed analysis of the three unusual actions of the boy that McDermott and Roth found the interactions that create and construct the context, the social order. Seeing the success of the boy's actions in attaining his goal, they rejected the idea that his 'inappropriate' actions came from culturally based ignorance of classroom norms; he had in fact used them very skilfully.

Whether or not it is true that the use of politeness formulas and indirect discourse strategies are associated with good or effective teaching, each of the teachers I observed used both direct and indirect strategies, though in varying proportions.

Teachers choose discourse strategies of indirection when, instead of stating or telling directly what they want, they speak to their students in a more oblique way. These strategies included the following:

- using politeness formulas (these forms of speech are discussed in more detail below);
- using speech acts whose surface meaning was not the same as their meaning in the interaction;
- placing themselves with the class, rather than underlining their status as teacher (one way of doing this was using the pronoun *we*, rather than *you* or *I*; Brown and Levinson [1978] named this as a face-saving strategy);
- praising desired behaviour rather than criticizing undesired behaviour;
- stating general principles of behaviour, rather than scolding or giving commands;
- asking for student opinions about process decisions;
- correcting student behaviour unobtrusively, by a touch or silent gesture, rather than by giving a command;
- offering many choices to students (but always from a range of possibilities that they themselves had selected and approved).

Two of these strategies were used by all the teachers during my observations; they were politeness formulas and speech acts whose surface meaning was not the same as their meanings in the interaction. These strategies are described generally, with examples from all the teachers. The use of the other strategies differed among the four teachers (three classroom teachers and the student teacher), so they are discussed in the individual contexts where they appeared.

Politeness formulas

Politeness formulas used by the teachers included:

- questions in place of commands: 'Sally, would you like to sit down?' in place of 'Sit down, Sally';
- mentions in place of commands: 'Sally, your desk is messy', in place of 'Sally, clean up your desk';
- statements of preference in place of commands: 'It's really better if desks are tidy', in place of 'Clean up your desks';

- requests that use *please*, *thank you*, *excuse me*, and similar words, or are expressed conditionally (using modals like *would* or *could*) in place of commands: 'Please sit down', or 'Could you sit down?' in place of 'Sit down'.

The teachers I observed consistently used these polite forms in their speech to students, much more often than they gave direct commands. Yet, they seemed to expect that students would comply with polite requests without question, and were surprised or displeased if they did not do so.

Here are some examples of teachers using politeness formulas. They are taken from field notes and videotapes:

In a group discussion time, one of Ms Kaminski's students was speaking, but a number of other students were chattering.

> *Ms Kaminski:* Please do him the favour of listening to him. [meaning: be quiet]

> *Ms Anderson:* All right, boys and girls, will you open up your assignment notebook? [meaning, open your notebook].

The children are seated in a circle on the rug. Ms. Kaminski is showing them an ABC book. The page they are looking at has the word BARN in large letters to represent the letter B. Someone says, 'ABC'. One of the students who can read, says loudly:

> *Nick:* It's not BC. It's BA.

> *Ms Kaminski:* Nick, could you please use a gentle voice, because it's the main job of people in the first grade to try, and it's hard to try if people yell at you when you are trying.

> *Ms Anderson:* It's really better if I hear just one voice. [meaning, be quiet].

Indirect speech acts

In all three classrooms, I also saw teachers use speech acts whose surface meaning was not the same as their meaning in the interaction. A classic example of this occurs when two people are in a room: One says, 'I'm cold', and the other rises and shuts the window. 'I'm cold' can be interpreted as having meant, 'Shut the window'. Here are some examples of such speech acts; first, four ways of saying, 'Be quiet':

> *Ms Kaminski:* I have two children who need to work on their listening. [meaning, you two be quiet].

> *Ms Corvo:* I need your help. [meaning, be quiet].

> *Ms Anderson:* I wonder if you can hear Patel – he's got some good ideas. [meaning, be quiet].

> *Ms Bridgestone:* Excuse me. [meaning, be quiet].

When these strategies were used, it was not always completely clear to me, an outsider, whether choices were being offered to the students, or whether they had to comply regardless of how the teacher's wishes were expressed. My judgement on this question was based on the students' responses, believing that as regular participants in the power relations of their classroom, they were the experts on what the teacher 'really meant' (McDermott and Roth, 1978). Two incidents from Ms Kaminski's room illustrate how the students' responses clarified the teacher's meaning for me:

Carlton is sitting directly in front of a child who is having a reading turn when the students are gathered on the rug.

> *Ms Kaminski:* Carlton, why are you sitting in front of him? [meaning, move over, Carlton].

Carlton moves over.

> *Ms Kaminski:* Than you very much. [Her thank you confirms that he has complied with her concealed command].

The students are gathered on the rug.

> *Ms Kaminski:* Noah, you have something in your hand. Would you look at it and see what you need to do? [meaning, get rid of what you are holding].

Noah looks at his hand, leaves the rug, and puts whatever it is in the bin. (Obviously, he has understood her meaning.)

I noticed considerable variation among the four teachers in their use of other kinds of indirect discourse strategies and in their willingness to use more direct strategies. Because of this variation, the next sections emphasize the particular strategies and choices of each teacher in turn. It was especially interesting that Aileen Corvo and Courtney Bridgestone, working with the same group of children, often on the same day, were quite different in their choices. In some cases, there was an opportunity for the teachers to give reasons for the variations in their practice that I observed. When these explanations were available, I have included them.

Sunny Kaminski, the teacher in the first-grade classroom, selected discourse strategies that covered a range from highly direct to extremely indirect. She quite consistently shifted between direct statements of expectations for students' actions and indirect statements about the learning activities they should engage in. She seemed to prefer making more direct contributions to classroom power relationships in the realm of student behaviour and less direct ones in that of student learning.

Here are some of her direct statements concerning student behaviour:

> *Ms Kaminski:* Carlton, sit on your bottom.

> *Ms Kaminski:* Erin, stay here. Don't get up.

Yet, sometimes there was room for indirection, or even negotiation, in interactions related to student behaviour. As these examples imply, this was more common when interactions were close to the 'border' between behaviour and learning.

The students are gathered on the rug while Ms Kaminski reads a story to them. When she finishes the story, she says:

> Tell you what. If you would come over here and choose a book and then find someplace in the room to read it it would be just great.

On this morning, a monarch butterfly is emerging from its chrysalis in a terrarium. During readers' workshop, Carlton has become deeply involved in watching this process. When Ms Kaminski calls the children to the rug, he is very unwilling to come. She calls him several times without response, and then says:

> *Ms Kaminski:* Give me five minutes with these kids and at snack time we'll look at it, I promise. And you can tell me what you saw.

Carlton comes reluctantly to the rug and sits down.

Ms Kaminski often used the indirect discourse strategy of stating general principles of behaviour rather than criticizing the behaviour of a particular child. In the instance that follows, she could have tried to find out who had broken Charles's jet and punished that person. Instead, she waited until all the children were gathered and spoke to them generally about what had happened.

During clean-up, Charles discovers that someone has broken his jet [which he made earlier from plasticene]. He asks again and again:

> Am I allowed to fix it?

Finally the aide says he can do it later, and he goes to sit on the rug, looking distressed. He has not helped clean up.

Once the children are gathered on the rug, Ms Kaminski tells them that someone is unhappy because somebody messed up his work. She says that this really upsets people, and suggests what the children can do when they are finished cleaning up so they won't wander around breaking people's things.

The choice of this indirect discourse strategy had a number of benefits from Ms Kaminski's point of view. She was able to bring Charles' problem to the other students' attention and show respect for his distress without developing the kind of adversarial situation between herself and the students that would contravene the colluded-on agenda of co-operation. Also, because Charles' distress was potentially disruptive to the clean-up process that she wants to support, she was able to avoid giving him strong encouragement for his behaviour by making him the centre of class attention. And she has avoided the potentially unsuccessful process of finding out who is responsible for a misdeed that neither she nor Charles saw happening.

Ms Kaminski made many statements offering the students a choice with respect to their learning activities. In an interview, she said she encouraged students to negotiate with her to carry out their own choices. She told of a time three children approached her during reading workshop, when her stated expectation is that children will be involved in reading. These three children asked that they be allowed to write, pointing out that when they were writing they were reading the words that they wrote. She said she thought this was wonderful, and told them in a typical phrase to 'go for it!'

The next instance illustrates well the cautious indirection with which she approached issues around the children's work. She wanted to offer the students choices, but she also had quite specific intentions for them. One day I heard her seeking a delicate balance between the two impulses:

It is time for writers' workshop, and Noah, Jane, Janet and Pearl are working at one of the tables. At the moment, none of them is writing; all are drawing. One of the aims that Ms Kaminski has at writers' workshop time [she said in interviews and in statements to the class] is to encourage these first-graders to actually begin to write, using invented spellings, and often captioning or commenting on drawings they have made. Ms Kaminski comes up to the table and squats down next to Pearl.

> *Ms Kaminski:* What are you doing here? What's your topic?
> *Pearl:* My friend.
> *Ms Kaminski:* Your friend. So you like to draw first when you write?
> *Pearl:* Yes.
> *Ms Kaminski:* Do you ever write words with your drawing?

Ms Kaminski's choice of the word *topic* here is part of an indirect discourse strategy through which she suggests that writing is a preferred activity. Children's drawings are not usually thought of as having topics; pieces of writing have topics. Similarly, the question, 'So you like to draw first when you write?' has an indirect meaning; it implies that writing will take place, even if after drawing. Pearl could draw and not write at all, but that is not what Ms Kaminski wants her to do. In the final sentence of the text, Ms Kaminski uses a question ('Do you ever write words with your drawing?') rather than stating a rule, such as 'We write words at writer's workshop time', or giving a command like, 'Write, don't just draw'.

Aileen Corvo, the supervising teacher in the fifth-grade classroom, used far fewer indirect discourse strategies with students than the other teachers. It is hard to be sure to what extent this contrast was a matter of style or philosophy, or was a more temporary result of the negative experience she said she had with her class of low-achieving students between September and March, when my observations began. Clearly, she was at this time far less committed than the other teachers to the colluded-on agenda of co-operation and courtesy.

Ms Corvo used strategies that asserted her power directly, minimized student power, and separated her relationally from her students. She made little attempt to conceal her view of herself as the most powerful person in the classroom. For example:

Ms Corvo goes to the front of the room and calls for attention.

> *Ms Corvo*: I don't have you with me and I can't function if I don't have you with
> me and I don't have control. I [she taps her chest audibly] must have control.

Ms Corvo stands in the front of the room, ready to begin the lesson.

> *Ms Corvo*: Give me your attention. That's right, your undivided attention – only
> on me, the Golden Girl. [aside to Ms Bridgestone, the student teacher:] I love
> that show. I need your attention and I'm not waiting much longer.

Ms Corvo is telling the class what to do next.

> *Ms Corvo*: Peter, none of you are talking while I am. Peter, I am an important
> person.

Ms Corvo used pronouns designating her own separateness from the group of students, as well as asserting her ownership of classroom supplies and naming the purpose of an activity as 'providing her with information about what students know' (rather than, perhaps, 'giving students opportunities to learn').

Ms Corvo: If *you* play with *my* rulers I'll have to take them from you.

Ms Corvo is introducing a lesson in which the class is to make 'story frames' concerning the novel they are reading. This is an activity they have done before for other novels.

> *Ms Corvo*: What skills do the story frames show me you have?

She used vigorous control statements and even threats to assert her own position of power:

A student returns from the bathroom and replaces the large wooden key which serves as a bathroom pass on its hook. Lewis stands up while Ms Corvo is at the front of the room talking and picks up the key, apparently heading for the bathroom.

> *Ms Corvo*: (sounding furious) Excuse me sir, how dare you? I am teaching a
> lesson. You know my rule.

She takes the key from Lewis and bangs it down on the table next to her.

Ms Corvo has opened the morning with a lecture on proper behaviour in the halls. Students, she says, are not to yell back and forth or speak rudely to teachers.

> *Ms Corvo*: You know I'm crazy enough so you don't try it with me. Just try
> loudcapping me and you'll hear Mean Joe Greene. Don't try it with me. [Later,
> she said in an interview that the reason for the lecture was that Donald, one of
> the students in the class, was rude to her in the hall on the previous day.]

Yet, there are still instances in my observations of Ms Corvo using politeness formulas and indirect disclosure strategies. Even for her, the colluded-on agenda was still in place at times:

> *Ms Corvo*: Let's not call out.

Some of the students are talking.

> *Ms Corvo*: No one is talking. [meaning, be quiet].

Courtney Bridgestone used a number of indirect discourse strategies as she worked with the children. Her personal style in the classroom was quiet, cool, almost self-effacing, and the colluded-on agenda seemed natural to her. She typically placed herself *with* the class through the discourse strategies she employed; she used indirect statements in asserting control over the class; her speech suggested that she and the class were working together, and that the class had important contributions to make to that work. For example, she often chose to use the pronoun *we* in place of *I* or *you*:

The class is in the midst of a discussion and has become quite noisy.

> *Ms Bridgestone*: I can't hear you when you all speak at once. OK, let's not call out so we can hear each person.

She openly took the students' opinions into consideration when making process decisions:

They are doing the practice tests for the Iowa Test of Basic Skills.

> *Student*: Can we go ahead to do the rest of the problems?
> *Ms Bridgestone*: Hmmm, yes, do the whole page. That makes sense to me.

Ms Bridgestone chose a number of other strategies that placed her with the group. For instance, she used humour quite frequently, laughing with the students at the jokes she made:

In reading the novel [*The Cybil War* (Byars, 1981)] they have come to a part in which the fifth graders in the story find a magazine on an older sisters' bed. The magazine is open to a 'love test', which they decide to take.

> *Ms Bridgestone*: Now listen to this, guys. You can find out if you're in lo-o-ove.

Students and teacher laugh together.

She sometimes called for a reading turn as if she were one of the students:

> *Ms Bridgestone*: Let me read a minute [. . .], let me read.

On occasion she asked for their help and even expressed admiration for their possession of skills she did not have:

Darin has made a cover for a story he has written and has lettered the title using glitter and glue. He has done a very neat job. Ms Bridgestone praises him:

> *Ms Bridgestone*: I could never have done it that well. I have trouble with the glue.

Ms Bridgestone sometimes defined assignments in terms of what the students would gain from them, rather than simply stating that they had to be done. For example, she told them that the purpose of one assignment they were doing was to help develop their self-confidence as they read by proving to them that they were able to figure out the meaning of words from their context.

When she stated a rule, it was often as a class norm or general principle, rather than as a command of her own:

At the end of one day's reading, Ms Bridgestone passes out slips of paper on which each student is to write a sentence of 25 words or less to add to the 'Simon Newton Sad, Sad Sentences Collection' [mentioned in the novel they are reading]. The response to this is fairly silly and Ms Bridgestone has trouble keeping a straight face about it herself. When the students start reading their sentences aloud, the first sad sentence read is, 'I came to school and I saw Marlon' [a student in the class]. The students find this extremely funny. Ms Bridgestone scolds them in these terms:

> *Ms Bridgestone*: That kind of thing is not appreciated in this room and laughing when someone says something mean is not appreciated either.

Ms Bridgestone also had other strategies for promoting the public agenda of co-operation by controlling children's behaviour silently and unobtrusively, while allowing the flow of classroom interchange to continue uninterrupted. Sometimes she simply moved to stand next to an offending student, or touched a student lightly on the head or shoulders as a reminder to be quiet or to turn around:

> Marlon is wiggling and is half out of his seat. He sits in the front row, so Ms Bridgestone can simply reach down and touch his shoulder without moving from her place. He sits all the way down in his seat at her touch.

Except for one doubtful instance . . . I never saw a class member who seemed to be confused by her indirect discourse strategies. It would be easy to think that using direct discourse strategies is simply better, more effective communication than using indirection; direct strategies might reduce confusion. However, the lack of evidence to support that idea – and the frequent use of indirection in ordinary communication – suggests that people are accustomed to using and understanding such speech acts. In fact, it would seem that in their use and acceptance of these patterns, students and teacher were colluding on the agenda of co-operation and courtesy.

About two years before I began to observe her classroom, Sue Anderson had made a conscious decision to do what she called 'turn over some of the control of her classroom to her students'. She consistently used this phrase to describe what she was doing, and reflected on the personal benefits she was reaping from the decision.

Many of the mechanisms for this transfer of control had become a routine part of life in her classroom. One was her use of what she called 'positive language', which in most cases seemed to mean what I have called indirect discourse strategies, although it also included replacing direct criticism of students and their work with 'finding something positive to say'. In addition to frequent use of the politeness formulas and indirect statements previously discussed, she often told the students how she was feeling about what was going on in the classroom, wanting them to respond to her statement either by continuing their desirable behaviour or by changing their undesirable behaviour:

When Vincent starts to read there is a buzz of talk going on in the circle of children.

Ms Anderson: Excuse me, Vincent, may I interrupt?

She turns to William and Kevin, who were among those talking.

Ms Anderson: Boys, it's really hard for me to listen over here (she gestures toward Vincent) when there's noise over there.

The noise stops.

Like Ms Bridgestone, she used the pronoun *we* to place herself with the class, rather than in opposition to it:

Ms Anderson: What we need is one hundred per cent attention up here.

Because she had explicitly stated to the students her goal of sharing control of the classroom, Ms Anderson made statements in the classroom about this sharing process:

Ms Anderson: I don't know who to pick [for the next turn], so I'll turn the responsibility over to Damon . . . Damon, anyone whose hand is up.

Nevertheless, this was a classroom where the majority of decisions about what learning activities to do when and how to do them were in the hands of the teacher. It was quite different from Ms Kaminski's classroom, where the teacher believed that choosing what to do enhanced children's learning, and where a workshop atmosphere was encouraged. Unlike Ms Kaminski, who was more likely to use direct statements with respect to behaviour and indirect statements with respect to learning, Ms Anderson was more often direct about learning than about behaviour. Here, she is giving an assignment:

Ms Anderson: Now, I want you to get out your notes from watching the video and make a list. Write down at least twelve birds or animals that we might see when we visit the marsh next week.

There's nothing indirect about that.

Some common threads stand out in what has already been said about teachers' use of indirect discourse strategies.

Every teacher used indirect discourse strategies and politeness formulas. There were many areas of differences among these teachers: their personal styles; their beliefs about whether, when, and to what extent students should have choices in the classroom; the degree of their commitment to the public agenda of co-operation; the frequency and contexts of their use of the indirect and direct strategies. Yet, each one did include indirect strategies and politeness formulas in her repertoire during the observations. I might even say that in all the classrooms I have visited in the course of my work, this is universal. I haven't yet seen a teacher who is always direct.

There was little or no indication that the use of indirect discourse strategies was confusing to children. The idea that children were colluding with teachers in this agenda of co-operation was supported by the observation that children, regardless of their ethnicity, most often correctly interpreted the indirect strategies their teachers used, and responded to them as the teacher seemed to wish. This observation reinforces McDermott and Roth's (1978) contention that miscommunication is not a problem in classrooms – even cross-cultural classrooms, while countering the contention of Delpit (1988) and others that politeness formulas and indirect discourse strategies serve to confuse children who are not from the majority White culture.

Indirect discourse strategies were often used when the choice of response they implied was not intended to be, or could not possibly be, offered to the students. A clear example of such a situation in Ms Kaminski's classroom follows:

The children are gathered on the rug for a sharing time; each has brought a book to read during the preceding readers' workshop.

Ms Kaminski: Oh-oh, the gym teacher will be here soon.

[From her tone and facial expression, I conclude that she has just realized that there is not enough time for very many children to share an entire book.]

Ms Kaminski: Tell you what – why don't you just find your favourite page in your book? [meaning, you can only share one page of your book].

Clearly the constraints of time preclude Ms Kaminski from actually offering the choice of letting each child share his or her entire book. If they should treat her indirect command as open to question, rather than as being polite, she would have to refuse their choice.

The kinds of situation in which indirect discourse strategies were used varied among the teachers. For two of them, Ms Kaminski and to some extent Ms Bridgestone, it was possible to see that indirect discourse strategies were more likely to be chosen in the area of children's learning activities, as opposed to the area of their behaviour. Each of these teachers was more likely to use a direct statement or command to control children's behaviour; indirect strategies appeared more often in the area of choices about learning. Ms Corvo, who rarely used indirect discourse strategy, seemed not to favour them in either area. Ms Anderson used such strategies more often in the area of behaviour and less often in that of learning. It seems likely that this reflects each teacher's beliefs about teaching and learning. Ms Kaminski stated clearly (in interviews) that she thought children learn best when they have choices about what to learn, so she tried to use discourse strategies that would not seem to impinge on the children's ability to choose. Ms Anderson, on the other hand, believed that children should be able to choose more freely in the area of interpersonal actions, although she said (in an interview) that she was 'not ready' to turn over to them many choices about what to learn.

There was an element of concealment in the use of the indirect strategies. Although students were offered, or appeared to be offered, choices, the teacher was fully in control of the range of choices available. This was most true for Ms Kaminski, who believed that having choices would lead to more learning for the children. She stated strongly in interviews that she felt intensely responsible for students' learning and that her moves in this area were more carefully planned than those in the area of student behaviour. She remarked that she regularly offered choices to students in the area of learning, but it was obvious that these were always choices between actions that were desirable from her point of view, and she said she believed that students learn better when they have the opportunity to choose.

Children did sometimes refuse to accept the polite or indirect discourse that was being offered to them and instead required the teacher to make a more direct statement. In this way, they forced the teacher's agenda to the surface so they could oppose it and prevented the teacher from maintaining the pretence that what was going on was co-operation and mutual politeness. [. . .]

Up to this point, I have tried to lay out what I saw, and what sense I made of it, but the questions I raised at the beginning of this chapter remain elusive. Why is it that teachers use indirect discourse strategies? Why do teachers choose to hide their agenda for children's learning behind the public agenda of co-operation and politeness? Why do teachers, who are supported in their contributions to building classroom power relationships by many of the institutional regularities of the school, seek to soften the edges of that power? Why do teachers make such heavy use of politeness formulas and discourse strategies as they further the colluded-on agenda of co-operation in learning?

According to Brown and Levinson (1978), politeness formulas are used to protect the 'face', or public self-respect, of the listener. If the speaker is in a position of authority over the listener, saying 'please' or using the conditional makes it less obvious that a command is being given to a person who is required to obey. Inversely, if the speaker is subordinate to the listener, using politeness conceals the fact that the speaker is telling the superior what to do.

This understanding of teachers' motivations is echoed by White (1989), who said: 'Thus, persons higher in status often treat persons lower in status with deference to ease the constraints of their inequity and to encourage a more free-flowing interaction and exchange of ideas . . . [The teacher] uses deference to reduce the social difference between her and her pupils' (p. 303). Such an analysis could suggest that teachers use politeness formulas because of their desire to protect the self-esteem of their students. These formulas allow them to avoid a continual emphasis on the strong contribution to the development of power relations that they make as teachers, adults, and possessors of greater knowledge. They might do this either because they wanted to preserve that self-esteem or because they wisely did not want to subdue students' thinking or provoke them to the point of rebellion.

A more subtle version of this analysis, as outlined by Cazden (1988), suggests that teachers do not feel so superior to their students, but in fact live in fear of an outbreak of student opposition, and use politeness formulas to steer clear of confrontations that they fear they may lose. Cazden recounted an incident in which she approached a student very cautiously, much concerned about his possible loss of face, but discovered with surprise that he was ready to be far more compliant than she expected.

Similarly, Courtney Bridgestone (a heavy user of indirect discourse strategies) discussed in an interview her concern that the children in Ms Corvo's classroom, who reminded her of the ones who had bullied her when she had attended the very same school as a junior high school student, would refuse to obey her. She described how careful she tried to be to avoid provoking such incidents and to handle them well on the few occasions when they occurred.

This analysis could also reflect, not the fearfulness of teachers, but their sense that time wasted on putting down student rebellion is time lost from learning. Thus, the motivation for the use of indirect discourse strategies could circle back to the teachers' agenda of controlling student behaviour in the interest of student learning. Sunny Kaminski and Sue Anderson talked about their belief that children do best when they have choices. I understood them to mean that the process of choosing was itself educational, that students show increased commitment to learning activities they have chosen themselves, and that they learn even from their errors, or 'approximations', as Ms Kaminski liked to call them.

Yet, a parallel interpretation could be that student choice is more efficient than teacher imposition – efficient in producing student learning. An alternative analysis could show that time on-task and seriousness of effort were increased by such teacher behaviours as offering choices and using indirect discourse strategies.

If this analysis were adopted, then the public agenda of co-operation and politeness (McDermott and Tylbor, 1986) that I have hypothesized would disappear, revealed as only a manifestation of the teacher's own agenda of maximum student learning. And students could quite simply be seen as either collaborating with the teacher's agenda, possibly because they had discovered that commitment to learning was one way to have 'an interesting day' (Fraatz, 1987, p. 31) or, at other times, promoting their own agenda of freedom from adult control.

My sense is that this last analysis is oversimplified, reducing complex classroom interactions beyond their lowest terms. Even the most reflective teachers, like Ms Kaminski and Ms Anderson, are not planning the smallest details of their daily actions to lead to a single, unified goal. Yet the point remains, the same point made by Mishler (1972), that indirect discourse strategies may be a sign of good teaching.

References

Brown, P. and Levinson, S. (1978) Universals in language usage: politeness phenomena, in E. Goody (ed.), *Questions and Politeness: Strategies in Social Interaction* (pp. 56–289), Cambridge: Cambridge University Press.

Byars, B. (1981) *The Cybil War*, New York: Viking.

Cazden, C. (1988) *Classroom Discourse: The Language of Teaching and Learning*, Portsmouth, NH: Heinemann.

Delpit, L. (1988) The silenced dialogue: power and pedagogy in educating other people's children, *Harvard Educational Review*, 38, 280–98.

Fraatz, J. (1987) *The Politics of Reading: Power, Opportunity and Prospects for Change in America's Schools*, New York: Teacher's College Press.

Grice, H. (1975) Logic and conversation, in P. Cole and J. Morgan (eds), *Syntax and Semantics*, Vol. 3, *Speech Acts* (pp. 41–58), Cambridge, MA: Harvard University Press.

McDermott, R. and Roth, D. (1978) The social organization of behavior: interactional approaches, *Annual Review of Anthropology*, 7, 321–45.

McDermott, R. and Tylbor, H. (1986) On the necessity of collusion in conversation, in S. Fisher and A. Todd (eds), *Discourse and Institutional Authority: Medicine, Education and Law* (pp. 123–39), Norwood, NJ: Ablex.

Mishler, E. (1972) Implications of teacher strategies for language and cognition: observations in first-grade classrooms, in C. Cazden, V. John and D. Hymes (eds), *Functions of Language in the Classroom* (pp. 267–98), New York: Teachers College Press.

Searle, J. (1966) *Speech Acts: An Essay in the Philosophy of Language*, Cambridge: Cambridge University Press.

Swidler, A. (1979) *Organization without Authority: Dilemmas of Social Control in Free Schools*, Cambridge, MA: Harvard University Press.

White, J. J. (1989) The power of politeness in the classroom: cultural codes that create and constrain knowledge construction, *Journal of Curriculum and Supervision*, 4, 298–321.

8

The Literacy Hour: a Case for Listening to Children

Roger Hancock and Melian Mansfield

Introduction

The idea that teachers should show respect for children as individuals and a regard for their ideas and opinions in the learning process is well reflected in the educational literature. Various reasons are given for teachers consulting children. For instance, children can:

- inform teachers about their teaching (Abdullah and Scaife, 1997);
- give teachers feedback on how school is being experienced (Cullingford, 1991);
- feel more involved in school (Levin, 1994);
- be more motivated to learn (Dearing, 1994);
- be partners in school improvement (Myers, 1996);
- be action researchers with teachers (SooHoo, 1993);
- help professionals better understand the qualities and shortcomings of institutions (Armstrong and Sugawara, 1989).

Despite this recognition in the literature, there is much to suggest that many teachers disregard children's views and perspectives in practice. For instance, in a recent study of 2,272 seven to seventeen-year-olds (see Alderson, 1999), only a quarter of those interviewed thought their teachers took their opinions seriously and many were angered by the way teachers dismissed and mistrusted their views. It was reported: 'Students made the point repeatedly in the research that they want more opportunities to express their own views' (*TES*, 1999, p. 5).

This chapter takes as its central theme the idea that teachers need to listen to children if education is to have any meaning for both parties. There is a particular reason for highlighting this well-founded principle at this point in time. The nature of recent changes in education policy and classroom practice in England and Wales, and the way teaching is being conceptualized, give rise to concern that the feelings and opinions of children (and their teachers) are being overlooked. There is a growing tendency to assume that good teaching is a matter of telling children what is the case – that it is simply a matter of 'delivering' a centrally determined curriculum. This view of teaching is strongly reflected in the government's notion of a 'literacy hour', a central feature of the National Literacy Strategy (DfEE, 1998a). The Strategy, which is aimed to raise standards in literacy, is a widespread innovation affecting all primary schools in England and Wales.

The case for listening to children is made through a small-scale interview study of their experiences and perceptions of the literacy hour. This chapter has three main aims:

1. to present reasons for thinking that teachers are unlikely to take account of children's views if they are expected to implement a tightly defined and highly centralized syllabus;
2. to offer a rationale for teachers consulting with and listening to children;
3. to show how comments made by children can serve to inform the thinking and practice of teachers.

A Profession that Does Not Consult Children

In the UK, over a period of 30 years, there has been a notable shift from a situation where primary teachers were almost totally responsible for what was taught in classrooms to one where they increasingly receive a great deal of government direction. The former position could be seen as professionally empowering; the latter as professionally de-skilling. The net result of the government's intervention has been a marked reduction in a teacher's right to be involved in the process of curriculum development at local education authority (LEA) and school levels, and much less autonomy to determine the day-to-day content and quality of children's learning experiences in the classroom.

Quicke (1999) comments that the national curriculum reifies subjects, sets up strong and questionable boundaries, and also encourages 'highly ritualised and hierarchical teacher–learner relationships' (p. 12). In 1988, the first version of the national curriculum specified the content of what should be taught in schools in some detail, but, it can be argued, in a way that asked teachers to select and interpret. More recently, the National Literacy and Numeracy Strategies (DfEE, 1998a, 1999) have greatly increased the level of specification. In both strategies, government has prescribed pedagogy as well as content.

The literacy hour increases subject reification yet further – mainly through the curiously restrictive notion of 'dedicated time to literacy'. It also increases the sense of teacher–child hierarchy by prescribing a particular pedagogy, i.e. 'whole class interactive teaching'. When teachers are told what to teach and how to teach it, they may come to believe that expertise and knowledge lies outside the contexts in which they work. This will make them less inclined to look to themselves or colleagues for ideas and solutions, or indeed, to see children as partners in the educational process.

Within a command and control structure, teachers are likely to command children in the way they themselves are being commanded.

The Literacy Hour

The idea of a 'literacy hour' stems from the yearly total for English (180 hours) recommended by the Dearing Review of the National Curriculum (Dearing, 1994). Given a school year of 36 weeks, that works out at five hours a week or one hour a day. According to the *National Literacy Strategy: Framework for Teaching* (DfEE, 1998a) the structure of the literacy hour should be as follows:

1. 15 minutes of 'shared text work' when the teacher leads shared reading or writing with the whole class (e.g. reading a big book together, writing collaboratively on a flip chart);
2. 15 minutes of 'focused word work' for 5- to 7-year-olds, and for 7- to 11-year-olds, a combination of either 'focused word or sentence level work' e.g. spelling, punctuation, grammar;
3. 20 minutes of 'Independent reading, writing or word work' for 5- to 7-year-olds, while the teacher works with at least two ability groups each day on 'guided text work' (reading and writing);
   or
   20 minutes of 'Independent reading, writing or word and sentence work' for 7- to 11-year-olds whilst the teacher works with at least one ability group each day on 'guided text work' (reading and writing); and finally,
4. 10 minutes when the class is brought back together for a 'plenary' when the teacher reviews what has been taught and learned.

The timings are said to be 'flexible' but they are unlikely to be regarded as such in practice because the Framework for Teaching emphasizes the need to keep the four time elements of the hour 'in balance'.

Glancing through the Framework, one can't help noticing the amount of detail that is provided. It sets out lists of teaching objectives for 5- to 11-year-olds on a term-by-term basis. It gives high and medium frequency word lists, provides a summary of objectives for phonics and spelling and a summary of the 'range of work' for each term. It also includes a 'technical vocabulary list' and a glossary of terms to be found in the Framework.

The Framework's theory of teaching literacy is a blend of approaches used by teachers in the UK, USA and Australasia in the past 30 years (see Beard, 1998). However, the Framework itself contains no mention of research studies or educational theorists and no bibliography.

The Framework reveals a very firm commitment to a view of learning in which children acquire skills in an incremental way. In reading, for instance, this is portrayed as learning about the smallest elements (e.g. the letter names and sounds) and then combining these to make words that enable the reading of phrases, sentences and texts. It is a beguilingly logical theory but it is probably more an account of how government would like learning to read to be, rather than how those children inside the process variously experience it. Solar (1998), writing of the politics of learning to read in New Zealand, draws attention to the way in which literacy instruction is rarely a neutral, apolitical endeavour. And Dombey (1998, p. 129) suggests the prescribed teaching method of the literacy hour is 'a pedagogy of untried formality'.

A Rationale for Teachers Listening to Children

The idea that teachers should consult children in order to be better informed professionals has, according to Davie and Galloway (1996), been increasingly recognized. However, the authors go on to suggest that education lags behind some other child services in terms of heeding what children have to say. It seems that there is a tendency for all child-focused professionals to consult children when they encounter difficulties and when they feel their existing knowledge and expertise is insufficient to deal with the issues confronting them. This is also echoed in professional–parent relationships. In education, children have been consulted, for instance: when teachers need a better understanding of the reasons for their alienation from school (Barrett, 1989); when they are deemed to be failing at reading (Lawrence, 1996); and when they are seen to have emotional and behavioural difficulties (Armstrong and Galloway, 1996).

Professional motivation to listen to children should not just be based on pressing professional needs. It is essential to consult children openly and sincerely, in an ongoing way, when things are going well and when they are proving difficult. Indeed, if this sort of collaboration is built firmly into practice, the perplexing pupil responses to learning may be reduced.

So, why should teachers listen to children? First, there is the ethical principle which is expressed in the 1994 *Code of Practice on the Identification and Assessment of Special Educational Needs* (DfE, 1994). This concerns children's 'right to be heard' in educational decision making. The right to be heard receives firm backing from the Children Act and the UN Convention on the Rights of the Child.

Secondly, there are personal and psychological benefits for children if they feel their opinions and feelings matter to teachers. Teachers should show respect for children as persons with points of view even if their views may not seem informing or helpful in terms of teachers' immediate interests.

Thirdly, if one accepts a view of education as a highly individual experience, it becomes quite pointless and meaningless if learners have no say and no opportunity to comment on what is being presented. Teachers must listen to children if their teaching is to make sense.

Finally, school life and the curriculum stand to be enriched if children are given the opportunity to influence and shape it.

Talking to Children about the Literacy Hour

Those who have written about interviewing children for research purposes, tend to see it as a bit of a methodological minefield in terms of, for instance: the general problems of engagement (David, 1992); reliability (Moston, 1987); and the effect of 'adult power' on the child's ability to offer voluntary consent (Hall, 1996; Evans and Fuller, 1996).

Forty-eight children between the ages of 6 and 13 years were interviewed for this study. However, the term 'interviewed' probably gives a false impression of what actually happened when we met children and invited them to talk to us about the literacy hour. The first point to be made is that most children do not readily respond to the standard question and answer format that characterizes an interview. Scheurich (1992), although referring to adults, captures the way most children were with us: 'Interviewees do not simply go along with the researcher's programme . . . they carve out a space of their own' (cited in Ball, 1994, p. 96). It was our experience, that we had to relinquish some of our controlling and directive power as adults in order to facilitate open and spontaneous comments from the children (see Hall, 1996). Children need time and space to get to know adult motives and personalities – Potts (1992) talks about an interviewee's need to trust the curiosity of the interviewer.

The children mainly came from the London area, although five were interviewed in Manchester. The sample was very much an opportunistic one which arose from our own family, school and professional contacts in London. There were a greater number of boys (28) than girls (20). A number of cultural backgrounds were represented. Generally, we formed the impression that the sample contained children who were mostly doing well at school. They were interviewed in a variety of ways – individually, in pairs, in small groups, on the telephone, in schools, at home and during after-school clubs. Some, mainly the younger children, were accompanied by a parent. A schedule of interview questions was drawn up and used in a loose way. Once we had established the focus of discussion, we encouraged the children to lead and offer their own themes and comments.

Quite a number of the children were not particularly interested in talking about the literacy hour and ways had to be found of engaging and maintaining their interest. However, most enjoyed the experience of having a listening adult who wrote things down and tape-recorded what they said. One or two children were quite surprised that their comments were of such interest. As one 8-year-old boy said, 'You mean you're going to write down what I'm saying?'

Discussion of Findings

Children's comments about the literacy hour are considered under four headings: what is the literacy hour?; the hour and its structure; learning the new language; how does the teacher teach?

What is the literacy hour?

> *Interviewer*: Why is it called the literacy hour?
> *Amarjit* (11 years old): I'm not very sure.

Amarjit's tentative answer was doubtless related to the form of the question, which may well have been interpreted by her as requiring an 'official' or 'right' answer. In her own way, during discussion, she was able to tell us a lot about her experiences of the hour and showed that she had many insights into why it is called 'the literacy hour'. Wood and Wood (1983) suggest that questioners quickly take control of a verbal exchange and this means respondents take the risk of appearing ignorant when a question isn't easily answered.

We found that most children were able to address the more open approach, 'Tell me about the literacy hour', and give us a sense of their various experiences. We should emphasize that many had positive things to say about the hour and literacy learning at school. For example, an 11-year-old girl commented, 'I've become better in my punctuation'. An 8-year-old girl said, 'I love it because I love interesting things' and a 7-year-old boy said, 'Literacy, there are some good things – we write stories about other people'. One or two children speculated about the reasons for the hour. For instance, 10-year-old Vita had this to say:

> *Interviewer*: What is the literacy hour?
> *Vita*: It's a thing that children have to do. You have, like English work, and like – I can't remember what it is.
> *Interviewer*: You said you have to do it?
> *Vita*: Yes, it happens in the morning, and what's that thing called where you have to read something and then answer questions about it? Anyway you have to do English. It's a new programme that the government set up to help children, like, learn more about English, because they thought they were doing too much maths. So we have to do it every week or something.

Younger children sometimes needed help to enter a discussion about the hour. For instance, we might ask them: 'Tell me about the writing you do at school?' or 'Do you do any reading at school?' Most children experienced the literacy hour as a time for reading, writing and spelling. Indeed, many responses had an almost timeless feeling to them. For instance:

- 'we have quiet reading';
- 'it's when you read a book';
- 'we write all the time';
- 'we do different spellings';

- 'we have to listen to the teacher';
- 'you read when you've finished your writing';
- 'we have to sit on the carpet and read with the teacher';
- 'we make up stories and the teacher writes them for us';
- 'we do handwriting every morning, we also do punctuation';
- 'she gives us spelling homework';
- 'we do hard writing work';
- 'we read together in groups'.

With regard to understanding what literacy is, both younger and older children tended to give very straightforward answers. Brian, a 7-year-old said, 'It's reading and writing'. Bala, who was 6, said, 'It's writing', and Stephen, also aged 6, said, 'It's mostly reading and spelling'. Older children often talked about literacy as 'English work'. Tony, who was 8, gave this response: 'Literacy is pieces of writing, anything to do with reading – we can do it in the afternoon or in the morning.'

We noted how an innovation that had been preoccupying government, teachers and the press for well over a year seemed not to have captivated the children we spoke to in any substantial way. Very few children seemed to have a strong sense of the literacy hour as a significant curriculum structure, or as a whole new programme. Norris (1998, p. 217) points out, 'from minister to classroom, from minister to child is a long way'.

Comments on the hour and its structure

Sometimes it's too long and sometimes too short. (11-year-old girl)

Most children did not respond to our invitations to comment on whether or not the idea of an hour, as a period of time for literacy, is a good thing, and if the recommended timed slots are helpful to their learning. This, in itself, seems to suggest that children do not expect to comment on how they are taught. The above statement from Ghazala, an 11-year-old girl, was mainly related to her feelings of involvement rather than a judgement about time. One boy, 6-year-old Fergus, gave us a sense of the status surrounding literacy at his school by commenting, 'We're supposed to do literacy work all day'.

James, Jenks and Prout (1998) comment that adults have a lot to learn about children's experience of time. When adults spend time with children – in schools, in the home, out and about – it soon becomes apparent that they both occupy somewhat different temporal frameworks. Adults invariably take responsibility for organizing time (mostly as they want it) whilst children easily 'lose sense of time' or 'get lost in time'. Although the theme of time didn't seem of direct interest to the children we talked to, they did have things to say that had a bearing.

One 9-year-old boy, Leon, said he thought his teacher was 'always changing it'. It wasn't clear if he meant the changes within the hour's structure or the day-to-day changes in content that he was experiencing.

However, he went on to say that, for him, it was sometimes very difficult to complete his work. This made him worry because his father had said he must try to finish it. Another child, Rita, who was 7, mentioned that her teacher 'rushes through it sometimes'.

Obviously, when designing a curriculum, with competing subject demands, it is important to think about the amount of time that should be given to its component parts, if only to achieve a sense of balance and variety. However, it is also important to remember that, although an institution like a school will organize time in a certain way for teachers and children, as individuals they will relate to and use this time in various ways. Campbell (1992) in a discussion of the use of personal time, quotes Hawkins (1988): 'In the theory of relativity there is no unique absolute time but, instead, each individual has his own personal measure of time . . .' (p. 343).

The Framework (DfEE, 1998a, p. 8) suggests the hour should be 'well-paced' with a 'sense of urgency' and 'driven' by the need to help children make progress and succeed. These are highly problematic associations to make with successful learning. This was confirmed by the comments of a number of children who expressed the need for more time to do their work. Some of the teaching principles embedded within the Framework are not in line with teachers' values (see Dadds, 1999). For instance, the literacy hour's emphasis on 'pace', would seem to run counter to much professional wisdom about how teaching should be adapted to meet the range of children's learning styles.

A further difficulty concerns the way in which the Framework plays down the exacting nature of differentiated teaching when the teacher is teaching the whole class. Without teacher spontaneity, empathy and a preparedness to come off the planned lesson when the collective feedback from the class indicates that this is required, there would be concern that children like Ghazala, Leon and Rita will not have their learning needs met.

Learning the new language

She did loads on roots and suffixes a few weeks ago. (Suresh, 8-year-old)

Although most children talked about the literacy hour in ways that related to what they had come to expect in English lessons, a minority did talk in ways that indicated something slightly different was happening. In the main, these were older children. One 11-year-old girl said, 'We have to think more about stories, characters, what they mean and metaphors behind the book'. Another said, 'I was doing prefixes and then read my book'. A 10-year-old boy, commented, 'We learnt about homophones, I think, and before that we did phonemes and vowels'. An 8-year-old boy said, 'We talk about adjectives and nouns, non fiction and fiction'.

We didn't feel it appropriate to probe children's knowledge when they mentioned such technical terms, unless they offered further information.

However, we did get the feeling, from the way some children used such 'subject-specific' terms, that they were using them in very tentative if not confused ways. The following two exchanges with 8-year-old Josh, and 9-year-old Sara, illustrate this:

> *Interviewer*: You know the haiku poems that you mentioned when we first started to talk? Tell me how you do these?
>
> *Josh*: Well, the poem has to have three lines and some words. I think it's nine or something. Also you need the 'synables'. I can't remember how many of those. I don't think it has to rhyme – I'm not sure. It's just a poem that Japanese people like.
>
> *Interviewer*: And do you like doing them?
>
> *Josh*: Yea, they're OK.
>
> *Sara*: Last week she told us about trigraphs and some kids didn't get it.
>
> *Interviewer*: What was the problem?
>
> *Sara*: Well, they kept getting them mixed up with digraphs. You know what they are? Anyway they weren't listening to her so they didn't get it. Well most of them didn't. It's mostly the same kids.
>
> *Interviewer*: Did you get it?
>
> *Sara*: I think so but I can't remember them now.

Through the literacy hour, primary children are introduced to a range of technical terms that have traditionally been used to analyse the English language. For instance, the Framework's 'Technical Vocabulary List' suggests that 5-year-old children should understand terms like 'grapheme', 'onset', 'recount' and 'title', whilst 9-year-olds should know terms like 'diminutive', 'superlative', 'cinquain' and 'epitaph'. Putting aside the debate about the relevance of this kind of explicit meta-language to primary children, it needs to be recognized that such terms will require considerable conceptual learning if they are not to become superficially acquired.

There is a substantial literature about the relationship between children's language learning and curriculum understanding at school. Some 30 years ago Barnes, Britton and Rosen (1969) raised the alarm about primary children's difficulties when they first come across 'the language of secondary education'. They write:

> Much of the language encountered in school looks at pupils across a chasm. Some fluent children adopt the jargon and parrot whole stretches of lingo. Personal intellectual struggle is made irrelevant and the personal view never asked for. Language and experience are torn asunder. Worse still, many children find impersonal language mere noise. (p. 12)

The literacy hour does court similar difficulties by introducing technical language to primary children from an early age and, moreover, advocating the learning of these terms within a time-limited framework. The Framework expects teachers to differentiate children's learning, however, there is a strong expectation that classes of children will cover the laid-down learning at a given rate.

One of the mothers (previously a nursery teacher) of an 8-year-old boy who was interviewed said at first she was impressed that Jamie was doing homework on themes such as alliteration and verb tenses. However, increasingly she found she had to spend time helping him make sense of these terms and this had made homework an emotional experience for them both. She commented, 'Surely, at his age shouldn't he just be reading books with me and enjoying them?'.

How does the teacher teach?

She's always talking. She's cross when we don't listen. (James, aged 8 years)

We didn't assume that the children would have things to say about their teachers' teaching styles during the literacy hour, however, a number made interesting comments as, for instance, in the following exchange with 8-year-old Jackie:

Interviewer: So, you were saying that your teacher is different in the literacy hour?

Jackie: Yea, she's sort of different. She speaks different and moves around a lot – a bit like she's worried or something.

Interviewer: Worried?

Jackie: It's like she's cross if we don't do it right and don't concentrate. She makes us concentrate, especially on the carpet, and kids muck around a lot. She talks too much and goes over the same things too much.

Other children also had comments to make about the style of teaching they were experiencing in the hour. One 6-year-old child talked about liking it when her teacher did 'numbers on the carpet' but her older sister quickly corrected her and reminded her that she was thinking of the numeracy hour.

Generally, there were several references to 'work on the carpet – now a key place for listening and literacy learning. A 10-year-old girl explained how her teacher used the carpet in her literacy hour: 'She talks about what we have to do and she explains it thoroughly. She goes through what we have to do and then we have to get on by ourselves and we can't ask any questions unless it's really, like, urgent. We're supposed to get through eveything on the carpet.' It seems that the classroom carpet may have undergone a significant change of function. Hitherto it was a place where children could relax and 'choose', maybe after they had finished their work. Now, with the arrival of the literacy hour, as a 7-year-old girl said, 'We do hard learning on the carpet'.

The pedagogy advocated by the National Literacy Strategy is one in which the teacher is a very prominent feature of a lesson. The Strategy's training videos (DfEE, 1998b) are very focused on teaching and the teacher's performance – not so much on learning and what the children are thinking. Although the Strategy talks of 'interactive whole class teaching', the advocated style of teaching requires that children do a lot of listening to a lesson that is being led by a teacher.

Two main factors seem to be reducing the opportunity for children to initiate interaction (with the teacher or with other children). First, there is the emphasis on the teacher getting through a tightly specified set of activities within an hour and, secondly, the highlighting of 'pace' as a key element in a successful lesson.

Thus, we have a classroom context in which the teacher:

- is required to talk a lot whilst children listen a lot;
- is driven by a need to get through the prescribed content of the literacy hour;
- is required to segment the hour into four timed mini-lessons;
- is urged to do this 'briskly' and with pace.

This amount of structure and control makes it very difficult for children to introduce their impromptu comments. It also makes it unlikely that the teacher will feel there is time to consult children in any 'open' way which is not directly related to the immediate agenda (as laid down in the required literacy hour lesson plans). Indeed, the form of child participation depicted in the literacy hour training materials is one where the teacher formulates questions which children are to answer. Wood and Wood (1983) warn that when the teacher is highly controlling of pupil-teacher exchanges and employs an approach that simply uses question after question, children are unlikely to spontaneously elaborate on a theme or go beyond the question (see also, Skidmore, 1999; Whitehead, 1999).

Some of the children we interviewed were clearly wanting to understand why their teachers needed to adopt this particular approach to teaching them. Some, it should be noted, tried to see things from the teacher's perspective. Suresh, aged 8, gave the following rationale for the teaching he was experiencing: 'Sometimes literacy hour is hard because our teacher is trying to get our brains into our heads and make us smart – he just gives us hard work.'

Conclusion

We have suggested that children have a right to be heard when they are at school. We have argued that teaching stands to be enriched if teachers consult children and that education will have more meaning for children if they are respected and their opinions valued. We have also argued that, at a time when the primary school curriculum is increasingly defined by those outside the classroom, children are at risk of not being seriously considered or consulted. As with teachers, there is a danger that children simply receive and absorb what is handed down, without any opportunity to influence or change it.

Through loosely structured interviews with 48 children we have tried to show how their comments about the literacy hour are significant to professional understandings. We believe the children in our small-scale study raise important theoretical and practical issues that require attention. Candid responses from children can help us become more effective teachers in the literacy hour and, more widely, in all our work as primary teachers.

It is essential that we learn to see school learning through the eyes of those who directly experience what we teach and how we teach it. If we don't give children the opportunity to tell us how they feel, and a chance to influence how they spend their time with us in school, then we make it difficult for them to engage with us as people and with education itself. We could have a situation where we, and they, are wasting our time. Quicke (1999) makes the salient point that despite some 11 years of formal schooling many children continue to leave without any strong sense of an 'academic self'. Here is one compelling reason for listening to children.

The National Literacy Strategy regards teachers and children as passive recipients of an outsider's curriculum. We believe, nevertheless, that classroom teachers are in a very strong position to listen to children. This, we think, is essential as it will stand to improve any present or future curriculum initiative that has to be adopted by primary schools.

There is evidence from the Office for Standards in Education (OFSTED) (Carvel, 1999), and the 1999 Standardised Assessment Tasks for 11-year-olds, that the literacy hour is having a favourable impact on the literacy skills of some children – assuming that these gains will be sustained over time. However, there is also evidence to suggest that the hour is not helping children with special educational needs, those who speak English as an additional language, and those who are high achievers (ATL, 1998). So it seems that the literacy hour may not be the complete panacea. We think children can help us make it better.

References

Abdullah, A. and Scaife, J. (1997) 'Using interviews to assess children's understanding of science concepts', *School Science Review*, 78, 79–83.

Alderson, P. (1999) *Civil Rights in Schools*, Children 5–16 Research Programme, Hull, School of Comparative and Applied Social Sciences, University of Hull.

Armstrong, D. and Galloway, D. (1996) 'How children with emotional and behaviour difficulties view professionals', in R. Davie and D. Galloway (eds), *Listening to Children in Education*, London, David Fulton.

Armstrong, J. and Sugawara, A. (1989) 'Children's perceptions of their day care experiences', *Early Child Development and Care*, 49, 1–15.

ATL (Association of Teachers and Lecturers) (1998) *Survey of Teachers' Attitudes Towards 'Literacy Hour'*, London, ATL/Opinion Research Business.

Ball, S. J. (1994) 'Political interviews and the politics of interviewing', in G. Walford (ed.), *Researching the Powerful in Education*, London, University College of London Press.

Barnes, D., Britton, J. and Rosen, H. (1969) *Language, the Learner and the School*, Penguin Books, Harmondsworth.

Barrett, G. (ed.) (1989) *Disaffection from School? The Early Years*, London, Falmer Press.

Beard, R. (1998) *National Literacy Strategy: Review of Research and Other Related Evidence*, Suffolk, DfEE Publications.

Campbell, J. (1992) *Managing Teachers' Time: Concepts, Evidence and Policy Issues*, Stoke-on-Trent, ASPE/Trentham Books.

Carvel, J. (1999) Poor teaching threatens writing targets, *Guardian*, 6 July, p. 5.

Cullingford, C. (1991) *The Inner World of the School*, London, Cassell.

Dadds, M. (1999) 'Teachers' values and the literacy hour', *Cambridge Journal of Education*, 29(1), 7–19.

David, T. (1992) 'Do we have to do this? The Children Act 1989 and obtaining children's views in early childhood settings', *Children and Society*, 6(3), 204–11.

Davie, R. and Galloway, D. (eds) (1996) *Listening to Children in Education*, London, David Fulton.

Dearing, R. (1994) *The National Curriculum and its Assessment: Final Report*, London, SCAA.

DfE (Department for Education) (1994) *Code of Practice on the Identification and Assessment of Special Educational Needs*, London, DfE.

DfEE (Department for Education and Employment) (1998a) *The National Literacy Strategy: Framework for Teaching*, DfEE, London.

DfEE (Department for Education and Employment) (1998b) *The National Literacy Strategy Literacy Training Pack*, Cassette 2, Side 1, DfEE, London.

DfEE (Department for Education and Employment) (1999) *The National Numeracy Strategy: Framework for Teaching*, DfEE, London.

Dombey, H. (1998) 'Changing literacy in the early years of school', in B. Cox (ed.), *Literacy Is Not Enough*, Manchester, Manchester University Press/Book Trust.

Evans, P. and Fuller, M. (1996) 'Hello. Who am I speaking to?' Communicating with pre-school children in educational research settings, *Early Years*, 17(1), 17–20.

Hall, N. (1996) 'Eliciting children's views: the contribution of psychologists', in R. Davie, G. Upton and V. Varma (eds), *The Voice of the Child: A Handbook for Professionals*, London, Falmer Press.

Hawkins, S. (1988) *A Brief History of Time*, London, Bantam Press.

James, A., Jenks, C. and Prout, A. (1998). *Theorizing Childhood*, Oxford, Polity Press.

Lawrence, D. (1996) *Enhancing Self-esteem in the Classroom*, London, Paul Chapman.

Levin, B. (1994) 'Improving educational productivity: putting students at the centre', *Phi Delta Kappan*, 75(10), 758–60.

Moston, S. (1987) 'The suggestibility of children in interview studies', *First Language*, 7, 67–78.

Myers, K. (ed.) (1996) *School Improvement in Practice: Schools Make a Difference Project*, London, Falmer Press.

Norris, N. (1998) 'Curriculum evaluation revisited', *Cambridge Journal of Education*, 28(2), 207–19.

Potts, P. (1992) 'Approaches to interviewing', in T. Booth, W. Swann, M. Masterton and P. Potts (eds), *Curricula for Diversity in Education*, London, Routledge/Open University.

Quicke, J. (1999) *A Curriculum for Life: Schools for a Democratic Learning Society*, Buckingham, Open University Press.

Scheurich, J. (1992) 'A post modernist review of interviewing: dominance, resistance and chaos', paper presented at the Annual Meeting of the American Educational Research Association, San Francisco.

Skidmore, D. (1999) 'From pedagogical dialogue to dialogical pedagogy', paper presented at British Educational Research Association Conference, University of Sussex. Available from the author: d.w.skidmore@reading.ac.uk

SooHoo, S. (1993) 'Students as partners in research and restructuring schools', *Educational Forum*, 57, 386–93.

Solar, J. (1998) 'The politics of learning to read: 1940s debates over literacy instruction in the New Zealand primary school', *New Zealand Journal of Educational Studies*, 3(2), 155–66.

TES (*Times Educational Supplement*) (1999) 'Pupils demand civil rights', 26 November, p. 5.

Whitehead, M. (1999) 'A literacy hour in the nursery? The big question-mark', *Early Years*, 19(2), 51–61.

Wood, D. and Wood, H. (1983) 'Questioning the pre-school child', *Educational Review*, 35(2), 149–62.

9

Silence as a Fortress and a Prison

Karen Gallas

[. . .]

Silence and Gender

The topic of silence in schools has often been associated with problems of gender and equity in the classroom, and if my experience as a teacher is common, I can see why. I have never seen truly silent boys, with one exception of a child who was severely disturbed. I have seen boys who are quiet and shy, but not silent. On the other hand, I have worked with truly silent girls, and in fact, I was a silent child, so I bring extensive personal experience to this discussion. Some girls are silent for only a few months. They can eventually be coaxed and reassured out of their silence and will participate in the social life of the classroom. But some, like Rachel, are silent for almost a year, and if they have different teachers every year, could potentially be silent throughout their entire education.

Many gender studies have implied that girls, most girls, are 'silenced' in the classroom by ineffective teachers and biased curricula. (See the 1993 AAUW report.) They tend to lump girls into one category – all equally disempowered and unequal. And all boys – that is, the culture's seditious favouritism toward all things male – becomes the reason that all girls are disempowered and unequal. I know what I think about that idea: it's simplistic. Yet gender studies have never, to my knowledge, explored *truly* silent girls, although some have self-consciously pondered why they were omitted (Best, 1983). Why not? Is it because we assume that their silence originates only in the classroom, and that therefore, by readjusting a class-room to be gender-neutral, we can put the voice into these girls? Or is it that lack of attention to silent girls occurs simply because they *are* silent – that is, that they are outwardly such good little girls that they are not interesting enough to merit study, or even (as I have found at times), to keep track of?

Studying Silences

[. . .]

For teachers, and perhaps even for researchers, it is so easy to overlook and forget about 'good', silent girls. The forgetting, in fact, is what these girls come to rely upon; it is what makes their life in school easier, though at the same time less fruitful. But as philosophers and linguists have pointed out, one cannot consider speech without studying the silences. Thus although the essence of classroom life is formed around talk, the form and purposes of silences must be documented and explicated.

When I encountered Rachel, I was struck by her silence both because of my own history as a silent girl and because of the difficulties her silence placed in my way as her teacher. As I worked with her over a two-year period, however, the issue of her silence became much more complex. On one hand, I wanted to break it, to pull her out of it so that I could teach her better, but when she finally began to pull out of it, Rachel revealed what was behind the silence, showing me that it concealed not only fear and a desire for personal power, but a richly imaginative private world. I found that I became her accomplice in protecting her silence even as I was asking her to give it up. This chapter will describe how the layers of Rachel's silence revealed a distinct approach to the world, and further, how a performance based on silence can have a very powerful effect on the dynamics of a classroom.

Rachel

When she walked into my classroom as a first grader, Rachel appeared to be the perfect little girl: beautiful, healthy, and intelligent, except for one pervasive problem. She was completely silent. All autumn, I worked to bring her out: I was gentle, caring, cajoling, reasonable, sensitive, soft spoken, patient; I expanded my wait time from ten seconds to half a minute. The other children encouraged her, reassured her, spoke more softly, and waited with me. Nothing. Rachel simply would not speak or participate in classroom discussions of any size. She would not respond to teacher or child questions about anything. She would not work co-operatively with any child other than her best friend, Yukiko, also silent, but with a reason – English was her second language. When pressed by me to speak or at least participate, Rachel was absolutely immovable. I decided that I needed to try and record what was happening to see if I could make some sense of it, but even that decision to look more closely at Rachel presented me with immediate problems.

A Data Gap

First, if you are using talk as one of your primary tools to study children and yourself and you are studying a silent child, you basically have a data gap. For example, on several occasions when I tried taping early morning work time, I would very casually set the tape recorded down on the table where Rachel and Yukiko were drawing and come back later only to find I had a blank tape. This strategy, when used with a table of boys, would result in tapes filled with unusual and complex language samples. These two girls, however, simply didn't talk, except for a few very minimal comments on each other's pictures, or questions about which colour marker to choose. Further, in taping class discussions or sharing times, Rachel was never on the tape. I then had to resort completely to field notes, texts Rachel had written, occasional transcripts when I would basically force Rachel to speak to me, and copies of her artwork. Not until my second year with her did I get any sense of what her spoken language was like. Was she inarticulate? Did she have ideas that made sense? Did she understand the main ideas we were working on? What were her interests, dislikes, confusions? Hers was a very hard track to follow.

In early November of 1992, however, as I became more determined to document her persona in the classroom, I obtained snippets of data that helped me begin to think about the issue of her silence. As time passed, I gathered more and more data, and gradually Rachel broke her silence. Time, however, has only increased and complicated my questions and observations. In writing about her, I have decided to work chronologically through my thinking as it has evolved, describing the themes that emerged over time.

Silence as a Problem

To begin, I will describe the dynamics that made Rachel's silence problematic for myself and for the other children using both field notes and one of the few transcripts I obtained from Rachel in the first year.

Girl's only science talk: 12 November

In this talk, from the start, Rachel was extremely resistant. How do I know that? As soon as the group of seven girls sat down to talk, Rachel began to move. She was plopped right in the middle of the circle, almost leaning on me and Yukiko, then rolling away like a top to the back wall until she was completely outside the group. Her body was turned away from us, and if she turned toward the girls, her head would be turned away so that she didn't have to make eye contact. I said directly to her (on tape):

> *T*: And Rachel, this is going to be a small group, so you really will have to help us. You can't, we're going to expect everybody to speak, and you're going to have to face the children in the group. Can you show me that? Right at them, so that they'll know you're talking to them. That's the only way they'll know. (I walk away to get a pencil, and leave the tape running.)

Dierdre: Science questions: it's going to be hard. (Rachel laughs nervously.)

Molly: Don't think it's so hard. There's thousands of things.

Dierdre: I know, but those thousands of things are going to be very, very hard.

Molly: They're all *hard*, Deirdre.

Dierdre: I know. They're very hard because we weren't even born in that time of day. (Rachel continues to roll around, picking at microscopic lint on the rug, not speaking. Teacher returns.)

T: Rachel, we can't speak if you're not sitting and looking at us. (She settles for a minute, and then I ask her if she has a question.)

Rachel: (in a whisper): Yeah. How did volcanoes begin?

T: Do you want to talk about how volcanoes happen?

Rachel: How did volcanoes begin? (She uses her hand to sculpt the shape of a volcano, with the hand topping off the volcano in a flat, sweeping motion.)

T: Ah. That's a different question. How is a volcano made? When you do the shape like that, it makes me think that you're thinking. 'How is it made?' (We review all the questions the girls have suggested. Rachel is still moving agitatedly. I mark an X on the floor in chalk to give her a firm space to settle on. We decide to talk about the question 'How did things get their names?' Rachel sits on the X. Later, at the end of the talk in which Rachel has been silent, continuing to turn and play with specks on the floor, I speak to her directly.)

T: Rachel, what do you think? Tell us what you think, 'cause we want to hear from you, too.

Rachel: What? (She almost seems like she hadn't been there. The intonation is up, but slightly puzzled.)

T: What do you think about the way words got their names?

Rachel: Words got their na–uh . . . uh . . . I'm still thinking about it. Uh . . .

T: Well, just try to help us. We need everybody's help. (Later, I asked each girl to give me a word they might have needed to say if they were living millions of years ago. Each girl said something. Then I asked Rachel.)

T: What do you think, Rachel, what's something you might have named? (Rachel is moving, almost on her belly on the X.)

Rachel: I still can't think of it.

T: No, you can tell us something. (Very long silence, perhaps 30 seconds.)

Rachel (very softly): I don't need to think it. I don't feel like it. (Later, I asked her again, the same question.)

Rachel: I'm still thinking.

T: No, you can't be still thinking. You've got to say something.

Rachel: But I don't know how. (After the science talk, I spoke to Rachel and asked her why she didn't talk in the talk. She told me she 'didn't want to . . . 'cause I don't feel like it'.)

Field Notes: November 16

Rachel and Michael are working together on a math assignment, weighing classroom objects. Michael takes a turn weighing an object. It's Rachel's turn and she weighs a toy polar bear. Michael jumps up and gets something else, brings it over, and puts it on the balance. Rachel pulls it out and puts her bear back in. They repeat the sequence. Michael comes over and asks for help (he's been told to do that). When I go over, Rachel is weighing her polar bear again, hunched over the balance so Michael can't get in. I ask her to take the bear out. She mumbles something under her breath and crouches over the bear, putting her hand on top so I can't remove it. I try to lift her hand, explaining that it's unfair to Michael, but her grip on the balance is like steel. I have great difficulty moving her hand with any dignity, and it angers me that such a 'nice girl', so feminine and lovely, can be so hard. I explain, trying to control my anger, that she and Michael are working together, and so she needs to let him have a turn. She very slowly and steadily turns her body away from my hands, which are resting on her shoulder. I can feel that her resistance to my control is located in the centre of her body. She is literally withdrawing into herself, almost moving into the furniture like a snail moving into its shell. I wonder if she hasn't even closed her ears.

So our struggles continued. I found in group meetings that Rachel absolutely would not give any indication that she was listening to anyone. If someone was talking, she would be playing with a speck on the floor, spinning her body in circles and semicircles, or whispering silently and continuously to Yukiko. I felt compelled to try and break through this wall. It seemed intentional, differing substantially from the random activity of children I have taught in the past with attention problems or emotional issues. When Rachel twirled, I noticed she would periodically glance at me out of the corner of her eye. I would stop discussions and ask her to look at me, to stop moving, to come sit by my feet, to give me some sign that she was engaged and thinking. This generally had a very short-lived effect. Soon she would be twirling and twiddling at my feet, eyes on the floor, body bent in two like a little frog.

Field Notes: Late November
In a break-off science talk just for girls in which six other nonthreatening girls are speaking together about a question (in effect, we are practicing how to speak in a group), each girl is taking a turn saying one idea about our question. I give Rachel a cue that in six turns we will ask her to say something. I think perhaps she needs time to be mentally prepared, to steel herself, as it were, for this ordeal. When we come to Rachel, she begins to twist and turn, tracing circles on the floor with her hand, gradually turning away from us. We wait, and the girls very softly reassure her that they won't laugh at her or hurt her feelings, that this is a safe place, but she can't speak or make eye contact with any of them or me. We go another round, and this time we wait again for a long time. It is a gentle and tender silence, so clearly without threat, and suddenly she blurts something out so quickly and without any volume that we can't make out what she said, but we are relieved that she tried, and we tell her so. I suppose that's a start.

Silence and Power

After a few months, I realized that Rachel was doing exactly what the bad boys did, but from a different vantage point. Bad boys typically manipulate language, including both verbal and non-verbal communication, in such a skilful way that they can often gain control of most classroom discussions and instructional activities. Their understanding of the relationship between language and power is sophisticated and extensive, developing more subtlety as they gain more experience in school.

Rachel's silence had a similar effect on my efforts as a teacher and on other children's efforts to work with her: by refusing to communicate with myself and others, she stopped the reciprocity of social discourse. We were getting a very clear and deliberate message that she would not join us, would not respond to my cues to speak, would make us wait forever to hear one sentence or observation, and that she knew I couldn't *make* her speak. While she was not making a bid to control the dynamics of the entire class, she was effectively controlling the dynamics of our relationship with her. She was extremely powerful, and in some ways more powerful than my bad boys. When bad boys are disruptive, teachers can ask them to leave, or discipline them by keeping them in at recess, or send them to talk to the principal, or call their parents in to school. But how can one punish a child *for silence*?

Further, Rachel had a habit of disappearing without being noticed. In fact, sometimes I would look around the group of children at storytime or just before introducing a new activity and realize that she wasn't there, and that I hadn't seen her in quite a while. Her silence on some levels made her almost invisible. Let me illustrate that point by telling what I call the Bathroom Story.

The Bathroom story

Field Notes: April 15
Both my intern and I were out of the classroom today. The substitute reports that around noon, Rachel and Yukiko disappeared. She didn't notice for a while, probably about 40 minutes, and when their absence was reported to her, she found Rachel and Yukiko in the bathroom, cleaning the sinks. She identifies Rachel as the mastermind. The incident seems innocuous enough, but had it been Michael, Tom, or Tony, they would have been missed immediately and much more seriously reprimanded.

Field Notes: April 26
At around 12:30, after story, I move across the room as the children settle down to write and find Rachel and Yukiko casually walking up the back steps, drying their hands. I realize then that they've not been at story. When I ask them where they've been, Yukiko says, 'Washing our hands', I had given them permission to do that at noon, but 30 minutes of water play wasn't what I'd had in mind. I reprimand them both fairly sternly, reiterating 'rules' and the importance of being at story, and I really am annoyed that they've missed story again. Rachel doesn't flinch or look away. I am annoyed with myself at overlooking these girls because they are sometimes so invisible. At the same time I realize that part of *my* way of being in the world relies on slipping by, or slipping away when I'm not inclined to be involved in something or want to avoid doing something that's unpleasant or threatening.

Yet when we carefully examine the impenetrable silence of this good little girl, it becomes immediately apparent that Rachel's silence is instructive in a disturbing way. She magnifies the problems and outcomes of a closely guarded silence because she shows how powerful silence can be in interpersonal dynamics and how intricate the construction of an attitude of silence becomes over time. Initially Rachel provided the absolute contrast with others in that her manipulation of language pushed the issues of power and authority *and their connection with language* into the foreground.

On one hand, she was silent, and often it is assumed that little girls who are silent are helpless and vulnerable. On the other hand, when we examine the nuances of her silence, we see that it has many layers . . . it is also about power. Where others deftly manoeuvre their way by skilfully using tone, gesture, and semantics to control classroom dynamics, Rachel employed very subtle non-verbal devices. That is, she controlled the flow of spoken ideas by recognizing the mediating role of talk in the classroom, but not participating in it. Rachel was also the queen of shrugs, twirls, and other avoidance gestures, and she would use these communication techniques with differing levels of success. For example, her gestures, as they're described in the following observations, were loaded with meaning, but were not always intelligible to others.

Field Notes: February 11
As I watch her in a creative movement activity I realize that I need to film Rachel's non-participation. As her small group works on developing a performance, Rachel characteristically refuses to participate even when begged by the children. Rather, she spends her time turning, leaping, skipping around and around her group without making eye contact, but always keeping her eye on what they were doing.

February 22
During the early morning exercises, when she is reading the daily schedule for the class, Rachel comes to a point where she doesn't know what to do next and falls silent. She shrugs very subtly (not at once noticeable to me), then again, and I realize suddenly that the shrug is very much her utterance for 'I don't know what to do'.

Rachel has taught me that shrugs, twirls, glances and hops, even if done for the purposes of *not* making contact, are communications worth studying for their implied meaning. I now see them as the *tone* in her silence. Thus comes my realization that Rachel's shrugs, whispers and possibly most of her gestures were utterances that while not voiced were 'said', and from my point of view should have been responded to in some way, much as I would respond to another child's voiced utterances, or a male child's direct verbal challenges.

Silence as a Prison

There was, therefore, an early point at which I knew that Rachel's silence was born within and outside of her control. I saw that she used silence for the purposes of realizing some personal power in her relationships, but she was also entrapped by her silence. Note, for example, her behaviour in the first science talk excerpt, where her physical resistance to participation is coupled with her statement as to why she did not speak, 'but I don't know how'.

When I observed Rachel in those few times that she said anything out loud, I recognized from my own childhood the terror behind her breathlessness, the way she blurted out short phrases and looked frantically for a place to hide. Silence as a personal position is a far safer place from which to maintain a sense of control over any situation, but silence is both a fortress and a prison. The threat to Rachel, in my opinion, lay in the public nature of the classroom: at some point each child must be able to stand up and say what he or she thinks. As her teacher, I kept pressing Rachel to take small steps toward that public discourse. I suspect that in Rachel's mind my pressure, however gentle and well intentioned, compromised her psychological safety.

Now that I reflect on her behaviour, framed as it was in a classroom filled with bad boys like Tony, Tom, Michael and Andrew, boys who scrutinized and judged every statement, *including the teacher's*, why would Rachel want to speak out loud? As Magda Lewis and Roger Simon point out, 'Being allowed to speak can be a form of tyranny', (1986, p. 461). The right to speak out loud and be heard, a dynamic that naive observers might place completely within the control of the teacher, in reality resides within the social dynamics of the classroom community. Those dynamics embody the subtextual and consist of undercurrents of status and dominance *among children* and, as we have seen, are rarely orchestrated solely by the teacher. Only when the teacher studies the development and process of those dynamics can she or he attempt to mediate them in the service of each child's development as a public person.

Finding a Public Voice

Still, in spite of all those factors and much to my surprise, in March of our first year together following an incident at recess, I observed a clear turning point in Rachel's classroom persona. For our class, that incident became the Stuck in the Mud Story.

Field Notes: Rachel and Yukiko Get Stuck in the Mud: March 23
Yukiko and Rachel are playing by the baseball diamond in what, after a week of rain, currently resembles a pond of mud. Yukiko wades in and gets stuck up to her boot tops. Rachel wades in to help her and also gets stuck. They are literally cemented in, and no one is around to help. Three boys from our class, Tom, Donald and Ian, come by and debate whether to help them, but none of them wants to wade in. Finally, they make an attempt, but realize that they'll get stuck, too, and back out of the mud. Rachel decides to try and get out, pulls one booted foot out, falls flat on her face and stomach in the mud, gets up, and (as the boys report to me, absolutely awestruck), 'She's still smiling, like she's having fun!' Rachel puts her boot back on her foot, manages to get out of the mud, and goes to look for help. The boys wander off. Rachel returns without help and wades back in to rescue Yukiko. This time, she gets really stuck, up to the very top of her boots. Another second-grade girl walks by and wades in to help. She, too, gets stuck. At this point I arrive to find the three girls stuck firmly in mucky, sandy mud. Rachel is absolutely having the best time. She's laughing and smiling at the predicament. Finally we manage to find the custodians, who rescue the girls, and their boots. A little later, Rachel and Yukiko return to class as we are

finishing story, having changed into spare clothes. I ask them to describe their adventure. Rachel, in a loud, clear, and expressive voice, retells the story (with the boys' interjections). She is so animated and articulate that I, and every one else, pay close attention. We are all completely amused by the whole event, and captivated with her energy *and* her voice. It is the first time I and many of the children have ever heard Rachel speak out loud.

Something about this adventure gave Rachel a new public voice. In the days that followed she began to initiate conversations with me and with other children in the class. One day, about a week later, she had a bottle of perfume from home that she was using to terrorize the boys. I note in my journal that

> now when she interacts, she is *so* alive: her eyes are wide open and lit up. Her face has a constant half smile on it. She chases those boys with the perfume leading the way. They return again and again to be chased, sort of hanging around her until she notices and then picks up the bottle in a threatening way. She is still very silent, but much more present. Instead of shutting us out, she's almost *prickly with attention and interest.*

Thus Rachel's movement into the public world of the classroom began. Although I never completely understood how her silence was broken, I had a suspicion that the transition was made precisely because she found an alternative position within the classroom from which to assert her authority. The Mud Incident became notorious in our classroom folklore, resurfacing as a point of admiration and wonder throughout the following year. Rachel attained in that event something of heroic stature, evoking kudos from even the baddest of the boys. The fortuitous Mud Incident had provided her with a bridge to public conversation with her peers and myself, showcasing her natural bravery and adventurousness, traits she could only reveal to us *outside* the confines of the classroom. Rachel had found a way out of her rigid persona, and the bridge that helped her negotiate that path was a story of risk that in many ways crossed a gender line, giving her a different kind of personal power both in her own eyes and in the eyes of her classmates.

About six months later I had an encounter with Rachel's kindergarten teacher that made me realize how far she had moved from her protected and isolated world into our classroom community. That teacher remarked to me, as she left our classroom after visiting for a few minutes, how Rachel seemed 'so grown-up. She has so much to say. I don't remember that at all'.

'That', I said to her, 'is because she never said anything'.

I remembered then how Rachel had not spoken for so many months and it was somewhat shocking to hear her speaking with her friends. But more surprising was the quality of her voice. It mesmerized: it was deep, rich and mellifluous, like a treasure. Perhaps it was so beautiful because it was so new. Or perhaps it was the life behind the silences that made her words so rich. Because even as Rachel made her entry into our community, she held on to a rich imaginal world, allowing us to see more of it but never abandoning it for too long. That story . . . reveals more of the 'threads of silence that speech is mixed together with' (Merleau-Ponty, 1964, p. 46), and expands our understanding of the interface between the child's strivings for control and autonomy, and the reality of the social world of the classroom.

References

AAUW (American Association of University Women) Educational Foundation and the Wellesley College Center for Research on Women (1993) *How Schools Short-change Girls*, Washington, D.C.: AAUW Educational Foundation.

Best, R. (1983) *We've All Got Scars: What Boys and Girls Learn in Elementary School*, Bloomington, IN: Indiana University Press.

Lewis, M. and Simon, R. (1986) A discourse not intended for her: learning and teaching within patriarchy, *Harvard Educational Review*, 56(4), 457–72.

Merleau-Ponty, M. (1964) *Phenomenology of Perception*, New York: Humanities Press.

Introduction to Section 3
Application of Practice

The influences and recent changes already described in the Introduction to Section 1 are discussed further in this section and issues are identified for consideration in a future curriculum. Wragg (1997) describes a model of curriculum that incorporates three dimensions: subjects, cross-curricular themes and forms of teaching and learning. He illustrates this as a cube (Wragg, 1997, p. 3) but believes that it might have more than three dimensions. However, he recognizes that 'the whole of what is experienced in schools . . . can make an impact upon those who attend' (Wragg, 1997, p. 2). The National Curriculum (DfEE/QCA, 1999) identifies ten subject areas plus religious education and sex education for primary schools as well as aspects of cross-curricular learning. It identifies the school curriculum as enabling 'us to respond positively to the opportunities and challenges of the rapidly changing world in which we live and work' (DfEE/QCA, 1999, p. 10). To achieve this, two aims are identified: 'the personal development of pupils, spiritually, morally, socially and culturally', and the 'opportunity to learn and achieve' which reinforce each other.

The practices of circle time and golden time are aspects of the curriculum that have developed since 1994 (e.g. Mosley 1996). Within these methods there is an overt recognition of children's power in the classroom, yet in practice this is not always realized. There is at least an acknowledgement that children are expected to have some ownership of the curriculum, evidence perhaps of teachers developing their own critical pedagogy. Many primary classrooms have 'Class Rules' or 'Golden Rules' displayed, which are developed and often signed by the children. Behaviour policies in school may include provision of the setting up of a contract between pupil and teachers when relationships have become strained. This has led to the statutory addition of 'citizenship' to the National Curriculum at Key Stages 3 and 4 with non-statutory guidelines about personal, social and health education and citizenship appearing in the Key Stages 1 and 2 texts (DfEE/QCA, 1999, pp. 136–41).

Legislation means that governors of schools have had to produce a home/school agreement for parents, teachers and children to sign. The legislation does not suggest what should be done if any party does not sign it as it cannot be binding in law, but it is expected that the agreement will clearly set out what children and parents can expect from the school, and vice versa.

Some would argue that teachers need to retain their own power by trying to exert control over pedagogy, and chapters in this section consider curriculum practices as aspects of this. The focus, however, is not on the knowledge or skills to be taught, but on ways of approaching the curriculum. This section explores curriculum and pedagogy in a number of ways.

The main themes in the section are:

- curriculum definitions;
- how the curriculum may be developed;
- approaches to the curriculum;
- citizenship, play, information communications technology (ICT) and literacy as examples of curriculum areas.

In Chapter 10 Alistair Ross describes the current curriculum. He explores aspects of it including culture and assessment issues before establishing a generic worldwide curriculum.

In Chapter 11 Mike Davies and Gwyn Edwards examine curriculum policies since 1997, arguing that 'standards' has replaced 'curriculum' in consideration of the development of educational policies. They suggest that government has established an even greater control over the pedagogy in order to 'deliver' these standards, so eroding the 'broad and balanced' curriculum established by the 1988 Education Reform Act. Like Pollard in Chapter 1 they make suggestions for a future curriculum.

In Chapter 12, Bob Jeffrey considers one school's approach to a 'subject-centred curriculum' using Bernstein's 'code theory' to analyse teachers' approaches both in ideology and practice. The teachers at the school believe in the importance of a 'child considered/child embracing' pedagogy. The chapter explores how it might be possible to include children's wishes and expectations in the curriculum.

Elizabeth Wood, in Chapter 13 examines the impact of the National Curriculum on play in reception classes. She considers the wider ideological, political and education context of the policy changes as well as reflecting on the realities of teachers' experiences. This gives rise to two themes: the teachers' perceptions of the impact of the National Curriculum on their practice, and their provision for play as part of the planned curriculum. This chapter also suggests implications for future curriculum development.

In Chapter 14 Don Rowe identifies a dilemma within a curriculum for citizenship in a democratic society. He suggests that there is no single view of what citizenship should mean therefore it is difficult to establish an acceptable model for teaching it. The chapter focuses on a wide variety of approaches towards citizenship education establishing models within three categories – the cognitive, the affective and the active.

In Chapter 15 Michael Bonnett, Angela McFarlane and Jacquetta Williams argue that interactive ICT has the potential to develop qualities of evaluation, independence and responsibility in children's learning and understanding. They suggest that ICT can challenge the existing culture of the classroom and stimulate teachers to devise teaching strategies. These will celebrate a reassertion of liberal educational values which have implications for the role of the teacher in interpreting the curriculum, teacher–pupil interaction and modes of assessment. They illustrate this through a drugs education programme with 10- and 11-year-olds.

In the final chapter Kathy Hall explores the concept of critical literacy, and seeks to assess its validity for the early years of the primary school. She examines the dilemma identified by Rowe and argues that children's views should be challenged and not necessarily accepted as was done in the 1960s. The pedagogy she suggests is not a comfortable one for it removes certainties from both teachers and children. She replaces these with the concepts of 'multiple realities' and 'multiple truths' suggesting these as the basis for developing a reflective curriculum.

References

DfEE/QCA (1999) *The National Curriculum; Handbook for Primary Teachers in England*, DfEE/QCA.

Mosley, J. (1996), *Quality Circle Time in the Primary Classroom*, LDA, Cambridge.

Wragg, E. (1997) *The Cubic Curriculum*, Routledge, London.

10

What Is the Curriculum?

Alistair Ross

Everyone believes that they know what other people should learn. Though they might not be able to express the precise detail, they could certainly advance the categories, whether in terms of bodies of knowledge, skills, or by an appeal to a higher or 'more educated' authority. The fact that defining the curriculum, like much of education, is seen by many to be part of 'common sense' does not make it any easier to engage in debate about purposes and priorities.

[. . .]

A curriculum is a definition of what is to be learned. The origins of the word are from the Latin *curriculum*, a racing chariot, from which is derived a racetrack, or a course to be run, and from this, a course of study. The term is often confined to formal definitions of what is to be taught in specific institutions – perhaps even as narrow as the notion of a National Curriculum that confines its coverage to the prescribed content of learning during the years of compulsory education. But even within compulsory education, it is also possible to refer to the 'hidden' curriculum: that which is not overtly stated, and which may be unintentionally passed on through the processes of education. Beyond this, curriculum exists in much wider domains, and it can – and perhaps should – include any socially constructed or prescribed activities, selected in some way from the culture of that society, that result in the transformation of the individual. It is possible, for example, to refer to a curriculum for parenting, in that in contemporary society there are a range of activities that, formally and otherwise, construct individuals as parents. [. . .] Though such a curriculum appears to be purely voluntary and informal, it is in fact governed not only by the socially accepted view of what constitutes 'good parenting', but through a series of laws such as the Children Act and Education Acts requiring parents to ensure the education of their children, and influenced by strictures from politicians and others about what they see as appropriate parental behaviour.

Perhaps the best brief definition of curriculum was that offered by HM Inspectorate (HMI) in 1985 as a contribution to the then current debate on curriculum aims:

A school's curriculum consists of all those activities designed or encouraged within its organisational framework to promote the intellectual, personal, social and physical development of its pupils. It includes not only the formal programme of lessons, but also the 'informal' programme of so-called extracurricular activities as well as all those features which produce the school's 'ethos', such as the quality of relationships, the concern for equality of opportunity, the values exemplified in the way the schools sets about its task and the way in which it is organised and managed. Teaching and learning styles strongly influence the curriculum and in practice they cannot be separated from it. Since pupils learn from all these things, it needs to be ensured that all are consistent in supporting the school's intentions. (DES, 1985, para 11)

This is a very broad conceptualization, but one that properly emphasizes that anything that schools do that affects pupils' learning, whether through deliberate planning and organization, unwitting encouragement, or hidden and unrealized assumptions, can all be properly seen as elements of the school's whole curriculum.

[. . .] Within formal educational institutions . . . many of the processes of teaching and learning take place outside the prescribed content. It has been argued that many of the aspects of schooling that are outside the material of lessons are more important than that material itself: uniforms and uniformity, timekeeping, subservience and obedience, the acceptance of orders and of roles imposed by others, social stratification and hierarchies – all of these, it has been held, are calculated to induce those behaviours and attitudes in adult life that are necessary to serve the needs of (capitalist) employers for a docile and tractable workforce (for example, Bowles and Gintis, 1976). Conversely, it has also been observed that the pupils' own counter-cultures – which are often created and transmitted within the boundaries of the schooling system – can sometimes be more powerful mechanisms for learning than any outcomes that were intended by the system's formal controllers, whether this was to produce complaisant workers or to transmit formal knowledge (Willis, 1977). [. . .]

Curriculum and the Reproduction of Culture

One of the key issues in the analysis of curriculum . . . is how a selection is made from a society's culture of the material that is to be included in the curriculum – what is chosen, by what processes, by whom, with what intent and with what result. Basil Bernstein suggested that 'how a society selects, classifies, distributes, transmits and evaluates the educational knowledge that it considers to be public reflects both the distribution of power and the principles of social control' (1971, p. 47), from which list the selection, classification and evaluation of particular knowledge are central to the definition of a curriculum. This is not a simple or deterministic model of social and cultural reproduction of the dominant ideology. There are many detailed studies of the growth of particular disciplines within the curriculum that suggest the processes are considerably more complex (e.g. Whitty, 1985).

There are two particular issues of cultural reproduction that are of note. First, society is no longer – if it ever was – possessed of an unmistakable and clear culture: we are now increasingly aware of a range of multiple cultural identities, each with its own necessary cultural impedimenta, from which individuals make their own selection. The individual constructs and projects a particular range of identities, utilizing an appropriate set of discourses. These cultural repertoires arise from constructions of ethnicity, gender, class, age-sets, sexual orientation and the like, and are often mutually exclusive. While individuals can adapt to their immediate chosen context and discourse – displaying different cultural traits, using specific language, selecting particular and specific identities – this can appear much more problematic when we are asked to do it on the scale of selecting a set of cultural attributes for conscious transmission, through the curriculum. The plurality of our society means that children come from a range of cultural backgrounds: they may come from different ethnic origins, have (or have parents of) different faiths, different attitudes, beliefs and experiences concerning gender and sexual orientation, come from homes with widely varied experiences of the nature of work, have different expectations of the efficacy of political systems. To make a selection for transmission through the school curriculum will necessarily be contentious, and the greater the scope of a curriculum definition – for example, at national level – the greater the degree of contention. There is a necessary tension between the narrowest of possible curricula and the widest. The narrowest would probably be a curriculum that was directly and exclusively selected from the culture of the parents or guardians of the child, in which the cultural reproduction of schooling directly mimicked the biological reproduction of the genes: few would argue for such a ghettoized curriculum, even if it were possible to deliver. But a national curriculum requires someone, somehow, to rule that certain cultural artefacts (selected, by very definition, from particular cultures) should be elevated to be passed on to all children, and that other cultural manifestations be excluded from formal education, even though they will probably be the principal cultural determinants of many children in the system. This leads to the second potential problem with simple cultural reproduction theory.

The very analysis articulated by Bernstein in the early 1970s has, in itself, altered the nature and processes of curriculum description. As with many aspects of the social sciences, the description and broadcasting of a social rule means that it becomes possible consciously to manipulate the situation that the rule purports to describe and, at least to an extent, the generalization that the rule represents is no longer valid. Once a policy-maker grasps that the act of defining the curriculum is a conscious selection of which culture shall be transmitted to the next generation, then it becomes possible to reverse the process: to decide what form of culture (or society) will be desirable in future, and to ensure that it is this which is included in the curriculum. For example, if a group of curriculum-makers feel that individuals should be more enterprising and responsible for their own social and economic progress, then they can ensure that the curriculum includes themes that emphasize individual initiative, that prioritize individual duties and obligations over social and communal rights, and that put a high value on entrepreneurial activities in schools (Ross, 1995). If curriculum-makers are concerned that their society is losing its sense of identity, then they can manipulate the curriculum so that – in the words of Nick Tate, Chief Executive of the Schools Curriculum and Assessment Authority for England and Wales – its key function becomes

> the explicit reinforcement of a common culture . . . Pupils first and foremost should be introduced to the history of the part of the world where they live, its literary heritage and main religious traditions . . . the culture and traditions of Britain should be at the core. Seen in this light, the central role of British history, Christianity and the English literary heritage are axiomatic. (Tate, 1994, p. 11)

If, as Tate goes on to argue, 'a national curriculum . . . plays a key part in helping society maintain its identity', then it is possible for those who have views about what that social identity should be to set out to construct a curriculum that does not just reproduce the existing diversities, dichotomies and contradictions in society, but produces the new order that they seek. [. . .]

The curriculum can be construed in this way as a way of constructing both individuals *and* society. The individual and society are created, by the processes of the curriculum, as related parts: society as composed of a set of individuals; individuals as existing through a set of social references; and society and individuals in contradistinction to each other. The curriculum is, therefore, a social construction, as individuals and societies decide what constitutes the processes and contents of the construction. The inevitable tension lies in the differences between what an individual learner (or their parent or guardian) might want from a curriculum and what a much wider social grouping might want – or indeed, what a narrower and more powerful group, such as curriculum authority, might want.

Curriculum and Assessment

One of Bernstein's key processes was the evaluation of educational knowledge. The mechanisms for assessing the curriculum often reveal as much about the motivations and ideologies of the educationally powerful as they do about the efficacy of the learning that has taken place. Decisions about what to assess, about why the assessment is to take place, and about how to conduct assessment are usually framed within the language of maintaining and improving standards, but this very often masks ways in which power is selectively transmitted to the next generation. Whatever the reasons for which assessment is carried out, however, it is clear that any kind of assessment has very far-reaching consequences for the nature of the curriculum, and consequently assessment is invariably seen as an aspect of curriculum design, rather than an independent variable. The dangers of this have long been apparent: the Spens Report (Board of Education, 1938) quoted a Board Circular (1034 of March 1918) that set out as 'a cardinal principle that the examination should follow the curriculum and not determine it': Spens also noted 'in practice, this principle has been reversed'. However much it is argued that assessment should be curriculum-driven, it seems almost inevitable that, even at the most straightforward level, it is inevitable that 'teaching for the test' will happen – that the curriculum is assessment-driven (Gipps and Stobart, 1993).

If an educational system is designed to be selective – to act as a filter – then assessment systems must be devised that only allow the necessary number or proportion of people to pass through to the next stage. Much of the educational system in Britain, and employers generally, demand that assessment (and thus the curriculum) be designed to select those students who are 'fitted' for further and more advanced study, or for particular employment needs. Such assessment systems must be norm-referenced; that is, the qualification level is related to the group taking the test. The old 11 plus examination system is an example of this: since there were, in a given area, only a fixed number of grammar school places, only that number could be awarded a pass. In a 'good' year, children would need to achieve a higher mark than would be necessary in a 'poor' year. Moreover, since girls as a group consistently outscored boys, and since it was held that an approximately equal number of each sex should receive grammar school education, the pass mark for girls was generally fixed at a higher level than the pass mark for boys. Other examinations also act as filters, though they are designed not to be norm-referenced. [. . .]

The effect on the curriculum is to value processes and content that are amenable to grading. This can mean that a curriculum is, at least in part, determined by its ability to filter: knowledge and skills (traditionally knowledge in particular) that are relatively inaccessible are given a more important place, because they will make it easier to construct filters that achieve the desired result. The use that was made of the study of classical languages is an example of this: irrespective of the merits of learning Latin and Greek, proficiency in one or both of these languages was used as a way of filtering applicants to university and to careers beyond this. [. . .] Mathematics and science (and, very recently, technology) have supplanted the classics in the pole position as subjects necessary for today's filtering mechanisms. Mathematical knowledge and ability have been accorded the status of high-level knowledge, suitable as a means of sorting out the elite from the non-elite. It can be argued that we have given this status to these subjects, not because of their intrinsic interest or usefulness, but because it is possible quickly and efficiently to grade people in their ability to perform, and to make appropriate categories in consequence. In view of the great difficulties that were encountered through the nineteenth century in recognizing science as a subject to be included anywhere within the school curriculum, the present reification of scientific knowledge as an essential element of the well-educated person is ironic.

Of course, it can be argued that mathematical and scientific knowledge is useful, in particular in contemporary society with its dependence on technology, and that this is why such forms of knowledge have now, rightly, acquired such high status. This leads to the second broad set of purposes of an educational system: to provide the necessary skills that will be useful to individuals, both in their immediate and future roles in society. This in turn requires an assessment system that can certify that a particular competence or level of knowledge has been reached: a criterion-referenced assessment. Such a system allows for the vagaries of a 'good' or a 'bad' year of students: all those who reach the standard will be awarded the grade, and only those students. It would be theoretically possible for all students to meet the required grade, or all to fail, in any given period. The argument for such testing is not simply that it is fairer and unambiguous: such assessment is related solely to the ability of the student to demonstrate that they can do or know something, irrespective of any other person's competence at the same task. The driving test or a swimming test are both simple examples of criterion-referenced tests. Once a description of the abilities necessary to be 'able to drive' or 'able to swim' have been determined, then one has only to meet these criteria to pass. There is no reason why virtually everyone should not be able to eventually learn to drive, or be able to swim. In terms of utility for employment and adult life, the advantages of such assessment are that one can, in theory, determine the skills and knowledge needed for a particular task, and then demonstrate competency at the necessary level. But it could be argued that an employer (or an educational institution recruiting) would find this system unhelpful, in that they find it easier to select on the basis of a norm-referenced system: they will take those judged best at a particular attribute, not those sufficiently able to perform the task successfully or take the educational course with advantage.

The effect of criterion-referenced assessment on the curriculum is to place special emphasis on measurable competencies. In practice, the setting of strict criteria may be too difficult, and the device of 'grade descriptors' (or 'level descriptors') is often used: an account of the standards expected of students reaching each grade. [. . .] These establish levels of abilities, and have marked a shift in the curriculum away from the idea of knowledge to one of competency: content becomes less important than standards of achievement, curriculum is defined in terms of desired outputs, rather than of inputs and processes, and competence itself is related to the whole work role. [. . .] But competencies are themselves constructs, and can only be assessed through observation, so that one set of cultural filters may merely be replaced by another (Wolf, 1995).

A third set of assessment purposes may be seen in what Gipps and Stobart (1993) distinguished as the managerial functions of assessment. While a professional assessment may be concerned with providing teachers with useful diagnostic material, with screening to detect special needs, or providing material that helps in record-keeping, managerial assessment is designed to produce data that will allow the comparison of teachers', schools' and local education authorities' performances. Assessments that produce direct comparisons over a wide range of the population are rarely sufficiently finely tuned to produce diagnostic feedback, or to provide more than the most crude ranking for the individual child, but do allow league tables to be constructed that – if everything else were equal – allow the direct comparison of the 'standards' or 'effectiveness' of different schools and LEAs. What effect will such assessment have on the curriculum? The introduction of this kind of assessment occurred in 1862 in England and Wales, when the revised code made teachers' salaries dependent on the results their pupils achieved, which resulted in an extraordinary narrowing of the curriculum to focus very largely on the tested elements.

The reasons why assessment is carried out thus have a very powerful effect on the content of the curriculum, and are very much associated with what are seen as the overall purposes of education, whether these are to limit the group who will have access to power in the future, or to ensure that individuals are educated towards particular levels of competence, or to enable individuals to gain access to as wide a range of knowledge and abilities as they are able to do.

Global Trends in School Curricula

The diversity of the ideologies that seek to create curricula might be expected to result in a great diversity of curricular patterns around the world, It would not be surprising to find some societies with wholly utilitarian curricula, geared closely to the local means of production, and other societies which valued and taught particular cultural forms to a stratified elite.

An important study of worldwide trends in the curriculum suggests that this may not be so. John Meyer's team at Stanford University has looked at the curricular categories used in primary education in over 70 countries since the 1920s. Instead of diversity, they discovered 'an extraordinary homogeneity across the extraordinarily variable countries of the world' (Meyer, Kamens and Benavot, 1992, p. 6). Comparing nationally provided accounts of curricular provision, it was perhaps not surprising that local influences on the curriculum appeared to be unimportant, as mass education overrode local cultural content: what was unexpected was the degree to which national pressures were also apparently unimportant, and that the broad similarities between curricula greatly outweighed the differences.

Meyer's team took official data from a variety of government and international sources, and from these analysed descriptions of the curriculum into broad categories, looking both at the lists of subjects taught and the percentage of total instruction time given to each subject. In some countries, they were able to trace accounts back into the earlier part of the nineteenth century; in other cases, they were looking at the educational systems of nations that have only achieved statehood since the 1960s. Admittedly the data is limited and superficial: it is not possible to discover what a particular curricular category might mean in any given country. There could be significant variations in the syllabus, in teaching materials, in pedagogy or in assessment; the implementation may differ from country to country, and it is possible that the category may in practice mean very different things for different children, when differentiated, for example, by class, or gender or ethnic grouping. But having allowed for all these caveats, their data still suggested that 'the labels, at least, of mass curricula are so closely tied to great and standardized versions of social and educational progress, they tend to be patterned in quite consistent ways around the world' (p. 166).

The world curriculum that they describe has changed through the period of their analysis, and local national variations have been ironed out as a pattern of international conformity has prevailed. The professionalized or 'tamed' curriculum generally now consists of

- One or more *national languages* (no longer classical languages): the reality of the nation state is that local languages and dialects are relatively downgraded in the teaching of a nationwide language. What variation that there is in language policy tends to be on matters such as which languages are to be regarded as national or official; how much use might be made of local languages or mother-tongue teaching in the early part of the elementary school; the methods and emphases used in language teaching; and whether and how to legitimize local languages. Very few systems now include at their core the study of classical texts or sacred moral texts (Cha, 1991).
- *Mathematics* is now found universally in educational systems: it has become 'a critically important element in the rationalistic modern world' (Meyer, Kamens and Benavot, 1992, p. 12). In some states in the nineteenth century, mathematics had been seen as either a speciality for an elite group, or as particularly necessary for those entering trade or commerce: now mathematics is seen as a requirement for everyone, and controversy in mathematics education is confined to matters of technique or emphasis (Kamens and Benavot, 1991).
- *Science* has also become canonical: as Meyer, Kamens and Benavot observe, 'all future little citizens are to learn that the world is empirical and lawful, governed by natural forces which can be scrutinised through rigorous investigations' (1992, p. 12). Science was introduced as a compulsory subject significantly later than the date at which mathematics became mandatory in different countries (see also Kamens and Benavot, 1991). The process began, it seems, in the primary curricula of European countries, and then spread around the world.

- The fourth curricular area that is found in all of the survey nations was some form of *social science*. This core area was generally taught either under the combined social studies rubric, or divided into separate subjects, such as history, geography and civics. The social world, like science, seems to be presented as having 'factual evidence and law-like properties' (Meyer, Kamens and Benavot, 1992, p. 12), taught not just to an elite group but to all future citizens. Wong (1991, 1992) has shown that the variations in social science teaching are greater than those in language, mathematics and science, and concern issues of categorization and organization as social studies gradually supplanted the separate subjects of history and geography (though this may be a trend that has recently been put into reverse) (Ross, 1996).
- Aesthetic education (in art and music) and physical education are not quite so ubiquitous as the four areas described above, but are still found in over 95 per cent of all national curricula.

[. . .]

Meyer, Kamens and Benavot conclude that in subject area after subject area . . . controversy is limited – matters of outline are settled, and national society is rooted in modern culture through universal socialisation schemes. True conservative protest, which might object to the whole system as an intrusion on the natural properties of society and communal life is dead . . . radical protest . . . focus more on styles of instruction . . . than on content categories. (1992, p. 13)

The data are not watertight – the categorizations may well conceal major variations in intention and in practice, and the sources used may well have put strains on responding government departments to make their practice 'fit' the requirements of the various surveys that were conducted. But the general conclusion is that there is what Ivor Goodson has described as an 'aggrandising world rhetoric' that has shaped the curricula of most countries (Preface to Meyer, Kamens and Benavot, 1992, p. x).

This does not, however, mean that analysis of the curriculum is inevitably confined within curricular category boundaries. Questions of cultural transmission and utilitarianism, of child-centred or subject-centred emphases are still valid. General world conceptions of curricula are not . . . as hegemonic as Meyer's team seems to suggest, and more local forces still have a pervasive influence on the forms and purpose of the curriculum. Such local forces are particularly to be found in the shaping of the UK's school curriculum, especially in the curriculum in England and Wales, where . . . there is a relative impermeability to international trends and forces in education.

References

Bernstein, B. (1971) 'On the classification and framing of educational knowledge', in M. F. D. Young (ed.), *Knowledge and Control: New Directions for the Sociology of Education*, London: Collier-Macmillan.

Board of Education (1938) *Report of the Consultative Committee on Secondary Education with Special Reference to Grammar Schools and Technical High Schools* (Spens Report), London: HMSO.

Bowles, S. and Gintis, H. (1976) *Schooling in Capitalist America: Educational Reform and the Contradictions of Economic Life*, London: Routledge.

Cha, Y.-K. (1991) 'Effect of the global system on language instruction, 1850–1986', *Sociology of Education*, 64(1), pp. 19–32.

DES (Department of Education and Science) (1985) *The Curriculum from 5 to 16: Curriculum Matters 2* (An HMI Series), London: HMSO.

Gipps, C. and Stobart, G. (1993) *Assessment: A Teacher's Guide to the Issues*, London: Hodder and Stoughton.

Kamens, D. and Benavot, A. (1991) 'Elite knowledge for the masses: the origins and spread of mathematics and science education in national curricula', *American Journal of Education*, 99(2), pp. 137–80.

Meyer, J., Kamens, D. and Benavot, A. (1992) *School Knowledge for the Masses: World Models and National Primary Curricular Categories in the Twentieth Century*, London: Falmer.

Ross, A. (1995) 'The rise and fall of the social subjects in the curriculum', in J. Ahier and A. Ross (eds), *The Social Subjects within the Curriculum: Children's Social Learning in the National Curriculum*, London: Falmer.

Ross, A. (1996) 'Curriculum, nationalism, identity and individualism: the roast beef of England', in S. Shah (ed.), *National Initiatives and Equality Issues: Papers Presented at the Inaugural Conference of the Centre for Equality Issues in Education, November 1966*, Aldenham: Centre for Equality Issues in Education, University of Hertfordshire.

Tate, N. (1994) 'Off the fence on common culture', *Times Educational Supplement*, 29 July, p. 11.

Whitty, G. (1985) *Sociology and School Knowledge Curriculum Theory, Research and Politics*, London: Methuen.

Willis, P. (1977) *Learning to Labour: How Working Class Kids get Working Class Jobs*, London: Saxon House.

Wolf, A. (1995) *Competence Based Assessment*, Buckingham: Open University Press.

Wong, S.-Y. (1991) 'The evolution of social science instruction, 1900–86', *Sociology of Education*, 65(1), pp. 33–47.

Wong, S.-Y. (1992) 'The Evolution and Organisation of the Social Science Curriculum', in Meyer, J., Kamens, D. and Benavot, A. *School Knowledge for the Masses: World Modules and National Primary Curricular Categories in the Twentieth Century*, London: Falmer, pp. 124–38.

11

Will the Curriculum Caterpillar Ever Learn to Fly?

Mike Davies and Gwyn Edwards

[. . .]

> Adding wings to caterpillars does not create butterflies – it creates awkward and dysfunctional caterpillars. Butterflies are created through transformation. (Stephanie Pace Marshall)

Any evaluation of New Labour's curriculum policies since assuming office in May 1997 has to be set within the wider context of the cultural politics of the last 30 years and against a backdrop of significant socio-economic transformations that we have witnessed during this period. Indeed, it was partly in response to the gathering momentum of these transformations that the previous Labour government (1971–79), under the leadership of James Callaghan, launched the Great Debate on education, the outcomes of which are clearly manifest in the curriculum today. Moreover, it could be argued that Callaghan's Ruskin speech in 1976, together with the Green Paper that followed (Department of Education and Science [DES], 1977), established the discursive boundaries within which all subsequent curriculum debate and policy-making at government level have been framed. The speech highlighted a number of concerns about schools which the government and public shared and, it was argued, had a legitimate right to air. Particular attention was drawn to complaints from industry that new recruits lacked the required skills and to parental unease about new informal teaching methods. To address the concerns raised in the speech, the government Green Paper (DES, 1977) proposed a review of curricular arrangements and, in the light of the review, to establish a broad agreement on a framework for the curriculum with the possibility of a 'core' or 'protected part'.

Over the next ten years numerous frameworks for a 'core' or 'common' curriculum were put forward (DES, 1976, 1980, 1981, 1984, 1985; Schools Council, 1981), but a statutory national curriculum was never formally proposed and there was no apparent support for any form of national testing. On the contrary, emphasis was given to arriving at a consensus on a broad framework for the curriculum without seriously undermining the professional autonomy that schools had always enjoyed in curriculum decision-making (DES, 1980, 1984, 1986).

By 1987, however, the mood had changed dramatically. With a general election on the horizon, the Conservative government announced its intention to legislate for a national curriculum should it be returned to power. In fulfilment of this election pledge, the 1988 Education Act (DES, 1988) legislated for 'a balanced and broadly based curriculum which: (a) promotes the spiritual, moral, cultural, mental and physical development of pupils at the school and of society; (b) prepares such pupils for the opportunities, responsibilities and experiences of adult life' (DES, 1988). As a general statement of intent, few would take issue with these broad aims. But their translation into a defensible and workable curriculum is a more contentious matter. What the 1988 Education Act failed to provide was a coherent rationale whereby its broad aims could be translated into a national curriculum which could be adapted to meet the needs of schools operating in a variety of contexts and circumstances.

In essence, the National Curriculum was constructed from a collection of already existing school subjects on the assumption that a coherent whole would emerge from the sum of the parts. Predictably, it didn't. Moreover, to comply with the model of assessment proposed by the Task Group on Assessment and Testing (DES, 1987), the subjects were broken down into programmes of study and these, in turn, were further fragmented into attainment targets organized hierarchically into ten levels.

Subsequently, the National Curriculum Council endeavoured to address what were seen as serious shortcomings by bolting on a framework of cross-curricular components designed to 'tie together the broad education of the individual subjects and augment what comes from the basic curriculum' (National Curriculum Council, 1990, p. 2). But this only compounded the problem by imposing an additional burden on an already overloaded curriculum. Not surprisingly, the cross-curricular themes have been marginalized to such an extent that their recovery is unlikely without a substantial revision of the National Curriculum subject orders (Whitty, Rowe and Aggleton, 1994).

Running alongside the demand for greater curriculum uniformity (culminating in the National Curriculum) – and to some extent in tension with it – there was also from the mid-1970s onwards a concerted effort to align the school curriculum more explicitly to the perceived needs of the economy, especially in the 14–19 phase. The Green Paper (DES, 1977) that followed Callaghan's speech highlighted 'the feeling that the educational system was out of touch with the fundamental need for Britain to survive economically in a highly competitive world through the efficiency of its industry and commerce' (p. 2). Young people, it was argued, were not 'sufficiently aware of the importance of industry to our society' and they were 'not taught much about it' (p. 2). Consequently, they left school 'with little or no understanding of the workings, or importance, of the wealth-producing sector of our economy' (p. 34). Henceforth, it was envisaged that education would 'contribute as much as possible to improving industrial performance and thereby increasing the national wealth' (p. 6).

The view that schools were out of touch with the needs of industry was reiterated in subsequent official government statements on the curriculum. *The School Curriculum* (DES, 1981, p. 18), for example, asserted that 'pupils need to be given a better understanding of the economic base of our society and the importance to Britain of the wealth creating process'. In a similar vein, the White Paper *Better Schools* (DES, 1986, p. 16) advocated a curriculum that brought education and training 'into closer relation in a variety of ways' and had 'preparation for employment as one of its principal functions'.

The most significant response to the demands for a more economically oriented curriculum during this period was the Technical and Vocational Education Initiative (TVEI), established by the Conservative government in 1982 to meet a 'growing concern about existing arrangements for technical and vocational education for young people' (Thatcher, quoted in Dale, 1989, p. 147). Despite its predominantly instrumental intent, in the hands of educational practitioners TVEI contributed significantly to a form of 'vocational progressivism' (Ball, 1990) which fostered new approaches to teaching and learning and went some way to bridging the traditional academic–vocational divide (Young, 1998). The innovative practices of TVEI, however, were strategically marginalized by the National Curriculum, which was configured and developed in compliance with a neo-conservative 'cultural restorationist' agenda (Ball, 1994).

In April 1993, in response to growing concern about content overload, John Patten, the Secretary of State for Education, invited Sir Ron Dearing to review the National Curriculum, albeit within the somewhat narrow remit of slimming down the curriculum, improving the central administration, simplifying the testing arrangements and reviewing the ten-level scale for recognizing children's attainment. Dearing's final report (School Curriculum and Asessment Authority, 1994), submitted in December 1993, recommended a substantial slimming down of curriculum content in Key Stages 1–3 and a reduction in the number of compulsory subjects at Key Stage 4 to create space for a vocational pathway. Needless to say, the casualties at Key Stage 4 were the arts and humanities subjects.

It could be argued that the general approval these recommendations received from the educational community was misplaced in that the underlying assumptions of the National Curriculum were never questioned – for it was not in the remit to do so – and its underlying structure survived virtually intact. Moreover, the changes at Key Stage 4 seriously undermined the principle of a broad and balanced entitlement during the compulsory years of schooling which almost universally has been accepted as one of the redeeming features of the National Curriculum legislation.

This, then, was the curriculum legacy inherited by New Labour in May 1997. Moreover, it was a legacy that was now firmly embedded, both discursively and structurally, in the educational system and, consequently, set strategic limitations on curriculum possibilities for the immediate future. Therefore, a useful way of analysing the subsequent curriculum policies of the New Labour government is in terms of the continuities and disjunctures with those of its predecessor. Perhaps the most obvious observation to make is that so far there appears to be no radical departure from the curriculum policies of the previous Conservative government. The post-Dearing National Curriculum settlement remains more or less intact and it is evident that the review currently being undertaken by the Qualifications and Curriculum Authority (QCA) will amount to little more than making the necessary adjustments to accommodate initiatives that are already under way. Indeed, the Secretary of State instructed QCA, albeit in response to advice given to him by this body, that the revision of the National Curriculum should 'avoid excessive disruption and upheaval in the curriculum' and 'must be limited to addressing what needs to be changed to allow schools to concentrate on raising standards' (quoted in QCA, 1999a, p. 2). Thus, it can be assumed that the review will be confined to cosmetic tinkering at the margins of the subject orders with the overall curriculum structure remaining essentially the same (QCA 1999a, 1999b).

This endorsement of the curriculum status quo does not square with pre-election promises of an alternative curriculum framework 'which values local flexibility and the professional discretion of teachers' (Labour Party, 1994, p. 15), provides 'a broad . . . entitlement ['in terms of areas of experience' (Labour Party, 1993, p. 28)] to all children without stifling a teacher's creativity and ability to respond to pupils' needs' (Labour Party, 1995, p. 24) and recognizes that 'development and innovation is essential if the curriculum is to be relevant in a modern and progressive society'. (Labour Party, 1995, p. 24). So, for the forseeable future, schools will continue to work within the confines of a 'prescriptive', 'content-specific', 'over-assessed', 'conceptually arid' (Labour Party, 1993) National Curriculum that, arguably, serves neither the personal needs of pupils nor the social, political and economic needs of the society in which they live.

Closer examination, however, reveals a number of distinctive features to New Labour curriculum policy that represent a significant departure from what went before. Most notably, under New Labour 'standards' has replaced 'curriculum' as the discursive hub of educational policy-making. And this discursive reorientation has legitimated the obsessive pursuit of a Thatcher-like 'back to basics' agenda. The stated educational priority is to 'ensure that every child is taught to read, write and add up' (Department for Education and Employment [DfEE], 1997, p. 9). This involves the setting of 'ambitious and challenging' (DES, 1997, p. 19) literacy and numeracy targets for 11-year-olds to be achieved by the year 2002.

While no one would seriously dispute the desirability of raising standards in literacy and numeracy – although many would object to this being seen as the predominant purpose of education – it seems reasonable to suggest that there will inevitably be a degree of contestation as to how this is best achieved. Not so for the New Labour government, which, despite criticisms and setbacks, remains dogmatically committed to both the appropriateness and the feasibility of its targets. Moreover, it simplistically assumes that the targets can be met by the application of what is taken to be 'proven best practice' (DES, 1997, p. 19). Underpinning this assumption is a discourse, emanating from the Teacher Training Agency and newly created Standards and Effectiveness Unit (SEU) at the DfEE, which perpetuates the view that teaching is a techno-rational activity, the underlying mechanics of which can be revealed through appropriate research and then universally applied in classrooms.

What the discourse avoids is any engagement with deeper questions relating to the complex, and inevitably contentious, relationship between educational purposes and the school curriculum and, in turn, the implications of this for what constitutes educational standards. There is an assumption that educational standards are unproblematical and, furthermore, that they can be raised without any consideration of curriculum content and pedagogical practice. So, the claim that the National Curriculum and its assessment, together with regular OFSTED inspections and league tables, are raising educational standards needs to be treated with a degree of scepticism in that it is premised on unquestioned assumptions about the nature and purpose of education. Within a pre-given, taken-for-granted curriculum framework, raising standards is seen simply as a matter of adopting 'proven ways' (DES, 1997, p. 12).

Consistent with the discourse are the attempts to exert greater control over pedagogical practice in schools by imposing on teachers tightly prescribed curriculum packages which are considered to be consistent with 'proven best practice' (DES, 1997, p. 13). The most obvious examples are the 'literacy and numeracy hours'. But of equal significance are the exemplar schemes of work that have been produced for other National Curriculum subjects at Key Stages 1 and 2. It is tempting to speculate that it will not be long before similar materials are produced for Key Stage 3.

Thus, whereas the Conservative government established tight control over the content of the curriculum and sought to influence pedagogy indirectly, it seems that New Labour might allow schools greater freedom over content but is adopting a more interventionist stance in relation to pedagogy. What both approaches share, however, is a profound mistrust of teachers: the former in relation to their ideological commitments; the latter their professional competence. And they also share a fundamentally distorted understanding of curriculum by permitting content and pedagogy to be separated and determined independently of each other.

Some teachers, of course, will 'read' government edicts and injunctions as open texts and reinterpret them in the light of their own values, understandings, experiences and circumstances. The danger is, however, that others – possibly the majority – will find it difficult to contest the new pedagogic identity being prescribed for them. Consequently, they will become little more than 'operatives' whose professional expertise is reduced to a command of the technical aspects of teaching and classroom management necessary to the pursuance of state sanctioned standards. Teachers, Stenhouse (1983, p. 189) argues, 'must be educated to develop their art, not to master it'. For him, 'close control of curricula and teaching methods in schools is to be likened to the totalitarian control of art' (Stenhouse, 1984, p. 68). If we extend his analogy further, the literacy and numeracy hours could be seen as the pedagogical equivalents of painting by numbers.

[. . .]

Further compromises and contradictions in New Labour's curriculum policies are evident in the recently established Education Action Zones. Here, local partnerships are being invited 'to put forward their own radical ideas and imaginative proposals to raise standards' (DfEE, 1998a). More-over, 'innovation and flexibility in curriculum organisation and delivery' (DfEE, 1998a) is encouraged, including the possibility of 'adapting the National Curriculum – or radically redesigning parts of it – to meet local needs' (DfEE, 1998b). Thus, while for the majority of schools standards will be raised through prescription, standardization and central control, in others it requires flexibility, experimentation and local autonomy. More-over, there is also the implication that in predominantly middle-class sub-urban and rural areas entitlement to a broad and balanced curriculum is maintained, while in working-class inner city areas it can be disapplied. Whether Education Action Zones will be catalysts for radical curriculum innovation remains to be seen. Indeed, evidence based on an examination of the 'first wave' of Education Action Zones applications suggests that so far the response has been 'safe' rather than 'radical' (Riley *et al.*, 1998) and the main emphasis has been on structure and provision rather than curricu-lum and learning.

For New Labour 'education is the key to personal fulfilment for the individual, to economic success for the Nation, and to the creation of a more just and cohesive society' (Labour Party, 1994, p. 3). What is lacking, however, is any appreciation of the complexities, tensions and contesta-tions that are endemic in the realization of a curriculum consistent with these three goals. Certainly there should be no serious obstacle, at least in theory, to the creation of a curriculum that facilitates the pursuit of per-sonal fulfilment of individuals and that contributes to the development of a more cohesive and just society. But creating a curriculum that achieves these two aims and, at the same time, ensures the economic success of the nation is far more problematical. Indeed, there are those who argue that there is an inevitable tension between educating young people for personal fulfilment and democratic empowerment, and preparing them for the world of work (Brosio, 1991; Jones and Hatcher, 1994; MacIntyre, 1987). And it is a tension that cannot be conveniently wished away. Thus, while in New Labour policy documents we get rhetorical gestures to the value of learning for its own sake and for democratic empowerment, it is clear that the overwhelming imperative is to recast education primarily, if not ex-clusively, as an instrumental means of ensuring economic success in an increasingly competitive global market.

It is beyond the scope of this chapter to pursue this issue further. Suffice to say that at the present juncture there might potentially be greater compatibility between New Labour's three goals. However, the realization of this in practice would require a radical reordering of the epistemological, pedagogical and organizational assumptions that underpin the school curriculum. Such an undertaking is unlikely to come about if schools are not given the necessary freedom, incentive and expertise to do so.

Research indicates that for a significant number of young people the school curriculum, in terms of both content and pedagogy, is not a pathway to enlightenment and empowerment but a source of alienation and failure, especially so in the later years of compulsory schooling and in inner city areas (Carlen, Gleeson and Wardhaugh, 1992; Kinder, 1997). Viewed from this perspective, current government policies are, ironically, causing the educational problems they are supposedly designed to address. Reassuringly, there is at least some official acknowledgement of the causes of disaffection and its consequences for the lives of young people. Douglas Osler, the Senior Chief Inspector of Schools in Scotland, for example, points out:

> There are an increasing number of young people who find school education to be an uncomfortable learning environment. We cannot write these young people off and say that they got it wrong. Young people can often be disaffected from school rather than from learning. Sometimes we speak as if the big idea is school. It is not. The big idea is learning and schools are just economical, collective ways of providing it. (Quoted in Munro, 1997)

In what follows we offer some tentative suggestions for a more holistic view of the curriculum which advances the view that 'the big idea is learning'. We seek a more sophisticated curriculum framework based on a better understanding of the relationship between content and pedagogy and on a recognition that educational standards are realised in and through the teaching-learning process itself, as well as being its extrinsic products. As Stenhouse (1967, p. 89) argues, 'A good curriculum is one which makes worth-while standards possible'. Of particular concern to us is the degree of control learners have over the contents and/or methods of their learning and how these might relate to what are considered to be worthwhile areas and forms of inquiry.

Within the traditional subject-based curriculum the norm is for students to be inducted into the various fields of knowledge and the conceptual structures that comprise each field. The learners are the recipients of the knowledge and have very little control over what they learn or how they go about learning. Regulation, prescription and testing stemming from the end of the last century have been the dominant features of this conception of curriculum.

In recognition of the fragmentation of experience embodied in such a curriculum various attempts have been made over time to combine subjects into integrated areas. But, within this format, the learner is still required to deal with thoughts and ideas mediated through a teacher, a text or, increasingly, a computer program. The contents, materials and methods of the curriculum remain external to the learner.

Looking back to an era when teachers were much more involved in curriculum making there was a strong disposition to viewing the curriculum more holistically. Indeed, this was very much the view that underpinned post-Plowden primary practice. [. . .] And there is a well-established tradition in some Scandinavian schools of involving students themselves in defining both the area of study and the method by which the study is undertaken.

These initiatives, and others like them, were imaginative responses to questions posed by the educational concerns and the socio-economic context at the time. What then are the questions the educational system should now be asking of itself in the light of the social, cultural and economic transformations we are currently experiencing – or anticipate in the future – and on the basis of new understanding about the nature of intelligence and learning? In relation to a number of 'sites' of educational organization and practice, we suggest the following.

- *Teams.* Is it possible to view the curriculum as large swathes which represent areas of common interest and complementary expertise between groups of teachers? Could the arts or the humanities, for example, be seen as a whole? And could the teacher be seen as both a resource and a coach and, additionally, as someone who continues to practice and research in his or her own field for part of the week as well as teach?
- *Time.* Is it necessary to bound learning by predetermined slots of time that are set on an annual basis irrespective of whether they meet the needs of learning and learners at a particular moment? How can we encourage greater flexibility over the use of time and effect greater collaboration between teachers?
- *Place.* With exponential developments in information and communication technology do we really need to have young people in school all the time or could we find greater flexibility in both the where and when of learning? Would there be merit in all young people being involved in learning which took them 'beyond the classroom' (Bentley, 1998) on a more regular basis?
- *Pedagogy.* What are the implications of recognizing that any group of people represents a broad range of human ability, motivation and need? How can we respond more creatively to all that we know about the multiplicity of human intelligence (Gardner, 1983), including emotional intelligence (Goleman, 1995), and the diversity of learning and thinking styles (Sternberg, 1997)?
- *Resources.* What are the curricular implications of ICT for the ways that we organize learning? How do we ensure that students engage critically with the knowledge made available to them through ICT? How can we use ICT resources to increase pupil motivation and develop in them a sense of esteem and human flourishing?

- *Relationships*. How can we encourage and strengthen warm, persistent and learning-focused relationships between different people? How can we break out of the stranglehold by which parents view themselves as possessive individuals interested only in what a school has to offer their child rather than as partners intent on getting the best education they can for all children? How can we mobilise local authorities, higher education institutions, businesses and schools to act as partners in a common struggle of improving learning for all?
- *Audience*. How can we develop more 'authentic' (Perrone, 1991) forms of assessment where the outcomes and products of students' work can be appreciated and celebrated rather than marked and graded and where the audience is seen not as an anonymous assessor but peers, the wider community or even the self?
- *Authorship*. How can we reconceptualize and reconstruct the curriculum in such a way that pupils have an opportunity for fashioning some time for themselves so that they can pursue their own ideas and studies?

In conclusion, it is our contention that the school curriculum is predicated on a seriously flawed logic that renders it ill-equipped to meet the challenges of the twenty-first century. Whether we like it or not education is caught up in the turbulence of exponential change, the outcomes of which are beyond prediction. Therefore, the principal purpose of education should be concerned with helping young people acquire the dispositions, skills, understandings and values that will enable them to live their lives intelligently, meaningfully, constructively and co-operatively in the midst of the complexity, uncertainty and instability they will increasingly encounter. There is no sense in a curriculum designed to predict and control in a world that is in a state of constant flux. What is required is a curriculum rationale and framework that seeks to rediscover the intrinsic purposes and principles of education and that gives schools the freedom and incentive to respond flexibly, creatively and responsibly to the needs of their pupils in an uncertain and rapidly changing world. If our aim is to produce butterflies rather than dysfunctional caterpillars then nothing less will do.

References

Ball, S. J. (1990) *Politics and Policy Making in Education: Explorations in Policy Sociology* (London, Routledge).

Ball, S. J. (1994) *Education Reform: A Critical and Post-Structuralist Approach* (Buckingham, Open University Press).

Bentley, T. (1998) *Learning Beyond the Classroom: Education for a Changing World* (London, Routledge).

Brosio, R. A. (1991) The continuing conflict between capitalism and democracy: ramifications for schooling-education, *Educational Philosophy and Theory*, 23(2), pp. 30–45.

Carlen, P., Gleesom, D. and Wardhaugh, J. (1992) *Truancy: The Politics of Compulsory Schooling* (Buckingham, Open University Press).

Dale, R. (1989) *The State and Education Policy* (Milton Keynes, Open University Press).

Department of Education and Science (1976) *The Curriculum 11 to 16* (London, HMSO).

Department of Education and Science (1977) *Education in Schools: A Consultative Document* (London, HMSO).

Department of Education and Science (1980) *A View of the Curriculum* (London, HMSO).

Department of Education and Science (1981) *The School Curriculum* (London, HMSO).

Department of Education and Science (1984) *The Organisation and Content of the 5–16 Curriculum* (London, HMSO).

Department of Education and Science (1985) *The Curriculum from 5 to 16* (London, HMSO).

Department of Education and Science (1986) *Better Schools* (London, HMSO).

Department of Education and Science (1987) *National Curriculum: Task Group on Assessment and Testing: A Report* (London, HMSO).

Department of Education and Science (1988) *The Education Reform Act* (London, HMSO).

Department for Education and Employment (1997) *Excellence in Schools* (London, DfEE).

Department for Education and Employment (1998a) *The Learning Age: A Renaissance for a New Britain* (London, DfEE).

Department for Education and Employment (1998b) *The National Literacy Strategy: Framework for Teaching* (London, DfEE).

Gardner, H. (1983) *Frames of Mind: The Theory of Multiple Intelligences* (London, Heinemann).

Goleman, D. (1995) *Emotional Intelligence: Why It Can Matter More Than IQ* (New York, Bantam).

Jones, K. and Hatcher, R. (1994) Educational progress and economic change: notes on some recent proposals, *British Journal of Educational Studies*, 42, pp. 245–60.

Kinder, K. (1997) Causes of disaffection: the views of pupils and educational professionals, *EERA Bulletin*, 3(1), pp. 3–11.

Labour Party (1993) Opening doors to a learning society. A consultative green paper on education (London, Labour Party).

Labour Party (1994) *Opening Doors to a Learning Society: A Policy Statement on Education* (London, Labour Party).

Labour Party (1995) *Excellence for Everyone: Labour's Crusade to Raise Standards* (London, Labour Party).

MacIntyre, A. (1987) The idea of an educated public, in G. Haydon (ed.) *Education and Values: The Richard Peters lectures* (London, University of London Institute of Education).

Munro, N. (1997) No 'radical surgery' 5–14, *Times Educational Supplement for Scotland*, 3 October.

National Curriculum Council (1990) *The Whole Curriculum (Curriculum Guidance 3)* (York, NCC).

Perrone, V. (ed.) (1991) *Expanding Student Assessment* (Alexandria, VA, Association for Supervision and Curriculum Development).

Qualifications and Curriculum Authority (1999a) *QCA's Work in Progress to Develop the School Curriculum – Materials for Conferences, Seminars and Meetings: Booklet A* (London, QCA).

Qualifications and Curriculum Authority (1999b) *QCA's Work in Progress to Develop the School Curriculum – Materials for Conferences, Seminars and Meetings: Pack B* (London, QCA).

Riley, K., Watling, R., Rowles, D. and Hopkins, D. (1998) *Educational Action Zones: Some Lessons Learned from First Wave Applications* (London, The Education Network).

Schools Council (1981) *The Practical Curriculum*, Schools Council Working Paper 70 (London, Methuen Educational).

School Curriculum and Assessment Authority (1994) *The National Curriculum and its Assessment: final report* (London, SCAA).

Stenhouse, L. (1967) *Culture and Education* (London, Nelson).

Stenhouse, L. (1983) *Authority, Education and Emancipation* (London, Heinemann).

Stenhouse, L. (1984) Artistry and teaching: the teacher as focus of research and development, in D. Hopkins and M. Wideen (eds), *Alternative Perspectives on School Improvement* (London, Falmer Press).

Sternberg, R. J. (1997) *Thinking Styles* (Cambridge, Cambridge University Press).

Whitty, G., Rowe, G. and Aggleton,P. (1994) Discourse in cross-curricular contexts; limits to empowerment, *International Studies in Sociology of Education*, 4(1), pp. 25–42.

Young, M. F. D. (1998) *The Curriculum of the Future: From the 'New Sociology of Education' to a Critical Theory of Learning* (London, Falmer Press).

12

Challenging Prescription in Ideology and Practice: the Case of Sunny First School

Bob Jeffrey

Introduction

The National Curriculum, the national literacy and numeracy programmes and OFSTED inspections place an emphasis on assessing direct teaching of a subject-centred curriculum in primary schools, a similar curriculum and pedagogy to that which operates in secondary schools. Many Early Years schools or departments have seen this form of curriculum organization and the proposed emphasis on direct teaching as running counter to their beliefs about the appropriate curriculum organization and pedagogy needed to satisfy the developmental needs of young children. They have, in the past, used an integrated curriculum organization and developed the 'teacher as facilitator', satisfying children's interests by providing a rich context and then following those interests to develop cognitive skills and understanding (Siraj-Blatchford and Siraj-Blatchford, 1995; Beetlestone, 1998).

These changes in curriculum and pedagogic policy direction have meant that it is possible to employ Bernstein's 'code' theory (Bernstein, 1971) more meaningfully than has previously been attempted in primary schools – with some notable exceptions (Pollard with Filer, 1996). Bernstein has defined curriculum as the principle by which units of time and their contents – how a period of time in a classroom is used – are brought into a special relationship with each other. If the various contents were well insulated from each other he would say that the contents stand in a 'closed' relationship to each other, whereas if there is reduced insulation between contents he suggests they stand in an 'open' relationship to each other. His fundamental premise is that the 'forms' of the 'contents' transmission, that is their classification and framing, are social facts that he sees as emphasizing the social nature of the system alternatives from which emerges a constellation called a curriculum. He suggests that there are two broad types of curriculum. If contents stand in a close relation to each other – if the contents are clearly bounded and insulated from each other – he calls this curriculum a 'collection' type. The second type describes a curriculum where the various contents do not go their own separate ways, but one in which the contents stand in an open relation to each other – an 'integrated' type. Bernstein argued that the two codes could not be reconciled since they reflected basic societal differences in the distribution of power and principles of social control. However, he did accept that they could include weak elements of each other.

He uses the concepts of 'classification and frame' to analyse the underlying structure of three message systems, curriculum, pedagogic and evaluation systems. The notion of 'boundary strength' underlies the concept of classification and frame. 'Classification' refers to the relationship between *contents*. The concept 'frame' is used to determine the structure of the message system – pedagogy. Frame refers to the form of the context in which knowledge is transmitted and received; to the specific pedagogical relationship of teacher and taught. In the same way as classification does not refer to contents so frame does not refer to the contents of the pedagogy. Frame refers to the strength of a boundary between what may be transmitted and what may not be transmitted in the pedagogical relationship. It refers to the range of options available to teacher and taught in the control of what is transmitted and received in the context of the pedagogical relationship. Strong framing entails reduced options; weak framing entails a range of options. Thus frame refers to the degree of control teacher and pupils possess over the selection, organization and pacing of the knowledge transmitted and received in the pedagogical relationship. It is important to realize that the strength of classification and the strength of frames can vary independently of each other. Another relevant aspect of the boundary relationship between what may be taught and what may not be taught is the relationship between the non-school, everyday community knowledge of the teacher or taught, *and* the educational knowledge transmitted in the pedagogic relationship.

Through focusing on a case study of one first school, with a reputation for environmental immersion and the active engagement of children in learning encounters this chapter will show how a teaching and learning ideology has been developed by teachers taking into account changing circumstances (Kellner, 1978) and how research practices focusing on the complexities of pedagogy (Watkins and Mortimore, 1999) in the primary school throw more light on the operation of Bernstein's theory of code.

The Case Study School

The current head teacher opened the school in 1971. She and the other adults in the school exude a collective, all-embracing ideology based on a continuous diet of multi-sensory experiences and appreciation of the social, spiritual and ecological environment. The school is internationally famous with reciprocal connections with schools in Sweden and relations with communities in Gambia, and the head teacher has lectured in the USA and recently visited China. All visitors are welcome at any time, including students, people on work placements, researchers, practitioners, community residents, officials and all varieties of performers and artisans, to name but a few. The head and deputy have published books on the teaching of science in primary schools and they and other teachers have lectured abroad. Nearly half of its 172 children come from a large army garrison nearby. Although there are fewer pupils receiving free school meals than the average nationally, the social context of the school is a mixed one.

Research

The current research was undertaken at the school from December 1998 for an initial period of a year using a range of ethnographic methods, the aim being to focus on the children's perceptions of the all-embracing ideology. This is described by Woods (1995), in previous research at the school, as being the involvement of children in a 'hands-on' process of learning and the involvement of the community in the school's educational practices; the promotion of holism in terms of the school and its environment – the cycle of seasons, festivals and special days – and the development of the whole child. The school was visited for approximately a week each half-term – seven in all. This chapter provides more detail about how the school's 'integrated code' curriculum operates in the light of the policy directions outlined above and how the teachers have reconstructed their ideology in the light of the recent educational initiatives indicated above. This is done, first, by examining the school's 'relational idea' – that which underscores a curriculum and pedagogic organization in an 'integrated code'. Secondly, by focusing on its classification and framing operation, we examine how the school operationalizes its 'integrated code'. Thirdly, the effects on the pupils are examined.

An Appreciative *Umwelt*

An 'integrated code' in Bernstein's terms needs a 'supra-idea': a relational idea that links the contents and the pedagogy employed. Child-centredness, holism and environmental engagement have been suggested by both teachers and researchers as principles that underpin the life at Sunny (Woods, 1995). However, there is another conceptualization that captures the distinctive features of the school, that of 'an appreciative umwelt' (Sebeok Thomas, Hayes Alfred *et al.*, 1964). An *umwelt* is a 'significant environment'. It is part of a wider environment that an organism, like a school, chooses to inhabit. It is the subjective universe of the organism. The latter acts as a sign of the *umwelt* in that the structure of the organism will in some sense be giving clues to the nature of its environment and conversely the *umwelt* also shows that it is, itself, a sign of the organism in that it is possible to make inferences about the organism based on an analysis of its environment. The organism enacts an ongoing process of interpreting its *umwelt* and it gives birth to new organisms which are born into the pre-existing *umwelt* but which contribute to further interpretation or change of the ongoing *umwelt*. Sunny's offspring are not only the children who it inducts into its *umwelt*, but also the teachers, students, parents and community friends who visit regularly. The latter are an integral feature of the *umwelt*.

Active visitors

The list of active visitors, those who talk about their lives, perform their skills, reproduce their craft, gives some indication of the extent of community involvement. Visitors included: Irish dancers; Scottish bagpipe performers; harpists; artists; stonemasons; a military band; a demonstration of sea shanties accompanied by an accordion; a bell-ringing group; a vet ministering to the sheep; a member of the Cromwell Society on a horse; an army helicopter; a juggler on a one-wheel bike; a specialist in children's playground songs and rhymes from America and a Muslim woman talking about her faith and culture. These talks, demonstrations or performances not only engage the children's interest and take them on something akin to 'the Grand Tour' of the world outside the school but they generate an '*umwelt* of appreciation'. Although some of the presentations are not followed up by the teachers, they contribute to the creation of a learning community (Woods, 1995), an *umwelt* that appreciates its world. The third feature of this *umwelt* – the first being the use of space (see Woods, 1995, for more details) and the second that of bringing the community into the school – is the grand topics that envelop the curriculum contents in the 'relational idea'.

Grand topics

These topics and themes stretch over periods of time from a week to a term and sometimes inevitably overlap. Again they all have a 'hands-on' element for the children, they permeate the subject-centred contents, yet they are explorations in themselves. Linkages are made across subject divisions through these topics and themes but the central engagement is one of 'appreciation'. Again, the list of topics is indicative of their purpose – a window on to the environmental, biological, social, cultural, historical, geographical and religious world. The majority of the topics are related to a particular national annual celebration or a particular point in the ecological year. They are repeated each year without excuse and with the argument: that cycles of life represent 'being'; that these narratives are relevant to young children (Jeffrey, 1999; Laing, 1999); that children at different developmental stages gain more understanding and insight in what the teachers call 'a spiral curriculum' and that children take ownership of these curriculum experiences as they are repeated.

Together with the creative use of space, in terms of the school grounds, the importation of community and cultural practices, the opening of 'windows on to the world', provides the teachers and the children with the contexts for enacting their 'appreciative *umwelt*'. Having established their supra 'relational idea', how does the school organize these contexts in terms of 'contents of time', national programmes and children's interests?

Sunny School's 'Integrated Code'

The school's contents organization provides an indicator of the extent to which they have reconstructed their ideology, adapted to current circumstances and developed their 'integrated code curriculum'.

'Contents' organization

The school has a nursery which has two daily intakes and organizes its own curriculum programme related to National Curriculum Guidelines for Early Years education and six vertically grouped classes in the rest of the school – the equivalent of a two-form intake. The decision to vertically group the children – a spread of 5- to 7-year-olds in each class – was taken in the early years of the school's history and was in keeping with their philosophy of holism, cycles, care and learning opportunities. Not only was the child seen as a whole person with a variety of interests, attributes and inclinations, but the responsibility of care and induction was also seen as a natural part of children's development. Not only did the elder children induct the younger ones into the classroom cultures, but they were also able to add depth to reception children's learning exchanges, founded on their own experience of the regular cycle of school events and celebrations each year – for example, offering informed perspectives on the causes and consequences of the Fire of London.

However, children did not in the past, nor do they today, remain in these vertical grouped classes (class groups) throughout the day. The current timetable, involving children moving to the other classrooms for specialist curriculum and teaching has evolved over many years. Although these are subject-designated sessions they do not constitute, in Bernstein's terms, a collection code, but are weak classifications within the 'integrated code'. Bernstein portrays his 'integrated code' as a process of declassification from the collection code, which, in the light of recent policy developments, makes the research as to how the school adapts its 'integrated code' more relevant given the strengthening 'classification' of the curriculum.

Table 12.1   *Weekly timetable*

Time	Area/Teacher	Monday	Tuesday	Wednesday	Thursday	Friday
08.50–9.10	*VG Class*	Class	Class	Class	Class	Class
	Groups–Sue R.	Groups	Groups	Groups	Groups	Groups
09.10–10.10	*Gill's class*	Literacy	Literacy	Literacy	Literacy	Literacy
10.10–10.30	*Hall*	Assembly	Assembly	Assembly	Assemnbly	Assembly
10.30–11.20	*Carol's class*	Numeracy	Numeracy	Numeracy	Numeracy	Numeracy
11.20–12.05	*Sue's class*	Class G.	Class G.	Class G.	Class G.	Class G.
12.05–13.10	*Lunch*	Lunch	Lunch	Lunch	Lunch	Lunch
13.10–13.15	*Sue's class*	Class G.	Class G.	Class G.	Class G.	Class G.
13.15–14.35	*Carol's class*	English		Class G.		
13.15–14.35	*Jo's class*					Science
13.15–13.55	*Hall – Jenny*				PE	
13.55–14.35	*Library – Sue H.*				RE	
13.15–13.55	*Hall – Gill*		Music			
13.55–14.35	*Judy's class*		Extension			
14.35–15.20	*Sue's class*	Class G.	Class G.	Class G.	Class G.	Class G.

The Sunny school's educational values are exemplified by their commitment to a vertical grouping, but reorganization of some teaching into subject-centred classes is still predicated on educational principles. It reflects a crucial element in the school's understanding of young children's desire for new and interesting experiences and the importance of engaging the physical and emotional alongside the intellectual.

> We are a whole school who fit together well but I also like constantly shaking the pieces and moving them around. I think the children gain from their experiences with every adult, that is why it is important to keep moving them. They can relate to many adults in this system and not only the one adult. You get changes of 'teaching temperature' all the time. I don't think they have much fear. I think they experience life in varying degrees and providing the teachers like them it is not a problem for them. (Sue)

To illustrate this, Jennifer, a Year 1 child, inhabited her 'class group' at the beginning and end of the morning and afternoon – four times a day. During these times the teachers followed up the humanities and environmental curriculum as well as art, design technology and information technology (IT). The 'class group' time totals 115 minutes a day but registration is included and sometimes there is a playground break time in the morning of 15 minutes, so class groups consist of about 75 minutes a day plus Wednesday afternoons. Wednesday has, in the past, been considered a 'class group' day with a special event in or out of the classroom. However, the introduction of the literacy and numeracy hours has reduced this 'topic day' to half a day (see Table 12.1).

The Literacy and Numeracy Groups are age cohorts but the Curriculum Groups (afternoon groups) are split into four roughly age-related cohorts where level of achievement is taken into account. There is a Year 2 group, a Year 2/1 group, a Year 1/Reception group and a Reception group. Children may be moved upwards after a review each term. The 'Extension' session could be any literacy, numeracy, humanities or science topic. The children have one 70-minute language and science session a week and one 40-minute session of PE, RE, Music and Extension activities per week.

As a 'national timetable' becomes more uniform, Sunny's timetable, in terms of time allocation – contents – differs little from many other primary schools or first schools throughout the rest of the country. However, the organization of the curriculum at Sunny may well differ considerably. First, it differs historically, for they 'have had curriculum groups for some time now' and they 'always taught basic literacy including phonics'. Secondly, there may well be significant differences in terms of the active movement of children and the number of teachers who teach them during the week. Thirdly, they operate a weak system of ability-related curriculum groups unlike most primary school classes. Fourthly, they have an extensive series of events (such as a 'lifelong learning' week in which community members of all ages are invited to join in learning experiences) that are not only used as a resource for some of the timetabled subjects, but one in which the whole school takes part. These 'events' sometimes overlap with the topics.

The active pupil

In terms of a learning environment the children's natural interest in a continually moving panoply of sensuous and cognitive engagements is supported by the opportunity to be mobile, albeit in an appropriate manner, around the school regularly. In this way they develop ownership of the school buildings and the rooms within, they anticipate something new and interesting each time they approach a classroom entrance. The school's principles about active engagement in learning permeate their entrances and exits of every session. Even the quiet reflective times sat at a table reading, writing, drawing and computing are felt by the children as 'active engagement'.

The children exhibited calm enthusiasm and engaged readily – almost routinely. The varied and extensive curriculum entailed frequent changes of focus, seen as appropriate for the pupils' age and consequently they saw writing exercises as another interesting activity instead of a debilitating routine. On the other hand there were many examples of sustained periods of activity, e.g. the writing up, for much of one day in one class, of a description of a Christmas pudding creation. There was an evenness of tone, never exuberant or heightened seriousness. The traditional end-of-day story was read by a teacher as parents quietly chatted outside the open classroom area without distracting the children.

> During the more 'active engagements' there were lots of shared smiles and laughter. They played with expressions as they: laughed at themselves and the situation; expressed amazement; made facial and verbal connections with peers; screwed up their faces with contorted smiles as they experienced strange noises

> like the bagpipes and tactile encounters such as making porridge. However, they did not overdo the excitement, they acted calmly with interest. Their engagement is with an infinite variety of experiences so one is not valued above another, i.e. one is not work and the other play. (Field note)

Sunny's subject-centred curriculum groups challenge aspects of the 'child-centred' rhetoric which emphasizes 'child chosen' activities or construction of curriculum based on children's current interests. The areas of investigation are not chosen by the children but by the teachers and the National Curriculum Authority. The children do not have control over the amount of time spent on an activity, in fact their activity may be changed frequently, depending on participation in activities of the week, such as exploring the harpist at work, or helping to plant daffodils in a bank of land in the school grounds. This is a 'teacher led' curriculum, or perhaps more accurately a combination of a national and teacher-designated curriculum but one in which particular attention is paid to the quality of the children's engagement with it. Subject boundaries, as in Bernstein's 'classification' theory, are delineated through the operation of the timetable, albeit weakly, and through an overt school discourse which encourages children to see themselves as linguists, writers, storytellers, mathematicians, scientists, ecologists, actors and musicians. Strong boundary maintenance between school subjects, as operated in the secondary school, eventually creates separate identities, e.g. arts or sciences, physician or lawyer, competition between departments and the possibility of a range of ideologies, but not here at Sunny where the staff feel united around one ideology of children's active engagement.

According to Bernstein weak boundary maintenance in terms of classification – in the integrated code – produces, an emphasis on *how* knowledge is created rather than concern with acquiring states of knowledge, social relationships between teachers and between teachers and pupils and a commitment by all the teachers to 'the relational thing'. Within Sunny's curriculum groups, the 'relational idea' – a central feature of an 'integrated code' – is paramount in the way the school's environment is used by each group as a pedagogic resource and the way the community events and the major school topics already described permeate the curriculum group's focus.

> The 50 or more houses that were constructed for the fire of London – most of them at least half a metre high – were laid out in the hall on a street plan for a week and the children conducted mathematical exercises relating to direction, map work, measurement and recognition, properties and use of geometric shapes. (Field note)

The Active teacher

Bernstein suggests that there are two types of integrated codes. The first type is 'teacher based'. This is where the teacher has an extended block of time, often with the same group of children, and where the teacher may operate with a 'collection code', keeping the various subjects distinct and insulated, or may blur the boundaries between the different subjects. It cannot be considered to be a 'collection code' existence in its full meaning because the teacher is not part of a subject discipline and institutional department: she does not get her identity from a specialism. The second type is 'teachers based' where integration involves relationships with other teachers. Sunny appears to operate both a 'teacher-based' and a 'teachers-based' system within the integrated code. The 'class group' would be an example of the first type where individual teachers decide how far to develop any particular theme or topic.

In the subject groups – the second type – teachers work in pairs, planning the contents, preparing materials, operationalizing the teaching – sometimes separate, sometimes together – collating record keeping and evaluation. They work very closely.

> You bring something to the group that the other person had not thought of and that feeds you. You bounce off each other. I couldn't say how we are doing it, but because we get on so well and enjoy what we're doing it comes naturally really. You share ideas. We are taking it in directions that the other might not have thought of. We share ideas and it gets you thinking about ways to develop and progress the situation. I love it. Because it happens so much you get to know each other so well. You play off each other. The children are sometimes able to choose between us, which is good for them. (Jo)

This would typify a weak classification code in terms of teacher relations. The 'integrated code' is operational at different levels. In terms of Sunny, teachers and pupils experience some teaching and learning in a 'classified form' albeit with weak boundary maintenance to community projects and school topics and a very weak experience when focusing on topics in their class groups. In terms of teacher boundaries, they develop both a 'teacher-based' and a 'teachers-based' identity.

Bernstein perceives a fundamental paradox that he believes needs to be faced and explored relating to the influences of collection and integrated codes on teacher identity. He suggests that the tacit ideological basis of the collection code includes a covert structure of mechanical solidarity within the subject discipline. Alternatively, the overt ideological basis of the integrated code – not being a condensed symbolic system like the 'collection code' – is verbally elaborated, explicit and an overt realization of organic solidarity made substantive through weak forms of boundary maintenance. (Sunny is a good example of this form of 'integrated code'.)

However, Bernstein goes on to argue that where there are strong collection codes it does permit, in principle, considerable differences in pedagogy and evaluation because of the high insulation between the different contents, in spite of the fact that the autonomy within the contents is the other side of an authority structure which exerts jealous and zealous supervision. An integrated code, on the other hand, he argues, will not permit the variations in pedagogy and evaluation which are possible within collection codes, on the contrary he suggests there will be a pronounced movement towards a common pedagogy and tendency towards a common system of evaluation. In other words integrated codes will, at the level of teachers, probably create homogeneity in teaching practice. Thus, the collection codes increase the discretion of teachers (within, always, the limits of the existing classification and frames) whilst integrated codes reduce the discretion of teachers in direct relation to the strength of the integrated code. Bernstein's paradox is that, on the one hand, the covert structure of mechanical solidarity of collection codes creates through its specialized outputs organic solidarity and, on the other hand, the overt structure of organic solidarity of integrated codes creates through its less specialized outputs, mechanical solidarity.

Sunny, it appears, has faced up to this paradox by encouraging its teachers to develop different subject experience, skills and knowledge and therefore creating some distance from the 'relational idea' – ideology – by asserting the particular and specific characteristics of subject specialism. Their autonomy is developed alongside the recognition of their insights and responsibilities to specific subjects in comparison with the development of other teachers' expertise in other subjects. The paradox is also resolved by accepting and encouraging teachers to move from one subject to another after two or three years' experience.

A 'Child-considered' Pedagogy

Framing is independent of classification and is the degree of control teacher and pupil possess over the process of the selection, organization and pacing of the knowledge transmitted and received in the pedagogical relationship. Overall, the constitutive nature of the Sunny 'relational idea' entails a fairly strong frame, albeit a framing that can be said to be indicative of an 'integrated code'. Within the subject groups the selection, organization and pacing of the knowledge transmitted is determined by national exhortations – albeit often in relation to the introduction by the school of topics, community practices, world pictures and cycles of cultural and ecological experiences. These curriculum mediums, many of which are directly relevant to children's experiences and interests are, nevertheless, teacher-led decisions. In terms of progressive pedagogies this approach could be described as a 'child-considered' approach rather than the 'child-centred education' rhetoric which espouses a curriculum content generated by the direction of children's interests. It is 'considered' in that the teachers recognize the necessity to maintain interest, the range of children's interests, the importance to children of a multi-sensory, 'hands-on' engagement and the necessity to differentiate the pace of learning relevant to their age and achievement levels. However, it is one where 'we don't choose what to do, the teachers decide for us most of the time' (Michelle).

A 'child-considered' approach could be seen as one that operates between strong and weak framing. Strong framing, as in pedagogies operated in some European countries, notably France, is one where the relationship between teacher and taught is distanced, learning what questions can be put at any particular time, placing the emphasis upon obtaining states of knowledge in terms of test results, rather than on ways of knowing and where the teacher and child have little choice. The receipt of the knowledge is not so much a right as something to be won or earned. At the weak end of the framing dimension there are a range of options for both teacher and pupil over the selection, organization and pacing of the knowledge transmitted and received in the pedagogical relationship. For example, in the nursery the children have opportunities to choose activities with which to engage but they are also introduced to initial letter sounds throughout the year. The former would be a very weak framing and the latter more heavily framed but at Sunny the practice is not at the other end of the dimension – it is more weakly framed. In learning about the letter 'm', the children would visit the maze, go on a walk in the grounds 'moving' differently, write the letters in chalk on the playground, be given 'Malteser' chocolates and construct models of their mothers – a 'child-considered' framing.

In their 'class groups' teachers and children had more control over the selection, organization and pacing of the knowledge to be transmitted and received. Children were more at liberty to choose a particular focus, to organize their engagement and to pace the work themselves. There was less pressure for individual performance and more emphasis on collective learning in these class groups. 'Ways of knowing' were prioritized over states of knowledge.

Uncommonsense Knowledge

Another aspect of framing focused on by Bernstein is educational knowledge as 'uncommonsense knowledge'. This is knowledge freed from the particular, the local, through the various languages of the sciences or forms of reflexiveness of the arts, which make possible the creation, or the discovery of new realities. He questions the relationship between the 'uncommonsense' knowledge of the school and 'common-sense' knowledge – everyday community knowledge – of the pupil, his or her family and his or her peer group, and invites us to ask how strong are the frames of educational knowledge in relation to experiential, community-based non-school knowledge. In polarizing this issue Bernstein suggests that where the knowledge frame is strong and discourages connections with everyday realities then the child experiences education knowledge as something esoteric which gives a special significance to those who possess it. Sunny's 'relational idea' – an 'appreciative *umwelt*' – is clear that 'common-sense' knowledge is a vital part of their school curriculum and in this sense they can be considered to have a very weak frame of control over what is defined as educational knowledge.

Pupils' Perspectives

A central feature of the research is to try and ascertain how the pupils perceive their experiences. However, pupils, like others in social situations, are socially constructed by the situation and cannot be totally objective, especially in a school like Sunny that organizes an integrated curriculum like an 'open text'.

'Open Text' learning

Learning is perceived of as 'mosaic learning' – listening, acting, engaging, writing (Carol). Umberto Eco (Eco, 1989) uses similar 'encyclopedic' definitions as opposed to dictionary definitions. The latter merely defines an object, phenomenon or experience in metaphoric terms, e.g. a dog is a carnivorous quadruped, this is a one-route maze to understanding. Encyclopedic knowledge is that which is seen through many different connected perspectives, like a net of understanding.

These are 'open texts' (Eco, 1989) that are woven together by the school to ensure that the 'reader/child' is drawn into the complexities and connecting threads of the experience. An 'open text' is one that works only when each interpretation is re-echoed by others and vice versa. The author/teacher/school sees the 'ideal' reader as one able to master different codes and eager to deal with the text as a maze of many entrances and exits. What matters are not the various avenues/issues themselves but the maze-like structure of the text. Sunny teachers explore light in terms of spirituality, religion, growth, energy, electricity, ritual and dance. Phonics as language phonemes are eaten, sung about, danced, found in the environment, and associated with playing detective.

In Eco's terms you cannot use the text as you want but only as the text wants you to use it. An 'open text', however open it may be, cannot afford a 'whatever' interpretation. In a closed text the author 'writes' for an average reader who can depart from the text at will because they are not intimately connected to it, the end is defined for him or her as for example, in a detective novel. The open text 'extrapolates' a reader by a tightly constructed text. The text author leads the addressee and then allows him or her to reflect on the whole experience. The reader is not 'persuaded' through textual contrivances or heightened emotional production but he or she experiences knowledge through a variety of related and integrated perspectives.

Recycling experiences gives new insights to children. The cyclical base to the curriculum experience fits within the school organization of vertically grouped classes, for each child is inducted by the older children as the school repeats experiences annually and the older ones gain new insights and confidences in turn. For example, the children rehearse the same nativity story at least four times in their school career and take different parts each year. Part of the process of gaining pupils' perspectives is to observe and empathize.

Umwelt *Engagement*

In terms of observation the children were sensitive to the *umwelt*, they involved themselves energetically, they reacted positively to the teachers' modelling and they indicated some understanding of the *umwelt*. During the day they moved to new places and spaces and never argued but were aware 'Is this anyone's place?' While they were working with their teachers on the carpet they knelt, sat, crept, did the splits, sat on boxes, leant against walls. They acted naturally within the *umwelt*. They fiddled with their hair, made quiet comments, whispered in other's ears. They talked, fidgeted, inquired and expressed themselves naturally. They were only 'encouraged' to take part in the 'learning' *umwelt* rather than disciplined or coerced to be still. The last pupil to respond to a gathering together after lunch in the playground was asked if 'he was stuck on some apparatus?' He was not told 'to hurry'. When a teacher did ask a child to quieten down a little, in a performance, she did it with a large smile and stroked the child's cheek. A collective discipline ensued. They did it with each other, like a gentle wind that the children explored as they 'energized'. There was minimal admonition, no lining up and few enforced silences. Consequently the children did not crave attention, covet particular seats or selfishly appropriate specific activities.

While a teacher heard children read one morning, the rest of the class engaged in carpet activities with apparatus consisting of puzzles, games and books. Two Year 1 boys, enclosed by boxes, looked at a book and discussed each page as they turned them over. They caressed their own faces slowly and generally fidgeted as they engaged intently on the book. When she had completed her group teaching the teacher gathered the children together and told them about everything that she was doing. She talked about a tray she must make up for a new child starting the next day and reminded them that they missed their break yesterday. These narratives are a form of tireless talking (Woods and Jeffrey, 1996) that gives meaning to the objects and events that constitute the *umwelt*.

There were lots of adults around the school and it was almost obligatory for them to join in – an expression of *umwelt* – similar to a 'least adult' role (Boyle, 1999). On one occasion the sea shanties were going on at the end of the day in the hall and all the parents who were waiting for their children joined in. There was music everywhere, nautical accordions, computers playing Vivaldi, a brass band and teachers singing instructions – an *umwelt* rhythm.

The staff modelled engagement with their visitors and the children mimicked their behaviour if they were so inclined. The staff ensured that everyone was part of the whole experience, e.g. engaging with the bell-ringers. The manner was one of quiet effusiveness and the staff, including the head, joined in these types of routine. Physical encounters permeate the school and tied elements of the *umwelt* closer together.

Psychologists suggest that the force of 'desire' can be translated into a 'love of knowledge' alongside and interwoven with the need for affirmation of the self. The subject, as a young person in particular, desires the same object that their 'loved one' desires mimetically for this will affirm them in terms of knowledge and their 'self' (Martusewicz, 1997). The children mimic the modelling, by the teachers and performers, of enthusiasm, emotion and intellectual engagement, as they satisfy 'desire'.

It was argued that it was important that the children knew 'who they were' (Carol). The opportunity to explore their given definitions and to develop their identity appears to be based in an *umwelt* of minimal fear and an abundance of security. This atmosphere is partly constituted by the extensive number of experiences that both teachers and children share. 'Eventing' is a central feature of the curriculum and as teachers and children anticipate them, a 'security of togetherness' envelops the whole class or school.

Pupils that had left Sunny were clear about its positive characteristics:

> Sunny Infant School is a lot more interesting. You went outside and did activities. It was like an extra classroom. In the juniors you mainly sit at your desk. The infant school had got the amphitheatre and the maze. We did a show in the amphitheatre to an audience. You learn in different ways. We learnt science and maths as we do at the Junior School, but for science we went pond dipping. Once we took a socket apart and learnt about it. We did much more fun stuff at Sunny than we do at the Junior School. Like making Christmas pudding.

The children did not condemn any part of their educational experience thus far (the children were Years 4 and 5) but they did indicate the kind of pedagogy they thought more interesting, one where it was more active. Although pupils are socially constructed within the context of the situation they are able to be reflective and evaluative.

Pupil Interventions and Reflections

Pupils intervene by: engaging individually; acting collaboratively – for example, a group spontaneously made a list of words that had an 'R' sound during a literacy hour – or leading actively. They bring experiences to events and employ imaginative links. They also reflect actively by making contributions to the teaching and learning situation, and by evaluating their experiences and acting critically (Jeffrey, 2000). Catherine uses her experience to describe the smell of some soapsuds doing science activity to establish 'a fair test' and Abigail uses her experience of categorization to organize a large counting exercise – by grouping sets of trees in tens.

Imagination plays a large role in children's learning experiences. Greg uses a torch as a medical instrument, a microphone and a lighthouse during a science lesson on the nature of light. These analogies can be seen as part of the learning process and not a diversion from the learning activity, for the connections are meaningful and consequently the 'knowledge that is to be transmitted' will be recalled more easily. Janet, after feeling the vibrations on a harp during the playing of it by a visitor describes the experience as similar to being 'whisked off into space and having some adventures'. Fiona described the daffodils she was about to plant as 'double deckers' – a reference to hamburgers – and in a class where the children were making three dimensional shapes with varied materials they transformed them into 'eyeballs, a hat, a clucking hen, a helmet, a salamander and a telescope'. These are imaginative perspectives brought to the learning process. Affirmation of these perspectives not only enhances the children's self-esteem but it should be recognized that these are 'connotations' (Barthes and Heath, 1984) that aid the learning process. Voluntary critical observations 'you haven't told us what is in the cup you are putting in the microwave, [during an examination of lighting processes], so we can see the light' may be few and far between unless there is weak framing and engagement is built in to that framing. As leaders and collaborators children again bring their experience or imagination to the learning process as did Charlotte who asked her friend if she could use her fingers as a counting tool. Calling out proposals and suggestions is an example of pupil leadership and incorporating them into the pedagogic relationship requires weak framing.

The combination of an 'appreciative *umwelt*', an 'integrated code' using strengths of classification and framing and the construction of an 'open text' displays the complexity of the pedagogy employed at Sunny School.

Conclusion

In terms of Bernstein's theory, Sunny School operates an 'integrated code' for they meet his four conditions, which if satisfied, ensure that openness of learning under integration produces a culture in which staff and pupils have a sense of time, place and purpose. First, there is a consensus about the integrating idea – an 'appreciative *umwelt*' and it is very explicit. Secondly, the nature of the linkage between the integrating idea and the knowledge to be co-ordinated is coherently spelled out as the teachers integrate community visitors and grand topics into the timetabled subject-centred contents. Thirdly, because it is a small school, all decision-making is carried out in the staff meeting and therefore they have created a sensitive feed-back system which also provides further agency of socialization into the code. Fourthly, the teachers use multiple criteria of assessment compared with assessments made in systems that operate collection codes, for example, the head teacher interviews every child when they are about to leave the school to ascertain their perspectives on their achievements and limitations.

However, the integrated code operated at Sunny School includes some secondary-school type operations redolent of systems operating a collection code. For example, the children move around the school to different classes for six subjects, each taught by a different teacher and the sessions are weakly streamed according to developmental ability. Nevertheless the subjects are taught with weak boundary maintenance in terms of classification as teachers use the space in their grounds, community visitors and their grand topics within each subject-centred activity and they employ their pedagogic 'integrating idea' of experiential learning.

There is one further central characteristic of an integrated code to which Sunny adheres. According to Bernstein, where an integrated code operates, emphasis is on *how* knowledge is created, rather than a concern with acquiring *states* of knowledge. In other words the pedagogy of an integrated code is likely to emphasize various *ways* of knowing in the pedagogical relationships. Through its 'relational idea' pupils at Sunny School are exposed to weak boundary maintenance in terms of knowledge and in terms of framing, the emphasis on experiential engagement also appears to be weak, giving the child some control over their learning. They learn *how* knowledge is created through the 'hands-on' approach that is adopted and through experiencing a variety of engagements they learn about various *ways* of knowing. Sunny School appears to have put some flesh on the bones of Bernstein's integrated code showing in particular how weak classification operates within the code. Schools wishing to remain within an integrated code of teaching and learning, rather than migrating to a collection code paradigm inherent within recent policy initiatives outlined in the introduction, will have to develop their own relational idea and meet Bernstein's four conditions but Sunny School appears to be showing how this is possible.

For primary teachers the concept of 'child-centred education' has been used by many teachers to mean many things and it may now need discarding or at the very least reconstructing (Sugrue, 1998). The teachers at Sunny have reconstituted their ideology due to changing circumstances and reconstituted 'child-centred education' as a 'child-considerate', teacher-led curriculum – one which the teachers would argue is appropriate for this age group. The danger of ideologies is not only that they mask differing interpretations but that those espousing the ideology find themselves unable to adapt when faced with different circumstances. This clearly is not the case for the teachers at Sunny who have developed and adapted their ideology in the light of changing educational policy and practice:

You've got to make the literacy hour work, you have got to be part of it, and change it to what you want it to be. Somehow you have got to make the SATs work, so that they are respectable in good honest terms. You have got to inform parents and ask them to work with you to get the results up and to consider homework. Otherwise you won't keep up your numbers and you wouldn't be allowed to do what you want to do.

Ideologies account for experience but they need reflexivity in order to maintain their existence (Kellner, 1978; Burbles and Berk, 1999).

The teachers at Sunny are not complacent. They are keen to develop and incorporate pupils' perspectives in the teaching and learning situation and to engage them as contributors to the pedagogic process to increase the possibility that pupils learn more about *how* knowledge is created and the various *ways* of knowing in the pedagogical relationships. During the next stage of the research we will consider together how we might develop children's 'critical perspectives' alongside their well-developed 'appreciative' ones by encouraging:

- children's use of and awareness of, opinions, feelings and factual observations and their differences;
- a wide range of questioning by pupils: of each other, about the subject matter and matters they want to consider or investigate. Responsive engagements could include possibilities, problems posing, problem solving, negotiation, conjecture;
- the evaluation by pupils of their experiences and activities in terms of knowledge gained, including process skills and the quality of engagement.

These objectives can be understood and operationalized by becoming aware of the classification and framing of curriculum and pedagogy and considering the appropriate circumstances for strengthening and weakening the boundaries between contents, curriculum subjects, teachers and between pupils and teachers. Sunny School is hard at work within its 'integrated code' but is not wholly determined by it nor is it ideologically blind to changing circumstances. They are a relevant contemporary model for other primary schools wishing to maintain any semblance of individuality as the national frameworks draw all primary schools closer together.

References

Barthes, R. and S. Heath (1984) *Image, Music, Text*, London, Fontana Paperbacks.
Beetlestone, F. (1998) *Creative Children, Imaginative Teaching*, Buckingham, Open University Press.
Bernstein (1971) On the classification and framing of educational knowledge, in M. F. D. Young (ed.) *Knowledge and Control: New Directions for the Sociology of Education*, London, Collier Macmillan, 47–69.
Boyle, M. (1999) Exploring the worlds of childhood: the dilemmas and problems of the adult researcher, in A. Massey and G. Walford (eds), *Explorations in Methodology*, Stamford, CT, Jai Press. Vol. 2: 91–108.

Burbules, N. C. and Berk, R. (1999) Critical thinking and critical pedagogy: relations, differences and limits, in S. T. Popkewitz and L. Fendler (eds), *Critical Theories in Education: Changing Terrains of Knowledge and Politics*, London, Routledge, 45–65.

Eco, U. (1989) *The Open Work*, Cambridge MA, Harvard University Press.

Jeffrey (1999) *Researching Pupil Perspectives: Beyond Reflexivity*, Ethnography in Education Conference, School of Education Oxford.

Jeffrey, B. (2000) *Analysing Pupil Perspectives of Teaching and Learning at Coombes*, Buckingham, Open University.

Kellner, D. (1978) 'Ideology, marxism and Advanced Capitalism', *Socialist Review*, 42: 37–65.

Laing, E. (1999) *Children's narratives and subject formation*, available from 68 Manor Ave, London, SE4 1TE.

Martusewicz, R. A. (1997) Desire and education, in S. Todd (ed.), *Learning Desire: Perspectives on Pedagogy, Culture and the Unsaid*, London, Routledge: 97–116.

Pollard, A. with Filer, A. (1996) *The Social World of Children's Learning: Case Studies of Children from Four to Seven*, London, Cassell.

Sebeok Thomas, A., Hayes Alfred, S., *et al.* (1964) *Approaches to Semiotics: Cultural Anthropology, Education, Linguistics, Psychiatry, Psychology: Transactions of the Indiana University Conference and Paralinguistics and Kinesics*, The Hague, Mouton.

Siraj-Blatchford, J. and Siraj-Blatchford, I. (1995) *Educating the Whole Child: Cross Curricula Skills, Themes And Dimensions*, Buckingham, Open University Press.

Sugrue, S. (1998) *Complexities of Teaching: Child Centred Perspectives*, London, Falmer.

Watkins, C. and Mortimore, P. (1999) Pedagogy: what do we know? in P. Mortimore (ed.) *Understanding Pedagogy and its impact on Learning*, London, Paul Chapman: 1–19.

Woods, P. (1995) *Creative Teachers in Primary Schools*, Buckingham, Open University Press.

Woods, P. and Jeffrey, B. (1996) *Teachable Moments: The Art Of Creative Teaching in Primary Schools*, Buckingham, Open University Press.

13

The Impact of the National Curriculum on Play in Reception Classes

Elizabeth Wood

[. . .]

Introduction

Following the implementation of the National Curriculum from 1989, it was widely feared that the child-centred principles which shape the early childhood curriculum would be eroded. Concerns were expressed that the National Curriculum would have a negative downward impact on this age group by formalizing children's early experiences and, in particular, eroding the commitment to play as the principal means of learning in early childhood (David, 1990). These concerns were particularly relevant to the quality of education provided for 4-year-old children in reception classes. This age group was left outside the remit of Key Stage 1 and, until the introduction of the Desirable Outcomes for Children's Learning (SCAA, 1996), had no legislated curriculum framework. [. . .] Concerns were already being expressed about the influences of educational reforms on reception teachers' practice, including the drive towards accountability, parents' expectations, and the impact of assessment and testing requirements at the end of Key Stage 1.

The aim of this chapter is to provide insights into how a group of reception class teachers responded to these policy changes in the years prior to the introduction of the Desirable Outcomes (SCAA, 1996) [. . .]

Principles and Ideologies

One of the central principles in the ideology which underpins early childhood education is the value of a play-based curriculum. This is based on a belief that there is a direct relationship between playing and learning, and that play is essential to children's cognitive, affective and psycho-motor development. Related principles suggest that the curriculum should be child-centred and developmentally appropriate, based on children's needs for play experiences which are matched to their current age and stage of development, as well as their interests and ongoing cognitive concerns (Blenkin and Kelly, 1994). Learning in early childhood is conceptualized as 'holistic' and integrated rather than being organized into discrete subject compartments (Nutbrown, 1994).

As the National Curriculum came on stream from 1989 onwards, concerns were expressed within the early childhood community about play being 'threatened' and 'attacked' (Tyler, 1991). Hurst (1994) identified the National Curriculum as a 'malign influence' because play was increasingly being seen as 'the enemy of education'. Blenkin and Kelly (1994) were unequivocal in their critique of the impact of the National Curriculum on early learning and identified a number of perceived threats. First, that play and the statutory requirements were incompatible; secondly, that assessment requirements would marginalize play; and thirdly, that direct instruction and formal activities would predominate at the expense of children's self-initiated activities and control of their own learning. They also perceived a division between the broad developmental aims of the nursery curriculum and the behavioural ones of the National Curriculum:

> Any curriculum which incorporates precise specification of what pupils should be able to do into each subject at each level has already petrified its curriculum around external objectives and has committed itself to the fulfilment of those objectives as itemized in the assessment structure. (Blenkin and Kelly, 1994, p. 51)

An assumption was made that child-centred and subject-based approaches to planning were incompatible:

> Young children cannot be taught effectively if planned learning is divided into man-made compartments called subjects. Children will explore science, learn about maths and develop language skills through activities and experiences which are planned to encompass these and many more elements of the curriculum. (Nutbrown, 1994, p. 3)

Such comments were a reaction to the increasing level of political control over curriculum content, and sustained critiques of the commitment to a child-centred ideology which was seen as a significant barrier to raising standards and improving practice (Anning, 1995). These negative standpoints assume that play did have a central place in the early years curriculum. However, the apparent commitment to play as *the* way of learning in early childhood must be questioned in the light of research into classroom practice.

Wood and Attfield (1996) argue that, although the rhetoric of play is highly persuasive, in practice play is lacking in both quality and quantity. Even before the implementation of the National Curriculum, there was a focus in reception classes on the basics of literacy and numeracy (Anning, 1997), with play being used predominantly as a time-filler or holding device

(Bennett and Kell, 1989; OFSTED, 1993). A review of research by Bennett, Wood and Rogers (1997) identifies a number of concerns about the quality of play in nursery and reception classes, including the level of cognitive challenge, the extent to which adults' expectations of different play activities were fulfilled, the work–play dichotomy and the role of adults in supporting children's learning through play.

The different standpoints on the rhetoric and reality of play reveal a range of tensions in early childhood education which have been expressed predominantly by researchers, educationists and politicians, with teachers' voices underrepresented. This omission begs the question of how the National Curriculum has impacted on play from the perspective of teachers. [. . .]

Teachers' Perspectives

The aims of the study (Bennett et al, 1997) were to elicit the teachers' theories of play, to ascertain the relationship between theories and practice and to examine the perceived impact of mediating factors on this relationship. Nine teachers took part in the study, all of whom were regarded as capable and committed practitioners in their use of play in the reception class. [. . .]

The impact of the National Curriculum

The perceived impact of the National Curriculum on play was by no means uniform across the group. Play was considered to be valuable for reception-age children because of their stage of development and all nine teachers integrated it into their daily planning and provision. The two most common issues were curriculum overload in terms of content and assessment procedures, and the 'downward pressure' on both the nursery and reception curriculum.

Eve was the strongest critic of these pressures. She would have preferred to implement a bottom-up, 'nursery style' curriculum, and was concerned to build on the good practice and 'nursery ideals' in the local feeder nursery school. She described the National Curriculum as 'bearing down' on the reception class:

> There is a danger of that filtering down and you getting squashed between the two. And one would rather it went along the nursery road than the other way around, because it should be building upon the nursery experience, not having a watered down Year 1 or Year 2 curriculum.

Eve was also concerned about the rolling programme of topics throughout the school and that the pressures from assessment would lead towards more formal activities. Similarly, Chris had to remind herself that the curriculum could be fulfilled through play activities: 'I think National Curriculum has made a difference, in that teachers have felt pressurized, including myself. I think it has put pressures on to look at the more formal bits.'

On the other hand, Chris thought that the National Curriculum had added breadth and balance but would have preferred a slower implementation. As a result, she prioritized structured play and formal work because of the need to 'move children on'. Her pressures stemmed from content overload and assessment requirements, particularly providing evidence of children's learning which was easier through more formal work.

Jennie also took a balanced view. She stated that the National Curriculum 'has some very good things about it', but had reservations about content and subject overload, especially in the early years. She referred to it as 'a huge weighty tome that sits on your shoulder'. However, she was able to 'work in the way that I think is right' because the headteacher valued the work of the early years teachers, and she was confident of the children's achievements and the quality of their play-based experience. Jennie felt that the National Curriculum and play are not incompatible:

> I think it does link with play . . . because certainly with attainment targets 1 in maths and science where they've got this exploratory, investigative emphasis, you can assess it . . . And also the programme of study for the current English National Curriculum has got a strong emphasis on literacy through play, so I was glad to see that.

She considered that the defining quality of the curriculum was whether it was developmentally appropriate to each child's age and stage.

Interestingly, the three novice teachers in the study were more accepting of the status quo. Gina, a newly qualified teacher, talked about the pressures of 'fitting everything in' and the wider constraints in providing good-quality play experiences:

> I don't think the National Curriculum should be constricting. I think it's there as a guideline, and I don't think you should necessarily be constricted by it. If there's a programme of study to follow, I think that you could use a play activity in order to present a topic.

Carly found it 'not at all constraining . . . It has always been there and I find it an extremely useful tool; I don't find it limiting at all'. Her planning incorporated activities which 'cover the content, the knowledge and the understanding of the National Curriculum and everything else'. Holly, another novice teacher, thought that it could be constraining if it was used exclusively to determine content:

> I haven't taught without it so . . . I think it's constraining if you just work to the letter on it, but if it's in the back of your mind and you know that what you're teaching is worthwhile, then it isn't too constraining because you will be fulfilling it just because of good practice.

Sara, an experienced teacher, thought that the National Curriculum 'had no effect'. She had a mixed nursery and reception age class, and although she was 'not governed by the National Curriculum', she was working towards it. Her planning was organized into curriculum areas with clearly defined learning intentions, and a firm belief in the value of play for achieving those intentions: 'I'm teaching the children the same basic skills that I would have been teaching before the National Curriculum came in.'

The teachers' theories about the value of play as a medium for learning predominated over the views of the impact of the National Curriculum, even where this was perceived as having a constraining influence. Their theories were influential in their conceptions and constructions of the learning environment and were translated into practice through the structure and content of the curriculum. Key features of this process were the design of curriculum models, structuring play, the role of the teacher and assessment. [. . .]

Curriculum planning

There was consistent evidence of teacher autonomy in making decisions about worthwhile activities and experiences, based on their pedagogical knowledge, wider beliefs, values and experience. All nine teachers had a framework for planning and provision which reflected the subject areas of the National Curriculum. Within this framework, they aimed to provide a continuum between adult-intensive and child-initiated activities which incorporated work, free play and structured play. [. . .]

According to the teachers' definitions, play served different, often multiple, purposes:

1. as exploration and investigation prior to a teacher-intensive activity;
2. as a free, unstructured activity with little adult direction or intervention;
3. as a context for developing skills and concepts introduced in teacher-directed activities;
4. as a context for realizing defined intentions.

Within this broad consensus, there were three distinct curriculum models:

- children have free choice within a structured environment;
- children are free to play with teacher-selected materials prior to formal teaching input;
- children are directed by the teacher to a succession of play activities throughout the day.

The first model was based on the plan–do–review system adapted from the High/Scope curriculum and was used by Jennie and Carly in parallel reception classes. Jennie felt that this approach enabled her to expand the opportunities for play because of the range of possibilities this offered for children's learning. They were able to exercise choice within a structured environment, with opportunities for reviewing their activities and reflecting on their learning. This approach was seen as supporting purposeful play rather than just having fun or choosing time. The second model was used by the majority of teachers in the study with play activities structured and resourced according to specific learning intentions. Within each activity, the children had some choices about how they used the materials. The third model, used by Eve, was more structured. Children rotated through both teacher-intensive and independent activities in sessions of 20 minutes.

For all the teachers, play was perceived as being valuable to all areas of children's learning, with language development and socialization most frequently mentioned. Accordingly, play was integrated into the curriculum through the ongoing theme or topic, and planning models included reference to the subject areas of the National Curriculum, particularly maths, English and science.

Structuring play

All play activities were structured to some extent through resources, space, materials and time. The rationale for structuring play was to integrate it into curriculum planning, organization and assessment. Play activities could be used to introduce, reinforce or extend learning, depending on each child's developmental needs. Within the broad structure, free play was distinguished as being determined more by the children's choices, allowing them to be in control of their own learning, and with less adult intervention and direction than in structured play. For example, Chris stated that as a result of the National Curriculum play was much more structured in her class, 'previously I had much more free play going on'. She distinguished between free play, which was based on children setting their 'own agenda', and structured play, where the activities would have a specific intention, 'for example, the play in the sand might be very much related to my maths or my science'.

There was a broad consensus that play was as valuable, if not more so, as formal, teacher-directed activities. One teacher did not distinguish between the two, 'because I like to think that children are learning as much through play as they are through formal work'. Jo linked play to curriculum areas for science and technology, art, writing, maths and a reading corner. Each of these areas was resourced and planned with specific learning intentions, but also with opportunities for free play and exploration. Eve described how she linked structured and free play experiences to the ongoing topic of the story of 'The Three Bears': 'You'd have different types of teddy bears for sorting activities and maths, letters written from Goldilocks to the three bears, so a lot of things would be topic-based.'

Provision for play was broad and imaginative in each of the classes. Sara provided a variety of media for tactile and water play with clear learning intentions: 'bark chippings, gravel, twigs and leaves, pebbles, lentils, pasta and sawdust. All are used to develop geography, mapping skills, technology, science and maths. Water is used with Aquaplay, funnels, bubble play and transparent containers to move water, siphon, and so on'. As well as specifying broad learning intentions, some teachers were clear about the learning processes which were integral to the subject areas. Chris described the links between role play and literacy development: 'when you hear them engaging in conversations and working together, working out a whole scenario, they're doing the very basics of story writing'. Similarly, Kate linked play to a developmental progression in writing. She provided formal sessions on handwriting, but saw the importance of children experimenting with emergent writing:

> They'll do squiggles and lines, or they'll do letters and numerals and symbols and slowly, as their knowledge of letter forms develops, they might use all letter forms and string them together, and they'll get directionality and then they'll slowly start to incorporate the phonics . . . So they're almost playing at writing.

The teachers revealed understanding of the processes which link play and learning with the content of the National Curriculum. Their role in integrating play into the curriculum was critical to sustaining this relationship.

The teacher's role in play

As part of the overall structure, all the teachers intervened in children's play for different reasons and by different means. The first level of intervention was in planning the curriculum and learning environment to incorporate play. In all classes the children were involved to varying degrees in setting up role-play areas, planning what resources would be needed and negotiating rules. This also involved teacher input, for example, setting up a café and explaining what a menu is, and making toys and games to sell in a class shop. The learning intentions were related to the National Curriculum, except in free play where intentions focused more on the socio-affective domain.

The second level of intervention was their direct involvement in play experiences. There was a reluctance among the majority of teachers to intervene directly in free play because of the commitment to respecting children's choices and 'ownership'. Thus intervention would be mostly *ad hoc* and in response to children's needs. At the same time, there was a recognition of the need to balance 'time for giving the children time to do what they needed to do', with specific inputs to check behaviour or 'move the play on'. This standpoint reflected a pragmatic recognition that young children do sometimes engage in repetitive play or lack the requisite social, cognitive or manipulative skills to play successfully. Interventions were often focused specifically on a child's individual needs, for example, playing at having telephone conversations with a child who was too shy to talk directly to an adult.

Strategies for achieving continuity between free play, structured play and teacher-intensive inputs included 'giving children ideas' and 'teaching children skills'. For example, Holly stated that 'you have to teach colour mixing for them to be able to do it properly', and Gina described how she helped the children to develop their role play by talking about themes, plots and characters. Chris saw some continuity between her role in formal activities and in play, and highlighted the importance of talking, questioning, explaining and helping. This sort of involvement was more likely to take place in structured rather than free play. Sara was quite confident about her collaborative role in learning, including play, which she regarded as 'a joint venture'.

Several teachers identified the problem of knowing the right moment to intervene and which strategies to use: 'Sometimes you go in and it's a disaster and you shouldn't have, but you can never judge.' They talked about 'going in with your size tens', 'making incredible gaffes' and 'getting it all wrong'. Eve felt strongly that teachers 'really shouldn't intrude and really, really take over the play', but recognized that appropriate interventions could extend the quality of play. Overall they relied on a degree of intuition and knowledge of individual children to guide their interventions. However, the amount of adult involvement was constrained significantly by time, curriculum priorities and the high ratio of children to adults.

There was a shared concern about the quality of learning through play. The learning intentions specified went beyond the subject framework of the National Curriculum. Many of these intentions were related to children's social and emotional development, with frequent mention of developing children's self-confidence and self-esteem, and positive attitudes towards learning and school. [. . .]

Assessment

All the teachers recognized the importance of assessment in terms of 'knowing the child' and informing planning and provision. Play was considered to have a revelatory function which could provide evidence of a child's developmental stage, needs, interests, knowledge and skills. Generally there was an emphasis on assessing the 'whole child' – social, cognitive, physical and emotional. Within this broad framework, the teachers focused on the child's individual characteristics, learning styles and attitudes towards learning.

Assessment was linked to planning and the learning intentions for an activity. These intentions could be broad, for example, developing social skills, or specifically related to the subject areas of the National Curriculum. Chris gave the example of assessing learning through sand play, focusing on: 'appropriate choice of materials, assessing whether they manage to organize themselves . . . whether they did the task independently of me . . . Whether they could explain what they did after and whether they could generalize.'

Carly talked about a child making a book and identified a range of design and technology skills, as well as knowledge about how books work: 'she was using a lot of real skills to do with writing and numeracy . . . she had also taken on board that the book should communicate . . . that books have a purpose.'

Assessment was more likely to take place in structured play activities, either through teacher observation and interaction or through feedback at review time, as exemplified by Chris: 'With my structured play activities I have an assessment agenda as well, so when they've been in the sand, they will come back and feed back to me, or feed back to the group and tell us what they found out.' Jennie saw assessment as a continuous striving towards deeper understanding of children's learning, 'getting to the heart of the learning that's taken place', in order to judge the quality of the activity and whether it had been beneficial to the child: 'I feel I'm beginning to understand more about why it's important to allow children to play and what is actually happening and how it's good for their learning. Rather than being recreational or emotionally satisfying, there is something deeper than that, something intellectual.'

While all the teachers placed a high value on assessment, in practice it was often difficult for them to find sustained periods of time for interaction and observation during play. Teacher-intensive activities tended to be prioritized because these were more likely to yield tangible evidence of the children's attainments, particularly in maths and English. A further problem to emerge was that children did not always play according to the teachers' expectations or intentions. The reasons for this were varied. First, children sometimes lacked the requisite social, cognitive and manipulative skills to engage successfully with the activities provided. Secondly, several teachers noted that they had both over- and under-estimated children, so that the play activities were not always well matched to their abilities. Thirdly, children often played to their own agendas in both free and structured play. This reinforced the view that learning through play is notoriously difficult to assess because of its open-ended, free-flow nature.

Discussion

The study indicates that the National Curriculum was exerting a 'top-down' influence on the curriculum for 4-year-olds in terms of shaping the content through the subject areas and focusing on assessment for entry into Key Stage 1. However, each of the nine teachers expressed a set of theories about the value of play to learning and development which influenced their commitment to play as an integral part of their practice. While the relationship between their theories and practice was not unproblematic, this commitment did prevail even among those who had identified the National Curriculum as a constraining influence.

The teachers provided quite complex models of curriculum planning and delivery in which they sought to integrate child-initiated and teacher-directed activities and track continuity between them. They planned for intended learning outcomes which were linked directly to the National Curriculum, but also allowed scope for unintended learning to reflect the free-flow nature of play, and children's individual needs, interests and learning styles. Provision was shaped by the subject areas of the National Curriculum but, equally important, was informed by their knowledge of children's learning and development. The data reveal the teachers' understanding of developmental progression, particularly in literacy and numeracy, which lead towards the Key Stage 1 requirements.

The teachers had accommodated this top-down influence, and did not see this as the main constraint on providing good-quality play experiences. Other constraints included space, resources and some aspects of the daily school timetable. By far the greatest problem for the majority of the teachers was class size, particularly as numbers rose across the two or three termly intake. The consensus was that large class sizes and the lack of classroom assistant support impacted on the quality of children's activities and on their learning. [. . .]

A further shared concern was the expectations of parents and colleagues who often valued more formal activities. The teachers felt that it was difficult justifying the importance of play to parents who think that, if the children are playing they cannot be working, and therefore are not learning.

[. . .]

Conclusion

This research study has provided some insights into the impact of the National Curriculum on play in reception classes, drawing on the perspectives of nine teachers. Although the sample is small, in-depth analyses were provided of the relationship between the teachers' theories and practice, and of the intervening constraints. While generalizations cannot be made from this study, it is evident that although the National Curriculum has been perceived as a threat to early years principles and practice, these teachers drew on considerable professional and pedagogical knowledge to provide what they considered to be an appropriate curriculum for 4-year-old children.

In the years between the introduction of the National Curriculum and the Desirable Outcomes, reception teachers were left in a hiatus. Given the pressures on early years teachers generally, it was inevitable that the National Curriculum would exert a downward pressure on reception classes. However, this study provides evidence that this influence was less negative than some commentators have suggested. The framework was seen as inappropriate for 4-year-old children, but while integrating free and structured play was problematic, it was not impossible. The novice teachers were more accepting of the National Curriculum than the more experienced teachers who had been used to greater freedom and autonomy. All the teachers were able to integrate child-centred and subject-centred approaches to planning, a process which was also informed by broader learning and developmental aims. There were concerns about content and assessment overload, with pressure to provide tangible evidence of children's learning for parents and colleagues, particularly in literacy and numeracy. Such evidence could be better provided through more formal activities. In spite of these pressures, play was not marginalized because of the teachers' beliefs about its value to learning, and there were accommodations between their beliefs and the National Curriculum requirements.

The teachers' perspectives revealed in this study are important for two reasons. First, they were able to articulate a rich store of professional knowledge, and to reflect critically on the relationship between their thinking and action. Their accounts of the realities and complexities of their practice provide a counterpoint to the assumptions outlined in the first part of this chapter which portray teachers as powerless recipients of curriculum change. Secondly, research that represents teachers' voices can present valuable insights into the situated nature of their knowledge about teaching and learning in relation to educational policy. Providing models of practice that are grounded in the everyday realities of classroom life is crucial in the light of current trends in the pre-school sector. [. . .]

A commitment to and belief in play as a learning medium remains a key issue when considering what constitutes good practice. Currently a weakness of play is that its relationship to pedagogy is not fully understood. It is argued here that a better understanding of this relationship could be achieved by further research on play in pre-school and school settings, with reference to teachers' professional knowledge and understanding of curriculum and pedagogical processes.

References

Anning, A. (ed.) (1995) *A National Curriculum for the Early Years*, Buckingham: Open University Press.

Anning, A. (1997) *The First Years at School*, Buckingham: Open University Press.

Bennett, N. and Kell, J. (1989) *A Good Start? Four-year-olds in Infant Schools*, Oxford: Blackwell.

Bennett, N., Wood, E. A. and Rogers, S. (1997) *Teaching through Play: Teachers' Thinking and Classroom Practice*, Buckingham: Open University Press.

Blenkin, G. and Kelly, A. V. (1994) *The National Curriculum and Early Learning: An Evaluation*, London: Paul Chapman.

David, T. (1990) *Under Five – Under Educated?* Buckingham: Open University Press.

Hurst, V. (1994) 'The implications of the National Curriculum for nursery education' in G. Blenkin and A. V. Kelly (eds), *The National Curriculum and Early Learning: An Evaluation*, London: Paul Chapman.

Nutbrown, C. (1994) *Threads of Thinking: Young Children Learning and the Role of Early Education*, London: Paul Chapman.

OFSTED (Office for Standards in Education) (1993) *First Class: The Standards and Quality of Education in Reception Classes*, London: HMSO.

SCAA (School Curriculum and Assessment Authority) (1996) *Nursery Education: Desirable Outcomes for Children's Learning on Entering Compulsory Education*, London: DFEE/SCAA.

Tyler, S. (1991) 'Play in relation to the National Curriculum', in N. Hall and L. Abbott (eds), *Play in the Primary Curriculum*, London: Hodder and Stoughton.

Wood, E. A. and Attfield, J. (1996) *Play, Learning and the Early Childhood Curriculum*, London: Paul Chapman.

Acknowledgement

The research on which this chapter was based was funded by the Economic and Social Research Council, award number R000 22 1397.

14

Value Pluralism, Democracy and Education for Citizenship

Don Rowe

Introduction: Citizenship Education as a Controversial Subject in Democratic Societies

Across the education systems of Western Europe, a resurgence of interest in citizenship or civic education is taking place. A number of factors are seen to be contributing to the urgency of the matter, including disillusionment with democracy, the threat to democracy from the mass media, the rapid pace of social and political change, the alienation of young people, rising crime rates and increasing ethnic intolerance (Newton, 1994). In Eastern Europe, too, many similar concerns are being expressed and are compounded by the need to introduce new approaches to civic education in response to the introduction of ideological pluralism and market economics (Valchev, 1992; Rachmanova and Severukhin, 1994). A recent report (UNESCO/CIDREE, 1993) emphasizes the critical role played by schools in promoting stable pluralist societies where coherence within the community is not threatened by value diversity. It suggests that schools must be places where 'peace, human rights, tolerance, international and intercultural understanding, solidarity and cooperation, peaceful conflict resolution and democratic organisation are fostered'.

Aims such as these are easy to express but they present considerable challenges to classroom teachers faced with children of different ages, abilities, attitudes and values. And the task is made more complex by the politically controversial nature of the subject matter (for an Austrian example, see Dachs, 1995). There is no single view of what 'society' and 'citizenship' should mean such that the content of the citizenship curriculum has often been a matter of heated debate between teachers, parents, politicians, church leaders and other interest groups. For this reason, it has been easier to implement programmes in non-democratic societies. Ironically, the very existence of value pluralism in society has tended to prevent liberal democracies from developing what I would call mature (i.e. pluralist) programmes of civic education because of the fear that such arrangements would be used by one group to indoctrinate the young in partisan values. The principal focus of this chapter is the wide variety of approaches towards citizenship education that have arisen in democratic societies in direct response to the presence of value pluralism. As we shall see, some models have attempted to ignore or suppress this pluralism, though in different ways and for a variety of reasons, whilst a minority have attempted what I argue is the necessary, but more challenging, task of facing up to the reality of pluralism and developing educational models that prepare young people for the essential role it plays in democratic systems (Dachs, 1995).

Many assumptions appear to underlie the teaching of social and moral values which often amount to working theories or models of citizenship education. These models are not necessarily clearly articulated or empirically validated and yet, I suggest, they influence the development of curricula in highly significant ways. For this reason, I believe it is important to be as clear as possible about the differences between these theoretical models, their functions and their implications. Because a principal claim of this chapter is that all democratic societies face these inherent difficulties, I shall support my arguments with references to civic education practices across Europe.

Broadly speaking, there are three main categories of citizenship learning that relate to the three domains in which social and moral development takes place – the cognitive, the affective and the active or experiential. However, within these broad categories a number of different models can be discerned and it is to these I now turn.

Cognitive Models

Constitutional knowledge model

This model adopts a descriptive approach to public institutions such as the constitution and the mechanics of local and national government. It recognises the need for citizenship education to foster social cohesion and civic virtue but tends to regard value pluralism as a potential source of confusion for children and young people. Therefore, it avoids or minimizes controversy and concentrates on 'safe' or consensus areas where pupils will encounter little or no value conflict. This model is more likely to be observed in secondary schools because of its relatively complex content but simplified forms are not unknown in primary schools, as in the French example described by Starkey (1992). Citizenship on this model is seen much more as a future political status than a dynamic set of rights and obligations encountered within one's daily life.

Because it avoids controversial issues, this model tends to lack relevance and interest for students. The methodology adopted by this approach is often formal and didactic, dominated by the one-way flow of information from teacher to pupil. Because there is little scope for discussion the model is weak as far as the development of democratic skills and attitudes are concerned. Its failure to address the affective domain of learning is also significant.

However, despite its grave limitations, this model does have some practical advantages which may account for the fact that it has been the single most common approach to be found in operation. For example, it is easier to implement than value laden approaches and there is some evidence that, because of this, it is reverted to by inexperienced or non-specialist teachers (Stradling and Bennett, 1981). [. . .] In addition, it has the advantage that it is less likely to bring the school into conflict with outside bodies such as parents or government.

[. . .]

An obvious objective of the constitutional model is to present a positive and clear account of society for young people but ironically, this whole approach has the potential to become counter-productive, since some commentators (Rowe, 1992) have claimed that the 'santized', problem-free view of society only leads to disillusionment when students begin to see for themselves that 'the world is not like that'. The failure of the school to offer students an adequate model of social conflict may leave confusion where there should have been understanding.

One further characteristic of this model can be observed. It appears to be favoured in circumstances where pupils are believed to be less capable of handling value conflict, as with younger and less able pupils. As already noted, primary school children are less likely to be presented with value conflicts and more likely to be offered a world view where social cohesion predominates and adults work harmoniously together for the common good. [. . .] A paternalistic desire to protect innocence may be at work here, despite much evidence that primary pupils experience moral uncertainty (Cullingford, 1992) and that the development of social and moral understanding is a continuous process throughout childhood (e.g. Dunn, 1988).

Patriotic model

This model regards the promotion of loyalty to the state or the community as the central concern of citizenship education. As such it stands in a very long tradition (Lister, 1988). In its militant or strong form this model becomes overtly propagandist, supporting the ideology of the ruling elite as was the case in Franco's Spain (Buxarrais *et al.*, 1994), the former Soviet bloc (e.g. Vari-Szilagyi, 1994) and Austria/Germany under the Nazis (Dachs, 1995). Dissent or criticism is suppressed and represented as socially unacceptable or subversive. Social control, as opposed to influence, is the central aim of the strong patriotic model. As such it fails to recognize the reality of pluralism, is anti-democratic and denies the fundamental human right to freedom of belief and expression. Yet it cannot be said that those who favour this model always do so for the cynical purpose of promoting state ideologies. It has been justified on the grounds that those being 'educated' will also benefit from it, although this can be seen as an extension of state control beyond the political into the field of culture. For example, Lister (1988) quotes Lord Macaulay who, in 1835, expressed the view that Indian education under the British should create people who were 'Indian in blood and colour, but English in taste, morals and intellect'.

The more subtle form of the patriotic model aims to promote civic cohesion by under-emphasizing, or sanitizing, issues that reflect badly on the good image of the state. For example, this model was influential in British civic and history textbooks in their treatment of the British Empire. [. . .]

It is probably fair to say that some aspects of this model are never entirely absent from citizenship education, though some teachers will be more prepared than others to acknowledge its subtle influence. Some observers believe strongly that the patriotic model is essential for the development of a sense of national identity. This is particularly likely to be prominent in the curricula of new nations, especially those emerging from a diversity of ethnic groups. As Osborne (1994) says of the Canadian experience, 'history was the major vehicle of the creation of national identity and patriotism. It told the national myth'. On the whole this model is now regarded with suspicion in post-colonial, multicultural Britain. Starkey (1995), however, compares the English approach unfavourably with the more patriotic French on grounds that, whereas the French civic education guidelines emphasize 'all that unites a nation, from symbols and mottos to President and Parliament', the English recommendations (NCC, 1990) make no mention at all of national symbols such as the monarchy, the flag or the National Anthem. Unfortunately, national symbols all too easily encourage attitudes of national superiority and xenophobia in the psychologically immature. The problem is that the patriotic model tends to place national allegiance above respect for justice, truth or universal human rights (Lister, 1988). It too readily encourages an uncritical view of the *status quo* and in this respect has much in common with the constitutional model.

Parental model

Parents quite properly have a desire and a right, under the European Convention of Human Rights, to raise children according to their own beliefs. This model openly acknowledges the difficulties of transmitting civic values that are in conflict with those of parents. This is one of the very clear points of tension between family values and those of the democratic state, and for teachers there may be no easy way to resolve the conflict this creates. This parental right to 'freedom of instruction' for children has, for example, been enshrined in the Spanish Constitution (Buxarrais *et al.*, 1994) making possible schools with a distinctive religious or ideological character where contact with democratic pluralism is minimized. This issue affects families in many different ways but is often acutely felt by parents for whom the maintenance of a distinctive culture is important. In Britain, the Muslim minority has long campaigned for state-supported separate schools (on a par with existing arrangements for Roman Catholic and Jewish schools) where their own cultural and religious traditions can be nurtured and respected. The British government, however, has long been reluctant to allow such schools, probably out of a fear of Islamic separatism or fundamentalism.

In her survey of teaching for conflict resolution in Europe, Walker (1989) quotes several instances, including in Northern Ireland, where teachers expressed reluctance to engage in activities that would encourage inter-community understanding (in this case between Catholics and Protestants) because they knew many parents would strongly object to any activity that appeared to erode their own strongly held beliefs.

Again, as in the constitutional and the patriotic models, the wish to protect children from contaminating ideas is present, though this model sees the school, and not society, as the main agent of contamination. The reality is, of course, that children in a plural society and in the age of the mass media are bombarded with a multiplicity of values from a very young age from which it is virtually impossible to protect them. Parents and teachers who fail to acknowledge the confusion experienced by children arguably make it more difficult for them, in the long run, to cope with it constructively.

A major difficulty with the parental model is, of course, that is leaves no role for the school in the development of democratic dispositions and fails to help young people deal with the fact that, outside of their own family culture, they will need to engage one way or another with a multiplicity of value positions. The kind of monocultural morality learned within the primary relationships of family and kin needs to be augmented by a secondary, but equally important, public morality, based on notions of rights and obligations rather than affection and loyalty. Quite obviously, schools are primary locations for the development of this public morality.

Religious model

The religious model of civic education reflects the widely held view that the best means by which to teach civic virtue is through religious education. No doubt the appeal for many is that religious beliefs are generally identified with clear and authoritative moral standards and it seems that many adults (even agnostics and atheists) believe religious teaching to be among the most effective means of inculcating moral values in children. Historically, this model was very strong with English pioneers of mass education, the first civic education textbook being the Bible. There is little doubt that where this model is firmly established it can obstruct the emergence of pluralist civic education. In England during the early 1990s, for example, whilst citizenship education languished on the margins of government concerns, the Secretary of State for Education suggested that religious education was the most effective vehicle for the promotion of values such as honesty and concern for others (NCC, 1993).

This model has a long history and dates from times when there was little or no distinction between the values of church and state and the dichotomy between public values and private beliefs was hardly recognized. It is an approach very deeply embedded in many cultural traditions and therefore is still highly influential, particularly in societies where the association between the state and the established religion remains relatively non-problematic, for example, in the Irish Republic and Spain. In Franco's Spain, according to Buxarrais *et al.* (1994) the State ethic *was* that of the Roman Catholic Church, and teachers were forbidden to promote moral views counter to those of Rome. Since the democratization of Spain and the embracing of pluralism, the legacy still remains and in only one region of Spain (Catalonia) has a secular form of moral education been introduced as an alternative to religious education.

Teaching 'good citizenship' by means of religious education is, of course, problematic. First, the model is philosophically flawed because, as White (1994) points out, the identification of the *moral* with the *religious* is untenable. Citizens should understand that the religious may not always be 'good' and the 'good' need not be religious. Second, the religious model fails to address many value issues that arise in secular societies. Its chief weakness is, perhaps, its lack of relevance or authority for those who hold a minority faith or no faith at all. For example, in England, the identification of British civic values with Christianity subtly promotes the view that to be, for example, a Sikh or a Buddhist is to be less than fully British. This does nothing to assist young people of minority faiths to come to terms with the problem of divided loyalties – and identification with the community is crucial to the development of positive, participative citizenship (Rowe, 1993).

There is a strong case for arguing that all state systems should teach citizenship education irrespective of the presence of religious education in the curriculum. This would provide a forum for the discussion of public issues (such as the death penalty or the role of women in society) in which religious and secular perspectives can be put forward with equal weight. In this way, classroom discussion becomes genuine 'democratic dialogue' where opinions and propositions are judged, not on the basis of the authority claimed for them, (which would be disputed outside of the faith community) but on their intrinsic merits (Haydon, 1995). This brings me to my final cognitive model of citizenship education.

Value conflict or pluralist model

This model openly acknowledges that humans experience many conflicts of value – both within themselves and in their relations with others – with the result that they take up widely differing positions on public issues. It bases its philosophical justification on the idea that each person has an inalienable right to freedom of belief and expression. On this view, the overriding aim of citizenship education is to develop morally autonomous citizens who can think critically and contribute positively to public discourse. It places value on personal development and individual integrity and recognises that the highest form of civic motivation is that which arises from principled commitment rather than coercion or persuasion. This is exactly the rationale underlying the Dutch social and political curriculum developed in the mid-1980s (Hooghof, 1987) and is implicit within the British government's guidance of 1990 (NCC, 1990). This model not only accepts, but is able to utilize, value conflict because, as Kohlberg has shown, this contributes to more mature moral reasoning (Kohlberg, 1984). It also develops better informed, more politically aware and tolerant citizens (Lipman, 1991). Further, as Tappan and Brown (1996) point out, acceptance of value pluralism is precisely what is demanded by a 'post-modern moral pedagogy'. This is to affirm the existence of many diverse socio-political perspectives, including those of the alienated and the oppressed of society. It is to argue that teachers need to acknowledge the authentic nature of each individual's perspective, which may be very different from that of the dominant ideology, and that such acknowledgement is potentially liberating.

Unlike the constitutional knowledge model, this approach is equally relevant to pupils of all ages. Even primary school pupils experience value conflict as they strive to understand their social world. The following example is taken from a discussion of fair and unfair rules with a class of English 7-year-olds (Rose, 1994).

> *Aaron*: I know a school rule that isn't fair.
> *Teacher*: Which one is that, Aaron?
> *Aaron*: The one that says if somebody hits you, you are not allowed to hit them back.
> *Teacher*: Why do you think that is unfair?
> *Aaron*: Well, if you hit them back they leave you alone.
> *Teacher*: What happens when you hit them?
> *Aaron*: They hit you back.
> *Teacher*: What happens then?
> *Aaron*: You hit them again.
> *Teacher*: And what have you got then?
> *Aaron*: A fight.
> *Teacher*: What would happen if everyone did that?
> *William*: It would be chaos. Everyone would join in.
> *Aaron*: [After thinking for a few seconds] It might not be a fair rule but it's probably a good one because teachers have to look after you and teach you.

This example demonstrates how Aaron's egocentric perception of justice is in conflict with the values underlying the school rule. If the teacher had not acknowledged the possibility of value conflict and encouraged her pupils to express their own ideas it would not have been possible to challenge Aaron's views with a broader perspective. The pedagogical requirement is to create a situation in which children's existing ideas come up against other perspectives and are modified. This is the importance of so-called 'active learning' techniques. Contrary to popular belief, pupils can be enabled to take part in discussions of this kind as soon as they begin school and research indicates that a weekly session can measurably raise the quality of children's socio-moral reasoning within a short space of time (Medrano and De La Caba, 1994).

However, the value conflict model creates significant problems for teachers concerning which values to encourage, which to discourage and on which to remain neutral. How, for example, is a teacher to react when a child expresses a racist attitude and reveals that this attitude is shared by its parents? There are two problems here. First, to what extent does the teacher have the right to undermine the parents' authority in the eyes of the child? Second, how far should teachers, in line with the free speech espoused by the value conflict model, encourage a classroom climate where harmful or antisocial views are permitted? Arguably, unless offensive opinions are expressed they cannot be challenged, but this position could deteriorate into a fully relativist approach where no opinions are held to be better or worse than any others. This is clearly not the case. Part of the function of this model must be to encourage students to understand that in democratic societies there is a core of essential beliefs to which prejudicial views do not conform, and yet, at the same time, there are many other ideas that are quite properly contested.

In fact, these contested ideas can provide a framework of concepts around which teachers can construct the content of the citizenship curriculum. Whilst being strong on process, this model should not be light on content, and should include issues that draw on curriculum areas such as moral education, social education, human rights education, law-related education and political education. The curriculum should help children develop an understanding of concepts such as justice, fairness, rights, responsibilities, rules, laws, power, authority, equality, diversity and community (Rowe, 1995) all of which are open to many different interpretations. These ideas permeate mature political debates but are also of keen interest to young children (Dunn, 1988). In my view, each of these concepts can and should be explored within the curriculum at a level appropriate to the children's age and maturity. [. . .]

This value conflict model is highly demanding of teacher skill and requires the creation of a classroom atmosphere where pupils can feel free to express themselves and engage constructively with the views of others. However, there is much research to suggest that teachers, albeit unwittingly, tend to suppress pupils' own views and inhibit their ability to take the intitiative in discussion. For example, Wood (1991) reports that the more questions teachers ask, the shorter are pupils' replies. Further, teachers rarely allow sufficient time for children to think before replying. In one study, when the teachers increased the pause after a question from an average one to three seconds, the responses of the children lengthened significantly. The teacher's style of language also influences that of the class – when she adopts a more reflective style of language herself (using fewer questions and more statements) then the children's discourse also becomes more reflective. In discussing social and moral issues, teachers need to use questions that encourage judgement rather than recall. They should elicit higher order thinking such as analysis, comparison and justificatory reasoning. Other techniques can also help, such as asking the whole class to vote on a pupil's statement and then analysing the reasons underlying the different positions generated.

Naturally, this conflict model is not without its critics. Indeed, all the previous models, with their emphasis on unitary values, implicitly criticize this approach. Watts, for example, quoted in Lister (1988), argues that acknowledging value conflict undermines civic loyalty in the young and O'Hear (1991) claims that its emphasis on critical thinking places insufficient importance on respect for the received wisdom of older generations. O'Hear, however, ignores the fact that value conflict is observable among earlier generations too, and that, in any case, successive generations cannot uncritically apply old ideas to novel situations. Even where a general precept is held to be true for all generations, for example that killing is wrong, there will be conflict generated by the different ways this rule is interpreted in any given set of circumstances.

Finally, the importance of the value conflict model in developing inter-community tolerance and understanding cannot be over-emphasized. The more young people learn to see value pluralism as normal, ubiquitous, and not simply ethnically or culturally based, then the less it will be seen as threatening or divisive.

Affective Models

So far in this discussion we have dealt with cognitive models of citizenship education. These develop social understanding, clarify values and create an awareness of rights, duties and obligations. These perceptions are very important in motivating citizens to take public action. Yet, as Gibbs (1991) argues, humans experience two quite distinct sources of moral motivation, the second being an empathic concern for others. Empathy has been defined (Damon, 1988) as the ability to recognize the feelings of others, the ability to take another's point of view and to vicariously share in another's emotional state. Empathy has both cognitive and affective components. Whilst the cognitive informs and activates the affective domain, the latter undoubtedly motivates and enriches cognition. Without the ability to empathize with others, moral decision making would be severely impaired and, according to Damon, higher empathizers are more likely to engage in pro-social actions. Citizenship education has therefore to address the question of educating the feeling, as well as the thinking, self. Students should be helped to see that citizenship education is ultimately about people and the quality of their lives in society. At all stages, therefore, pupils should be encouraged, through the use of case studies, narrative, video and other means, to enter imaginatively the experience of others as well as to consider and articulate their own feelings. So, in promoting empathic reasoning, the teacher will use questions such as 'why do you think X believed that?' or 'how do you think Y was feeling in that situation?'

Teachers are trained primarily to impart knowledge and consequently many find it difficult to address the demands of the affective curriculum. Its importance in the study of the arts and literature is clear but social studies and civic education have not wholly embraced affective approaches, being influenced, instead, by more empirical sociological and political models. Walker (1989) reports that during the 1970s the Luxembourg authorities considered the affective side of the curriculum so important that affective goals were included in a new curriculum planning model. Unfortunately, according to a government official, these goals were seldom realized.

Experiential Models

Experiential approaches to citizenship education emphasize the importance of delivering an holistic citizenship education in which both cognition and affect are fully involved, and in which citizenship skills are put into practice. I would identify two common models in this category – the school ethos model and the community action model. These are of relevance to this particular review because they also need to take account of value pluralism in different ways. I suggest that the controversial nature of civic education curricula has sometimes encouraged teachers to rely on these less contentious experiential models, rather than bite the bullet and deal with controversial issues. In the UK, this approach has been particularly true of primary schools (Rose, 1994).

School ethos model

In democratic societies, schools should ensure that their organization and ethos take account of value pluralism and respect the right of all members to be consulted on issues of concern to them. Power should be exercised responsibly, not in an authoritarian or despotic fashion. Values such as respect for persons and for justice are undoubtedly learned experientially and therefore they should permeate the whole of school life. Teachers encouraging respect for human rights in the classroom should, of course, act in a consistent manner (Best, 1992). Rules should be seen to be fair and should be enforced humanely. As Lister (1988) succinctly puts it, civic educators 'need to shape institutions and not just plan curricula'.

Many schools have worked hard on their democratic or consultative structures on the view that pupils need to experience democracy, not simply be taught about it (Best, 1992; Trafford, 1993). In the UK, for example, a survey undertaken in 1993 showed that about half of all state secondary schools and one-seventh of primary schools had pupil councils for the discussion of issues raised by pupils themselves (Ashworth, 1995), though this survey indicated that consultations often take place by other means, such as questionnaires. Walker (1989) refers to consultative procedures in Germany, Denmark and Italy where pupils can comment on curriculum matters, discipline, textbooks and the organization of learning. Harber (1995) quotes examples from The Netherlands and the UK where, even in primary schools, pupil participation in decision-making has genuinely enriched the quality of community life and contributed to more positive attitudes of respect and understanding between staff and pupils. In addition, pupil councils provide experience of important aspects of the democratic processes such as standing for elections, representing the opinions of others, campaigning for change, participating in formal meetings and reporting back (Rowe, 1997). A trend towards involving young people in municipal decision-making is also discernable in a number of countries, including the UK and France (see, for example, Rossini and Vulbeau, 1994; Starkey, 1992).

There are, of course, limits in the extent to which state schools can democratize. Indeed, some teachers are uncomfortable with the language of democracy in schools (Rowe, 1997) and others have preferred to think in terms of creating schools characterized by the more comprehensive values of justice or human rights. Kohlberg's 'just community' schools are the best known example of this trend, though Kohlberg's own experiments were carried out with specially selected groups of pupils, creating highly democratic, self-regulating 'schools within schools' (Power, Higgins and Kohlberg, 1989). A radical approach of this nature is very difficult to replicate in large mainstream schools. However, Walker (1989) describes the Loretto Catholic Girls' Schools in Ireland as basing their ethos on the 'specific philosophy of justice and peace', emphasizing the quality of relationships, structures and processes throughout the school. On this model even school discipline should take account of the high standards demanded by the justice concept (see, for example, Cunningham, 1992). In similar work, Rogers (1994), has developed a highly sophisticated approach to classroom control that is effective yet always maintains respect for the rights and responsibilities of students.

Community action model

Many schools encourage citizenship learning through community action programmes in which pupils are encouraged to identify a local or national issue and take appropriate action. Typical projects would include working to improve the environment, helping old people or supporting national and international charities (Best, 1992, refers to typical examples in Denmark, Portugal and France). Community action can be part of a structured learning programme or a voluntary activity undertaken in pupils' own time.

Another example of this action model can be seen when, during the study of a particular issue, such as environmental pollution or human rights abuse, the teacher requires each pupil, as classwork, to write a letter to a politician expressing concern and demanding action. However, if pupils are not given a free choice about the views to be expressed, there is a danger that work of this kind could become indoctrinatory. Where such activities are voluntary, as when they arise out of membership of a school society, this problem is avoided.

Conclusion

The central theme of this chapter has been that the very nature of democracy and pluralism poses complex problems for citizenship education. I am of the belief that some of the models described above are philosophically and educationally better than others, and I have therefore not presented this framework as a neutral observer. I have argued, in effect, that nothing that is controversial outside of the school, should be presented to pupils in any other light. Clearly, these models are not mutually exclusive – many of them certainly interact and overlap. Within a single course, several models might justifiably be present. For example, it will be important to ensure that a proper balance between cognitive, affective and experiential learning is maintained. However, it is important to emphasize that a number of these models are incompatible with pluralism. Models that emphasize consensus or unitary values, ultimately fail to prepare young people for full democratic citizenship, though I believe that teachers are not always aware of the implications of the pedagogies they adopt. In this respect, the analysis offered here may encourage curriculum planners at school, local and national levels to be more clear about which models of citizenship education are present within their own curricula, and to ensure they are there as the result of careful planning and not by default or accident.

At the present time, there is a resurgence of interest in citizenship education as the importance of schools in the socialization process, and not merely as producers of technologically competent workers, is rediscovered. As Skilbeck (1989) points out in his review of major international trends, 'education as a means of nation building or rebuilding is once again high on the agenda'. However, the potential pitfalls for such a project are many and, ironically, the gap between national and international rhetoric and the quality of delivery in the classroom is nowhere greater than in this field. In many countries citizenship education remains optional, fragmented, poorly resourced, lacking a sound theoretical base and taught by reluctant or poorly trained teachers. This is a situation that needs urgent and concerted attention at all possible levels.

References

Ashworth, L. (1995) *Children's Voices in School Matters*, London: Advisory Centre for Education.

Best, F. (1992) *Human Rights Education, Summary Work on the Council of Europe*, Strasbourg: Council of Europe.

Buxarrais, M. R., Martinez, M., Puig, J. M. and Trilla, J. (1994) Moral education in the Spanish education system, *Journal of Moral Education*, 23(1): 39.

Cullingford, C. (1992) *Children and Society: Children's Attitudes to Politics and Power*, London: Cassell.

Cunningham, J. (1992) Rights, responsibilities and school ethos, in E. Baglin Jones and N. Jones (eds), *Education for Citizenship: Ideas and Perspectives for Cross-Curricular Study*, London: Kogan Page.

Dachs, H. (1995) Civic education in Austria – a controversial issue, paper presented to the European Conference on Curriculum Development: Civic Education in Central and Eastern Europe, Vienna, October.

Damon, W. (1988) *The Moral Child: Nurturing Children's Natural Moral Growth*, New York: Free Press.

Dunn, J. (1988) *The Beginnings of Social Understanding*, Oxford: Blackwell.

Gibbs, J. (1991) Toward an integration of Kohlberg's and Hoffman's moral development theories, *Human Development*, 34: 88–104.

Harber, C. (ed.) (1995) *Developing Democratic Education*, Ticknall, Derbyshire: Education Now Publishing Cooperative.

Haydon, G. (1995) Thick or thin? The cognitive content of moral education in a plural democracy, *Journal of Moral Education*, 24(1): 53–64.

Hooghof, H. (1987) Curriculum development for political education in The Netherlands, paper delivered to International Round Table Conference on Political Socialisation on the Young in East and West, National Institute for Curriculum Development, Enschede, Holland.

Kohlberg, L. (1984) *The Psychology of Moral Development*, New York: Harper and Row.

Lipman, M. (1991) *Thinking in Education*, New York: Cambridge University Press.

Lister, I. (1988) Civic education for positive pluralism, working paper presented to the Conference on Education for Citizenship in Multi-Ethnic Societies, Rutgers University, New Jersey, USA: England: University of York.

Medrano, C. and De La Caba, M. A. (1994) A model of intervention for improving moral reasoning: an experiment in the Basque Country, *Journal of Moral Education*, 23(4): 427–37.

NCC (National Curriculum Council) (1990) *Curriculum Guidance 8: Education for Citizenship*, York: National Curriculum Council.

NCC (National Curriculum Council) (1993) *Spiritual and Moral Development – A Discussion Paper*, York: National Curriculum Council.

Newton, K. (1994) The causes of declining interest in public affairs and politics in the old established democracies of Western Europe and in the new democracies of Eastern and Central Europe, in *Disillusionment with Democracy: Political Parties, Participation and Non-participation in Democratic Institutions in Europe*, Strasbourg, Council of Europe.

Developing Pedagogy: Researching Practice

O'Hear, A. (1991) *Education and Democracy – the Posturing of the Left Establishment*, London: The Claridge Press.

Osborne, K. (1994) Democratic citizenship and the teaching of history, *Citizenship*, 3(2), London: The Citizenship Foundation.

Power, C., Higgins, A. and Kohlberg, L. (1989) *Lawrence Kohlberg's Approach to Moral Education*, New York: Columbia University Press.

Rachmanova, E. and Severukhin, V. (1994) Teaching human rights as the main trend in educational reform in Russia, *Citizenship*, 3(2), London: The Citizenship Foundation.

Rogers, B. (1994) *The Language of Discipline*, Plymouth: Northcote House Publishers.

Rose, G. (1994) (unpublished) A consideration of the primary project of the Citizenship Foundation in the light of curricular demands for citizenship education.

Rossini, N. and Vulbeau, A. (1994) Children and young people's city councils: an evaluation report prepared for the National Association of Children and Youth Boards (L'Anacej), in G. H. Bell (ed.), *Educating European Citizens: Citizenship Values and the European Dimension*, London: David Fulton.

Rowe, D. (1992) Law-related education, an overview, in J. Lynch, C. Modgil and S. Modgil (eds), *Cultural Diversity and the Schools, Vol 4: Human Rights, Education and Global Responsibilities*, London: Falmer Press.

Rowe, D. (1993) The citizen as a moral agent – the development of a continuous and progressive conflict-based citizenship curriculum, *Curriculum*, 13(3).

Rowe, D. (1995) Developing spiritual, moral and social values through a citizenship programme for primary schools, in R. Best (ed.), *Education, Spirituality and the Whole Child*, London: Cassell.

Rowe, D. (1997) *The Business of School Councils: A Study of Democracy in Schools*, report available from the Citizenship Foundation, London.

Skilbeck, M. (1989) A changing social and educational context, in B. Moon, P. Murphy and J. Raynor (eds), *Policies for the Curriculum*, London: Hodder and Stoughton.

Starkey, H. (1992) Education for citizenship in France, in E. Baglin Jones and N. Jones (eds), *Education for Citizenship: Ideas and Perspectives for Cross-Curricular Study*, London: Kogan Page.

Starkey, H. (1995) From rhetoric to reality: starting to implement education for European values, in G. H. Bell (ed.), *Educating European Citizens – Citizenship Values and the European Dimension*, London: David Fulton.

Stradling, R. and Bennett, E. (1981) *Political Education in West Germany: A Pilot Study of Curriculum Policy*, London: Curriculum Review Unit, Institute of Education, London University.

Tappan, M. and Brown, L. M. (1996) Envisioning a post-modern moral pedagogy, *Journal of Moral Education*, 25(1): 101–9.

Trafford, B. (1993) *Sharing Power in Schools: Raising Standards*, Ticknall, Derbyshire: Education Now Publishing Cooperative.

UNESCO/CIDREE (1993) *A Sense of Belonging: Guidelines for Values for the Humanistic and International Dimension of Education*, Paris: UNESCO.

Valchev, R. (1992) The civic education experiment: ideas, problems and prospects for Bulgaria, *Citizenship*, 2(2), London: The Citizenship Foundation.

Vari-Szilagyi, I. (1994) Values education in Hungary, in M. Taylor (ed.), *Values Education in Europe: A Comparative Overview of a Survey of 26 Countries in 1993*, Paris: Consortium of Institutions for Development and Research in Education and UNESCO.

Walker, J. (1989; reprinted 1992) *Violence and Conflict Resolution in Schools*, Strasbourg: Council of Europe.

Wood, D. (1991) Aspects of teaching and learning, in P. Light, S. Sheldon and M. Woodhead (eds), *Learning to Think*, London: Routledge.

White, P. (1994) Citizenship and 'spiritual and moral development', *Citizenship*, 3(2), London: The Citizenship Foundation.

15

ICT in Subject Teaching: an Opportunity for Curriculum Renewal?

Michael Bonnett, Angela McFarlane and Jacquetta Williams

[. . .]

We have entered a potentially seminal phase in the UK: the initiatives to consolidate and extend information and communications technology (ICT) in the curriculum are not only unprecedented in their scope, but also in the levels of funding being made available for both hardware and software provision and teachers' professional development. [. . .]

But what are the curriculum and learning gains which might result from such initiatives? Clearly there can be no global answer to this question: ICT is no more homogenous than programmes on television or books in a public library – indeed, even less so. Its potential is as varied as the huge – and ever growing – range of software and hardware devices that are available. Thus, while it becomes increasingly important in curriculum terms to evaluate the merits of ICT, because of its protean character, in many respects this must of necessity be piecemeal. (This is not to deny that there may be *some* fairly generalizable features: see, for example, Bonnett, 1997; McFarlane, 1997.)

This chapter reflects upon the findings of a recent piece of research into the effects on learning of using what has been regarded as a particularly potent kind of ICT: multimedia authoring. In 1997 Cambridgeshire LEA was awarded a GEST grant to develop a drugs education project in Key Stage 2, which would use multimedia authoring as a vehicle for developing pupils' knowledge of drugs and awareness of health-related issues. The application used was HyperStudio. This software is designed for use in schools and allows images and sound to be combined with text, and the resulting material to be organized in non-linear ways (i.e. as hypertext) through the creation of 'cards' (computer screens of material) which can be linked in a variety of ways to form 'stacks' (see Scrimshaw, 1993, for a useful discussion of the potential of hypertext). In principle, any card can be linked to any other through either one-way or two-way connections, thus enabling the creation of a highly flexible network for organizing and accessing material. The task of the pupils was to work in groups to produce a multimedia learning resource which could be used to help other children explore drugs issues.

The project was undertaken in 1997/8 with Year 6 children in seven schools. Prior to the project all the teachers had access to a programme of drugs education produced by Tacade and received training sessions in using Hyper-Studio. The pupils were taught how to use the software in separate sessions parallel to the drugs education lessons before embarking on the multimedia authoring in the context of drugs education. Like the pupils, none of the teachers had experience of multimedia authoring prior to the project, but throughout there was access to technical support provided by an advisory teacher. While the pupils reported experiencing some technical difficulties with operating the software – such as making links between desired screens both within and across stacks, saving recorded sounds correctly and in the desired place and drawing pictures with the mouse – these tended to be regarded as enjoyable challenges rather than insurmountable obstacles.

The objectives of the project were to:

- raise the levels of knowledge and information on drugs issues for a targeted group of staff and pupils;
- allow opportunities for the targeted pupils to consider a range of personal responses to drug-related situations;
- develop pupil and staff skills in the 'communicating information' strand of the National Curriculum;
- investigate the conditions needed for the successful development of multimedia authoring.

Two aspects of this project are particularly pertinent to evaluating the potential of ICT in more general curriculum terms. First, the view of drugs education taken in the project required the development of a number of attitudes and dispositions such as recognizing choice and responsibility and making autonomous judgements. These are important across the whole curriculum, involve higher order thinking abilities and extend the learning focus beyond the purely cognitive domain. Second, the facility to select and arrange media in non-linear ways is widely believed to be a powerful vehicle for the expression and development of a wide range of thinking qualities and strategies (Rodrigues, 1997a) and fits well with constructivist theories of learning. Thus the opportunity was presented for evaluating the potential of ICT to further some central educational aims in what was ostensibly a favourable context.

What Can Be Expected of Multimedia Authoring

Very little empirical research, as noted by Rodrigues (1997a), has focused on the use of multimedia authoring by pupils and extensive searches have revealed none in the context of drugs education. However, studies relating to the use of other information technologies in education, as well as the few evaluating multimedia authoring tools, make a number of claims. For example, the potential of ICT to support discussion and collaboration is frequently highlighted (e.g. Crook, 1994; Light, 1993). Rodrigues (1997b) found that children reviewed science information collaboratively when editing and collating it using multimedia authoring software, suggesting that such reflection and discussion are encouraged by the choices involved in selecting and presenting the information to be included. O'Neill suggests that 'Perhaps the most immediate advantage of multimedia authoring is that children's preferred medium can dominate' (1998, p. 147). Arguably this gives two main benefits: first, the opportunity to choose how they communicate will increase pupils' motivation to do so; and second, by selecting modes of representation they may develop an understanding of how photographs, drawings, diagrams, text and sound may contribute 'to the meaning making process' while taking part in that process themselves (O'Neill, 1998, p. 148). In addition, he suggests that the ability to link and sequence materials in a variety of ways when using hypermedia constitutes 'a representation of the thinking process itself' (p. 149). Hypertext has long been associated with non-linear representation of ideas and in turn with encouraging and extending the processes of integration and contextualization of knowledge by allowing the author and/or reader to structure knowledge as *they* understand it (Beeman *et al.*, 1987, cited in Mayes, Kibby and Anderson, 1990).

A related advantage frequently associated with multimedia authoring is 'ownership'. It has been suggested that by engaging in choices about modes of representation pupils might develop a sense of responsibility for what they are producing and might be more likely to assimilate new information with existing knowledge and experiences as well as communicate their existing knowledge and experience. This links with the increased motivation often associated with the more general use of ICT in education (Rodrigues, 1997a; Cox, 1997). Motivation can be characterized in a number of ways and Cox (1997) identified the following areas of gain in relation to students' experiences of ICT:

- increase in commitment to the learning task;
- enhanced enjoyment and interest in learning and the subject;
- enhanced sense of achievement in learning and pride in work produced;
- increase in self-directed learning and independence;
- enhanced self-esteem leading to expectations of achieving long-term goals.

In addition, an increased willingness to spend time and effort on something has been attributed to the development of active learning habits which ICT can encourage (Somekh, 1996).

While these latter findings do not refer specifically to multimedia authoring, given the kind of interactions that its use involves, it seems reasonable to assume that they are likely to apply equally to this implementation of ICT. Thus the overall picture that emerges suggests a considerable potential for multimedia authoring to enhance aspects of children's learning which extend well beyond simple knowledge acquisition.

The Project Evaluation

[. . .]

Teachers' and pupils' views on the contribution of multimedia authoring to learning

At the end of the project the teachers expressed views which closely reflected the potential benefits suggested by previous research. They identified the following main learning gains resulting from the use of multimedia authoring:

- in planning the content of their presentations, the pupils discussed and evaluated information;
- in turn, this encouraged a sense of responsibility for their own choices and actions when considering situations involving drugs;
- the awareness of an audience encouraged the pupils to review information and thereby consolidate understanding;
- the pupils enjoyed using the computer and the degree of choice facilitated by the multimedia authoring package increased their commitment to the task.

The children's own view of matters concurred closely with this picture. In the group interviews they spoke of how they needed to listen to each other in order to work together, to evaluate material for their audience and to take responsibility for the material they presented:

> If someone gives you an idea don't just forget it because it could be a really good idea, and don't just leave it and say 'No I'm not doing that – that's a really rubbish idea'. (Girl)

[. . .]

> We had to think a lot about the children . . . We've got to make sure and back up everything we've said because if we've said something wrong then it's not going to look very good because they might think what we've told them is right and so we've got to check all our information. (Boy)

What was interesting about their motivation was not simply that it was high, but its quality, which, in line with Cox's findings, celebrated engagement, learning and autonomy:

> I think it's good that we get a choice what to do in here. We got told that we were doing something and we normally get told that we're doing this and that and the

other, but we get a choice of what to do in this. It's good . . . We get to choose what we get to put in it, how it's presented, what colour it is and everything like that. (Girl)

I think it's much more interesting because we find things out for ourselves instead of the teacher telling us and we can do what we want the way we want because we find it out ourselves. It's much more interesting. (Boy)

[. . .]

A further aspect of their motivation – perhaps going beyond Cox's findings – was an enhanced sense of collaboration:

Some people might not get along and stuff, but while we've been working in groups people have got along because like, when you're doing something really good you just want to get on with it and have fun. (Boy)

In addition, the teachers observed that the multimedia authoring encouraged the development of a range of skills and attitudes which generalized beyond those involved in assimilating the drugs education information. These included the development of independent learning skills, IT skills and a confident attitude towards IT, and also social skills – a learning gain that the teachers had not anticipated at the start of the project. After the project several of the teachers emphasized how both within and across groups pupils had developed their ability to negotiate and to compromise and that they were already beginning to see these skills being applied by the pupils more generally throughout the curriculum.

However, one of the teachers was less enthusiastic about multimedia authoring, describing it as being no different to other traditional methods in terms of supporting subject objectives, except for the IT-related learning gains: 'The children were very interested in the drugs anyway. It provided a "purpose" but I would aim for a purpose anyway, i.e. presentation/drama to other classes, information booklet. The multimedia provided an extra "reason" for them to do it.' This observation raises the interesting question of the extent to which ICT is essential to achieving the learning gains commonly associated with it. There is also the complementary question of the extent to which the introduction of ICT provoked some radical rethinking of possibilities and approaches to the topic which made such gains more likely. We will return to these issues in the final section of this chapter.

Along with the gains, the teachers reported a number of organizational problems relating to the integration of ICT into classroom life as a whole and, more specifically, to the organization of small groups of pupils requiring access to a computer for relatively long periods of time. The solutions found to these problems – which basically involved giving more responsibility to pupils for their own learning in various ways – raised a predictable but interesting array of questions associated with managing a more open learning environment alongside more traditional teaching. Questions concerning the provision of support and guidance, the monitoring of individual progress and the reintegration of individuals who had been working on computers into ongoing class work loomed large. One thing that became very clear was that in various ways the demands of more interactive and independent learning can challenge the pre-existing culture of the classroom and stimulate teachers to devise new teaching strategies. Indeed, sometimes the very attitudes, abilities and the experiences which are centrally valued in such learning can be at odds with what classrooms can commonly accommodate, calling into question the underlying ethos of much teaching and the expectations generated by the National Curriculum. Teachers may have to rethink their practice in quite radical ways if they are to meet the challenge of this tension (see also, O'Shea, 1996).

This suggestion is reinforced by the observation of two teachers that using multimedia authoring requires a reorientation from product to process, while another teacher commented on the change that took place in her relationship with the pupils, describing the project as requiring a 'more open teaching style'. This was partly related to the nature of the drugs education programme itself, but engaging with a piece of software that is premised upon the user making choices and decisions about how to link material in non-linear ways inevitably challenges the teacher to at least acknowledge a more open approach to learning and to address the issues it raises.

The research revealed an interesting aspect of assessment. Performance on the formal multiple-choice test suggested that a large majority of the pupils understood most of the issues it raised, i.e. that medicines are drugs and consequently that not all drugs are harmful; that the danger of drugs can be related to their use for fun; that the dangers of drugs are not merely related to addictiveness; that drug users cannot be identified by what they look like; the identification of a volatile substance. This traditional measure of mastery of the information content of the drugs education programme suggested that the children's acquisition of factual knowledge was satisfactory. However, discussions with pupils which centred around their own multimedia creations revealed a certain lack of assimilation of some of the key ideas. For example, in the test 90 per cent of pupils avoided stereotyping drug users, but many of the pupils' presentations and comments made in the interviews suggested that certain misconceptions about drug users persisted. When asked why people might take drugs that are not 'good' for them only a few of the pupils could offer reasons that did not involve damning or demonizing the drug user. This is in line with previous findings about the attitudes and understanding of 10–11-year-olds, who tend to portray drug users as 'mad, bad and sad' (O'Connor, Best and Best, 1998, p. 54). This was frequently reflected in the presentations the children produced. [. . .]

One observation on this might be that the mere introduction of ICT had done little to enhance the development of the children's personal responses to such issues. Another, perhaps more salient point is that in contrast to the impression given by the more formal assessment, the introduction of ICT afforded an opportunity for an assessment which reflected what had actually been assimilated by the children into their 'everyday' thinking – the result of their own discussion, interpretation and evaluation processes. In this way, the increased level of genuine interactivity the use of such authoring prompted made the real character of children's thinking and understanding more overt and thus accessible for evaluation and formative assessment. (It should also be noted that notwithstanding their weaknesses, many of the projects displayed considerable attention to potential courses of action and, at times, the interpersonal issues that might arise, implying an acceptance of responsibility for one's actions.)

The Impact of Multimedia Authoring on Children's Learning – a Discussion

Many of the objectives set for the project were met to some degree:

- Despite some confusions and the persistence of certain stereotypes, the pupils' knowledge of drugs did appear to improve and there were substantial gains in their level of competence in ICT itself.
- The flexibility of multimedia authoring – in terms of the form of presentation, whether it be narrative or non-narrative, poetry or prose, voice sequences or song, pictures or photographs, or any mixture of the above, and in terms of structure – whether organization be linear, hierarchical or entirely interconnected – seemed to encourage pupils to explore drug-related situations using their own frames of reference and ways of communicating.
- The multimedia authoring presented pupils with many detailed choices about how to communicate and this did appear to encourage consideration of different media and ways of communicating. Teachers also reported being impressed by the extent to which pupils developed verbal communication skills in their attempts to come to agreements within and across working groups.

However, underlying these achievements were a number of further points. We will consider three of them here: structure; discussion and teacher intervention; and personal development.

Structure

Structure affected children's learning in two related ways:

- the way in which their preparation for multimedia authoring was structured affected their overall orientation to producing their presentation;
- the way in which their multimedia authoring presentation *itself* was structured could affect the focus of their attention when developing their ideas.

With regard to the former, an important structural element was the degree of pre-specification of content and its organization – and how this was decided. In some cases, in an effort by the teacher to manage an area that was new to them, there was a high degree of teacher direction from the start. In other cases more scope was provided for children to contribute to the decision-making process through class and/or group discussions and their own pre-planning. But by whatever route, in some cases the content and its organization was fairly fully specified in advance of incorporating it into the presentation, whereas in other cases this was done much more in conjunction with work on the package – ideas about content being reworked in the light of ongoing discoveries as the presentation developed, or as new discoveries were made about what the software facilitated. From this point of view, higher degrees of pre-specification might be thought to inhibit fuller utilization of the potential of the software to enhance the complexity of the children's thinking. However, examination of the children's work suggested an important caveat to this.

In so far as lack of pre-specification might lead to greater experimentation with the software and the possibility of more non-linear stacks, we found that card networks whose formal structures were apparently more non-linear (i.e. they contained more branching and connections between cards) did not necessarily contain more non-linear developed *content*. [. . .] From the point of view of the organization and representation of *ideas* there was little sense of *development* at all or linearity continued to dominate. On the other hand, *within* some cards which were part of a seemingly linear stack, divergent pathways for thought were sometimes more evident and content was sometimes expressed in a more balanced and sophisticated manner. [. . .]

Clearly there is a distinction to be drawn between the form and the content of children's networks and it needs to be recognized that a higher degree of development or non-linearity in one does not necessarily translate into the other. [. . .] Our evidence suggests that working within a simpler and fairly prescribed presentation structure led to a focus on the *content* rather than a focus on the *presentation structure* itself (which was encouraged by a more open approach). This in turn may actually have facilitated greater non-linearity of *thinking* in the sense of material being organized in ways that recognize potentially different pathways for understanding and decision-making. Thus, at this stage in the children's development, at least, closing some of the options available in software as open as multimedia authoring led to a greater exploration of content and ideas. There is a sense in which this finding seems to parallel the view of Wegerif (1997) who questions the claims of Anderson *et al.* (1993) and Fisher (1997) that more 'closed' software (such as adventure games), which both initiates the character of the pupils' activity and the feedback/follow-up, restricts the nature of pupils' discourse. Wegerif's work led him to suggest that computers can facilitate a new kind of educational interaction which 'combines structuring and directing children's learning with being used as a passive and infinitely patient resource for children's active exploration and discovery'.

It would seem that unless pupils already have experience of multimedia with a variety of routes through material, they are likely to stick to a straight linear sequence for developing their ideas. Providing the context of a series of decisions where there is more than one option available can act as a stimulus for developing a branched structure which is then understood as a vehicle for exploring complex issues. Established in this way, such a branched structure can give a focus for children's thinking about what the options might be and what consequences might arise as a result of making certain choices. We found that where teachers offered this scaffold, the children then used this to display more sophisticated thinking. In addition, where the intended audience for the presentation had been clearly identified and efforts had been made to enable the children to assess the needs of this audience (for example, by having the opportunity to conduct their own interviews of target groups), there was evidence of a greatly enhanced degree of interpretation, translation and evaluation of the original material. The virtues of deeper understanding associated with attempting to teach something to others really became apparent. The potential of this kind of motive may be greatly increased as the possibility of children publishing on the internet becomes a reality in schools.

Discussion and teacher intervention

It is likely that realizing the potential of multimedia in teaching and learning lies, in large part, in teachers anticipating and planning for discussion periods with pupils both during and after projects have been created. This aspect of the role of information technology in the learning process is discussed by Jones and Mercer who argue that computers ought not to be regarded as an 'impersonal tool for "autonomous learning" ', but rather more 'as a medium through which a teacher and learner can communicate' (1993, p. 22).

The simple introduction of ICT – even in a form as powerful as multimedia authoring – will not necessarily produce learning gains. The broader learning context and quality of teacher intervention are critical to outcomes. [. . .] For example, Wegerif and Dawes (1998) argue that teachers need to support effective interaction and collaboration around computers as exploratory talk is not automatic. Others have also expressed reservations about the claim that collaborative work with ICT necessarily evokes particular ways of interacting with material such as redrafting (Jessel, 1992). Crook (1994) stresses the importance of integrating computer use into the discourse between teachers and pupils and into the wider discourse of the classroom. [. . .] Such observations do not negate the potential value of multimedia authoring tools but, rather, make clear the integral role of teachers' introduction and supervision of such work to the quality of the processes in which pupils engage.

Personal development

Ostensibly, the approach taken by the project offered two kinds of benefit: enhanced quality of drugs education and the development of ICT capability. However, it was evident that other kinds of significant educational gain were also possible – particularly in the area of children's personal and social development. For many teachers, the opportunities – indeed the *need* – for children to discuss, negotiate, co-operate and devise decision-making procedures between themselves as they worked together in planning and constructing their presentations was very important. So, too, was the development of attitudes of respect, trust and responsibility involved. [. . .] In addition, the status afforded to the project as a whole through the use of such relatively powerful software and the aspiration to use the product for teaching other children notably increased the self-esteem in children whose previous level had been low. Such attitudes are not only germane to the ability of children to respond responsibly to drugs-related situations but, as previously suggested, represent central educational aims in their own right.

Conclusion: ICT and the Retrieval of Educational Values

We would like to conclude this chapter by raising some broader issues concerning the impact of ICT on education. A possible response to a number of the potential benefits described above is to ask – as one of our teachers did – whether the introduction of ICT was essential to their achievement. Could they not have been achieved by other, more 'conventional' means? Given the expenditure of time, effort and money that can be involved in employing ICT, this is clearly a very pertinent question. A full answer to it would require some close analysis of processes and outcomes, but in general terms it is important to note the following points:

1. To the extent that it is true that such outcomes are attainable by other means, it is none the less true that they *were* achieved through the use of ICT.
2. It may well be that the introduction of certain novel elements into the curriculum will disturb the status quo and provoke a re-evaluation of practice, but it remains the case that the introduction of ICT contributed to a fairly radical re-evaluation – even on the part of the teacher who ended up being relatively dismissive of it. The conventional alternatives already available had not done this.
3. Part of the reason for this re-evaluation is the philosophy of learning implicit in the software itself. Multimedia authoring, along with other more common forms of ICT such as word-processing, desktop publishing and constructing databases, clearly invites a significant level of pupil

choice, responsibility and independent learning. Teachers who are asked to interact with it are therefore confronted with this open approach to learning and are provoked to consider the possibilities it raises. They also have at hand a tool particularly adept for supporting such learning (granted previous caveats about the need for supporting structure and discussion).

4. As previously discussed, this element of re-evaluation of current practice is also reflected in the enhanced assessment which interaction with the software provided and which has the capacity to reveal to teachers aspects of the reality of children's understanding which belie the comforting impression which may be given by more formal modes of assessment. This is not to deny that more formal kinds of assessment have any value, but to make the point that they measure a different level of understanding – as it were, 'academic' understanding – which should not necessarily be taken as an indicator of that understanding which is authentic in the sense that is has become integrated into the real life of the child through the need to evaluate it personally and operate upon it (Bonnett, 1994).

In such ways the introduction of ICT into the curriculum invites us to address some fundamental educational issues not only at the level of classroom practice, but also at the level of policy. With regard to the former, there are important issues concerning the extent, timing and nature of teacher intervention and interaction with pupils which could have a considerable impact on their general relationship with their pupils and the whole ethos of the classroom. With regard to the latter, TTA requirements clearly see the potential of ICT not as something to be 'bolted on' to a previously existing curriculum, but as integral to the teaching of the different subject areas and as having pedagogical implications which will draw heavily on the professional judgement of teachers. The proper integration of ICT will require subject matter and pedagogy to be significantly *reconstructed*.

Thus notwithstanding the frequent instrumental/utilitarian association of ICT use with preparation for a 'high-tech' society and the world of work, there is a significant sense in which the introduction of ICT into the curriculum raises issues that are central to more liberal conceptions of education. It can act as a catalyst to return to centre stage significant elements of teacher and pupil autonomy in teaching and learning and in so doing represents a reassertion of values that lie at the heart of these more liberal conceptions, but which have long been overshadowed. If this is true, it presents an opportunity for the retrieval into practice of a conception of education which puts genuine quality of understanding and personal growth back on the agenda.

Recent years have been littered with extravagant claims about the potential of ICT to change schooling – indeed even to replace it. We make no such extreme claims in this chapter, but the potentially beneficial effects of its introduction into the curriculum need to be exploited while they are there – though it remains to be seen whether these will ever be anything like fully realized while the qualities of understanding and the levels of autonomy which result are not recognized by current formal assessment procedures. Here is another respect in which the introduction of ICT challenges the status quo – another set of potentially liberalizing implications as important as they are yet unacknowledged by those fervently legislating ICT provision in the curriculum.

References

Anderson, A., Tolmie, A., McAteer, E. and Demisne, A. (1993) 'Software style and interaction around the microcomputer', *Computers and Education*, 20(3): 235–50.

Bonnett, M. (1994) *Children's Thinking. Promoting Understanding in the Primary School*, London: Cassell.

Bonnett, M. (1997) 'Computers in the classroom: some value issues', in A. McFarlane (ed.), *Information Technology and Authentic Learning*, London: Routledge.

Cox, M. J. (1997) *The Effects of Information Technology on Students' Motivation. Final Report*. London: King's College, London and NCET (National Council for Education Technology).

Crook, L. (1994) *Computers and the Collaborative Experience of Learning*, London: Routledge.

Fisher, E. (1997) 'Children's talk and computer software', in R. Wegerif and P. Scrimshaw (eds), *Computers and Talk in the Primary Classroom*, Clevedon: Multilingual Matters.

Jessel, J. (1992) 'Do children really use the word processor as a thought processor?', *Developing Information Technology in Teacher Education*, 5: 23–32.

Jones, A. and Mercer, N. (1993) 'Theories of learning and information technology', in P. Scrimshaw (ed.), *Language, Classrooms and Computers*, London: Routledge.

Light, P. (1993) 'Collaborative learning with computers', in P. Scrimshaw (ed.), *Language, Classrooms and Computers*, London: Routledge.

McFarlane, A. (1997) 'Where are we and how did we get here?', in A. McFarlane (ed.), *Information Technology and Authentic Learning*, London: Routledge.

Mayes, J. T., Kibby, M. R. and Anderson, T. (1990) 'Signposts for conceptual orientation: some requirements for learning from hypertext', in R. McAleese and C. Green (eds), *Hypertext: State of the Art*, Oxford: Intellect Books.

O'Connor, L., Best, D. and Best, R. (1998) 'What "works" in drugs education?', in L. O'Connor, D. O'Connor and R. Best (eds), *Drugs: Partnerships for Policy, Prevention and Education. A Practical Approach for Working Together*, London: Cassell.

O'Neill, B. (1998) 'New ways of telling: multimedia authoring in the classroom', in M. Monteith (ed.) *IT for Learning Enhancement*, Exeter: Intellect Books.

O'Shea, A. (1996) 'Curriculum and information technology', *Curriculum Journal*, 7(3): 385–9.

Rodrigues, S. (1997a) 'The role of IT in secondary school science: an illustrative review', *School Science Review*, 79(287): 35–40.

Rodrigues, S. (1997b) 'Using multimedia authoring tools in primary science', *Primary Science Review*, 48: 21–4.

Scrimshaw, P. (1993) 'Reading, writing and hypertext', in P. Scrimshaw (ed.), *Language, Classrooms and Computers*, London: Routledge.

Somekh, B. (1996) 'Designing software to maximize learning: what can we learn from the literature?', *Association for Learning Technology Journal*, 4(3): 4–16.

Teacher Training Agency (1998) *Initial Teacher Training National Curriculum for the Use of Information and Communications Technology in Subject Teaching (Annex B of DfEE Circular 4/98)*, London: DfEE.

Wegerif, R. (1997) 'Children's talk and computer software: a response to Fisher', in R. Wegerif and P. Scrimshaw (eds), *Computers and Talk in the Primary Classroom*, Clevedon: Multilingual Matters.

Wegerif, R. and Dawes, L. (1998) 'Encouraging exploratory talk around computers', in M. Monteith, (ed.), *IT for Learning Enhancement*, Exeter: Intellect Books.

16

Critical Literacy and the Case for It in the Early Years of School

Kathy Hall

[. . .]

Critical Literacy in Action in an Infant Classroom

I will begin by summarizing some examples of critical literacy from one primary teacher's pedagogy (Comber, 1993) as a basis from which to explore its aims, assumptions and rationale. These examples come from Australia where education has been the site of various curriculum developments and experiments supported by the Labour government's social justice policies and where teacher educators and researchers seem to have made a major contribution to an ongoing debate on critical literacy (see Comber, 1994, for a review).

The teacher in this particular example typically problematizes the fiction texts which she reads to her 5 to 8-years-old, and which they read themselves. This means that instead of asking her pupils what they think of a story or what characters they like/dislike, she encourages them to consider the story as a crafted piece in which realities are represented in certain ways. Over the period of the school year children are encouraged to discuss the following questions:

1. What do writers say about girls, boys, mothers and fathers in the books you read?
2. What do adults think that children like to read about?
3. If you knew about families only from reading this book what would you know about what mothers do?
4. What would you know about what fathers do?

They are encouraged to consider the versions of reality presented and not presented, to relate the presented version to their own reality, and to imagine, discuss, create other possibilities. They are provided with opportunities to make a personal response to stories and to construct their own texts in the knowledge that there are multiple ways to present the world and to be in the world. There are two assumptions in this model of literacy. The first is that literacy cannot be separated from the use to which it is put. Lankshear with Lawler (1997) for example argue that literacy *is* the use to which it is put. The above questions require learners to consider how they are positioned by texts (and how they, in turn, position others and themselves in their own text productions). The second assumption is that to focus *only* on the plot and the characters etc. is an inadequate literacy. Issues of equity and one's own social reality and place in the text are highly important foci for evaluation in the literacy classroom. I will return to the assumptions of critical literacy below.

This approach is also used with non-fiction texts. The children examined, for example, mother's day catalogues and junk mail, undertaking the following tasks:

1. Draw and label six presents for mothers you expect to see in mother's day catalogues.
2. Draw and label some presents you wouldn't expect to find in mother's day catalogues.
3. What groups of people get the most out of mother's day?
4. Look through the catalogue. What kinds of presents can you find?
5. How are the mothers in the catalogues like/not like real mothers?

Through considering this cultural event and its link with marketing and advertising, the children begin to understand how they are positioned by texts, and specifically, the children realized that the shopkeepers make the most out of mother's day and that the purpose of the junk mail that arrives in their letter boxes is to sell products. With regard to the last in the list of questions above, the children decide who is underrepresented or misrepresented in the text and then they consider the text from this individual's or group's stance. By exploring the text in this way they are learning to answer the following questions:

1. What is this text asking you to think or feel?
2. Do you agree with the point of view offered?
3. What or who is left out?
4. Would you have left them out?
5. Why or why not?

Infant teachers are already familiar with some of the new versions of old tales where the roles have been reconstructed to ones where the characters themselves are aware of their own social positioning. Excellent examples include *Snow White in New York* and *The Real Story of Mr Wolf*. These new versions help to expose how identities and roles are socially created. With particular reference to gender roles and identities, fairy tales became the focus of much feminist writing because of their perceived function of acculturating young girls into passive sexual and social roles (Cranny-Francis, 1990, 1993). Writers such as Angela Carter and Tanith Lee created different versions of the tales, changing the female roles from ones where their only value was their physical appearance to one where they became active in determining their own fate. *The Bloody Chamber* by Angela Carter offers different versions of Bluebird, Red Riding Hood and Beauty and the Beast while *Red as Blood or Tales from the Sisters Grimmer* retells Cinderella, Red Riding Hood, The Pied Piper of Hamelin. The purpose of all these retellings is not to replace the traditional but to expose their ideologies, that is their patriarchal, taken-for-granted assumptions and their particular constructions of femininity (Cranny-Francis, 1993).

Teaching strategies with the above might include comparing the unconventional text with a conventional text, for example, the traditional and modern versions of Snow White, to explore how this offers the possibilities of multiple readings and getting pupils to make predictions at various points in the texts to examine how prior knowledge and assumptions (literary and social) influence the construction of readings (Kempe, 1993). Such strategies assist learners to begin to address the question 'why are things the way they are?' and thus, challenge the inequalities of the status quo. The next section further explores this theme in examining the conceptions and aims of critical literacy.

Critical Literacy: Conceptions, Assumptions, Aims

Many adjectives have been used to distinguish different types of literacy: basic, functional, higher-order, cultural, computer, musical, media, domesticating, liberating, proper, improper, and so on. Even literacy is a term used (Kintgen, 1988). I want to dwell on the distinction between functional and critical literacy (sometimes called proper or liberating or socially perceptive literacy). The ability to use literacy merely to cope with the demands of living in a print society is functional literacy, which is a minimalist type of literacy. The literacy competence to complete an application form, to read print in the environment, to follow instructions, to fill a tax return describes a passive and responding literacy. Critical literacy, on the other hand, proposes that literacy learning involves learning to understand the socially constructed nature of knowledge and experience as expressed in written and spoken language. It is essentially about being aware of the processes that produce knowledge. It aims at helping learners understand their own reading practices and to realise that their responses to texts are not really individual or personal but are socially constructed. So it means 'reading the social' as well as 'reading the words'. McLaren (1988) says it is wrong to assume that individual men and women from different social classes read texts in a similar manner, in the same way that it is wrong to assume that reading a work of literature remains the same throughout time.

Critical literacy does not, or tries not to, place cultivated expression on a pedestal. Rather it tries to demonstrate that the most valued forms of speaking and writing (and indeed knowing) are not universal, neutral forms of excellence but are outcomes of power and inequality – outcomes that have come down through the ages from societies that never provided equal learning to all their members. In their studies of the politics and history of literacy, Lankshear with Lawler (1987) shows that 'improper literacy' (functional literacy) within education is a major factor contributing to hegemony or what Lankshear terms 'the hegemonised consciousness' by which is meant the way subordinated or non-elite groups support, (or, at least, fail to oppose) their own subordination. Similarly, Graff's (1987) study of the history of literacy shows that the most striking continuity in its history is the way literacy has been used time and time again to consolidate the social hierarchy, to empower elites, but even more importantly, to ensure that those lower in the hierarchy accept the values, norms, and beliefs handed down by the elites, even when it is not in their interest to do so.

Critical literacy accepts that literacy is inescapably ideological, that as part of and integral to the school curriculum, it is not neutral or innocent but that what counts as literacy is the result of complex power relations and struggles among class, race, gender, religious and other groups in society. Apple says 'education and power are an indissoluble couplet' (Apple, 1992, p. 4). So, too, for literacy and power. Critical literacy assumes that attempts to link a text's meaning to a single 'reading' serve mainly the interests of powerful social institutions. The authority of many of these institutions (like some religions and political orthodoxies) depend on the controlling of social meaning, and so the exposure of such practices is a legitimate activity for the critical literacy classroom (Gilbert, 1993; Morgan, 1994; Comber, 1994). Critical literacy involves decoding the ideological dimensions of texts in order to reveal whose interests are being served – this is exactly what the children in the above example were doing in their exploration of the junk mail about mother's day.

The assumptions and aims of critical literacy are those of critical pedagogy: that to become ever more critically aware of one's world leads to one's greater creative control of it; that while certain groups in society are systematically better placed to promote their own interests, existing patterns of power and control are not fixed, but are historical outcomes that can be challenged and changed (Lankshear with Lawler, 1987; McLaren, 1988; Giroux, 1988, 1989). [. . .] Critical literacy, through acquiring a greater understanding of this historical and social process, is aimed at the construction of a more just and democratic social order. McLaren (1988, p. 214) summarizes it well:

> Critical literacy . . . involves decoding the ideological dimensions of texts, institutions, social practices, and cultural forms such as television and film, in order to reveal their selective interests. The purpose behind acquiring this type of literacy is to create a citizenry critical enough to both analyse and challenge the

oppressive characteristics of the larger society so that a more just, equitable, and democratic society can be created.

It should be acknowledged at this point that there is no consensus in the research literature that literacy is or ought to be social and political – the premise of critical literacy. Gough (1995) for example, subscribes to 'a literacy narrowly conceived as individual, psychological skills' and argues that literacy is neither social nor political. He justifies this on the grounds that 'the act of reading, that is, literacy itself, is one of the least social of human activities'. However, his argument does not sufficiently take account of the concept of 'social' as posited by critical literacy advocates and his style is, at times, flippant. For example, in arguing against Street's (1993) perspective that readers cannot be separated from the society which gives meaning to their uses of literacy, he retorts: 'Why not? When I watch a Wimbledon tennis match, I separate those players from the society which gives meaning to their uses of their racquets; I am interested in the players and their game, not that society. Why can't I do the same with readers?' (1993, p. 81). He rejects the political connection on the grounds that politics and education should be kept separate. Gough considers his work on literacy apolitical and unproblematic but this denial of the political does not mean that he stands apart from the politics of literacy education – which is what he thinks he is doing. Rather, his denial, like many practising teachers' political *naïveté* concerning literacy, teaching and schooling, serves to perpetuate the status quo. Politicians, policy-makers and educators with vested interests in current practice accept their non-action and silence as endorsement of current practice.

Implications for Classroom Practice

Critical literacy implies working with the learner's constructions and values as well as working *from* them. It means challenging their world views and not benignly accommodating them (Boomer, 1989) as was more typical of the 'progressive' approach of the 1960s. This is not a comfortable pedagogy for it removes certainty from the teacher and the learner. The teacher is not the final arbiter of knowledge or does not determine *the* meaning of the text. Studies of critical literacy in practice show that some learners find it disconcerting to realize that there is no one correct meaning of the text which the teacher or the text itself can determine and they continue to look to the teacher for a version of the text, believing that the teacher's reading is more acceptable (e.g. Kempe, 1993). However, I agree with Gilbert (1993) when she says that even quite young children can understand matters of equity, including matters like, say, sexist language practices and discriminatory social organization. Young children's sense of fairness is usually acute.

Critical literacy challenges the notion that the text stems from the creative powers, imagination, inspiration and personal vision of the individual author. Pam Gilbert objects to a conception of authoring as 'the natural and authentic expression of individual expression' (1994, p. 262) and she rejects the familiar terms used to describe it: personal, individual, spontaneous, natural, emotional, real and so on – terms associated with whole language or process approaches to language development. The lack of an explicit political and cultural dimension in process pedagogy raises concerns about the validity of process approaches to language development. This emphasis on authoring, in her view, fails to acknowledge that all texts are intertextual – all rely on other texts for their meanings. Gilbert's point is that concepts like authorship undermine the social nature of the text's production. This is echoed by Gee (1988) in his study on the history of literacy when he refers to 'thinking for oneself' as the 'culprit' as it obscures the social nature of interpretation. Gilbert concludes by saying: 'Rather than authorizing disadvantage by focusing on the mystique of authorship, could we not instead promote critical social literacy by focusing on the cultural construction of reading and writing practices?' (p. 275). However, I would argue that the latter can be achieved through authoring or having children write their own texts and providing them with opportunities to discuss the social and cultural influences on their production.

Denaturalizing what has been taken for granted is central to critical literacy. And herein lies the affective dimension of critical literacy. It isn't just one's point of view that is being challenged but one's way of life, family, and community, i.e. the heart of one's personal and social identity. This contrasts sharply with the more relaxed stance of the progressive approach, as represented in, say, the creative writing movement of the 1960s. The assumption here is that the culture all groups, including minority groups, bring to school may be interrogated and analysed (Giroux, 1988). The kind of interpersonal argumentation and discussion which such 'critical interrogation' would involve is bound to be risky and be emotionally, as well as, cognitively challenging. If, however, the teacher manages, through his or her interaction and discourse style, to treat the learners as partners in an inquiry and language researchers, rather than objects of pedagogy, the pupils are likely to appreciate its value.

[. . .]

The importance of critical literacy in the infant classroom

In this section I will propose a rationale for including critical literacy in infant pedagogy and go on to suggest in the next section what status it should have, relative to other types of literacy, at this stage of schooling.

The reason why critical literacy is important in the infant classroom is basically the same reason why it is important in any setting: that the literacy one practices powerfully influences, even produces (rather than merely reflects), one's consciousness, i.e. one's beliefs, values, assumptions and related behaviour. Consciousness, in turn, impacts on literacy, influencing one's literacy practices, thus a dialectical relationship exists between literacy and consciousness (see Lankshear with Lawler, 1987; Bennet, 1983; Giroux, 1989; Morgan, 1994). Examples of how language produces consciousness can be found in the way national languages are used as a precondition of the formation of a socio-cultural identity for 'the nation'. The hugely increased status of the Irish language and its designation as the official language of the people on the foundation of the new Irish State is one example. Another is the displacement of regional and class dialects in France by a standard French language, justified on the grounds of economic and legal necessity. Through the national language people's thought processes are organised by trying to forge a 'national–popular' identity (see Donald, 1983; Bennett, 1983 for a full discussion). A third is the status conferred on Standard English in the English National Curriculum – it not only discriminates between texts, it also sorts out people. Children may come to school as competent speakers of language and their competence takes the form of a variety of dialects. But what these dialects are affects how children are judged, not only in their speaking performance but also in matters of attitude and motivation (Cook-Gumperz, 1986; Gilmore, 1985).

Macedo points out that different English dialects 'decode different world views' (Freire and Macedo, 1987, p. 127). [. . .] James Gee says (1991, p. 5) that 'individuals do not speak and act, but . . . historically and socially defined discourses speak to each other through individuals'. Donald explains how political struggles around language involve the attempt to control these codes, to construct one set of meanings rather than others, 'literally to define a society's common sense' (Donald, 1983, p. 47). The point here is that language is politically important because of its ideological power – its meanings shape our experiences and our interpretations of the world. It is for this reason that critical literacy, in acknowledging and exposing the ideological basis and social-situatedness of language, is important and deserves a place in the curriculum for the early years of school.

Language is the vehicle for identifying, manipulating and changing power relations between people. In other words, power over language or critical understanding of the discourse is needed in order to elevate the needs and interests of non-elite groups above those or on a par with those of the elites. Frances Christie reminds us that success in school is largely a language matter, that is the 'capacity to interpret and manipulate the various patterns of discourse characteristic of the many kinds of knowledge, information and ideas schools value' (1984, p. 21; 1994). This is why critical literacy which acknowledges the power of language is so important.

The reason for suggesting that critical literacy should be included from the earliest stages of schooling is that it is a social practice rather than a developmental attainment. Children have to be code-breakers (how do I crack this?) text participants (what does this mean?) text users (what do I do with this here and now?) and text analysts (what does all this do to me?). It is as text analysts they can be said to engage in a critical literacy. According to Freebody and Luke (in Comber, 1994) children need opportunities to take on this text-analysis role from the beginning, as part of what counts as literacy, not as a separate component of literacy later on in their schooling. This seems highly reasonable. To assume that critical literacy is too complex for the youngest learners is misguided. Issues of fairness and having a fair go are within their experience as already noted, and what they need arguably is access to a language that names inequity, narrowness and unfairness. To summarize so far, critical literacy is politically, educationally and pedagogically important and therefore ought to have a role in all stages of schooling, including the early stages.

The relative *importance of critical literacy in the infant classroom*

The more difficult question to answer is: what relative status should be accorded this type of literacy in the infant classroom? How should the time and energy spent on critical literacy compare with, say, basic literacy. Let me conveniently define basic literacy as the ability to decode words and sentences and grasp, at least, their literal meaning. Let me also assume that basic literacy is a condition of being educated in the 1990s. For convenience, I confine myself now to one dimension of critical literacy, i.e. written text. It is reasonable to say that basic literacy enables critical literacy. One cannot grasp any meaning from a written text, let alone several meanings, unless one can decode it, that is unless one has moved beyond the logographic, to the alphabetic and then to the orthographic stage of decoding the symbol system. There is now a very substantial body of evidence demonstrating that alphabetic coding is a most crucial subprocess that supports fluent reading and that automatic, context-free word recognition skill is a necessary (though not sufficient) step for good reading comprehension. It is not my intention to summarize this considerable literature here (See Oakhill, Beard and Vincent, 1995; Adams, 1992; Barr *et al.*, 1991, for reviews) rather I refer to it to support my contention that basic literacy should be accorded priority in the early stages of school. This can also be justified on the grounds that since basic literacy, in the form of say, the alphabetic system, is fixed, formalized and codified, the young learner needs to grasp that code in order to apply it. It follows, therefore that this literacy ought to have first, though not exclusive, call on the available resources of time, materials and effort. Critical literacy, as defined in the early part of this chapter, should still have an important role to play. I do not see critical literacy as a variable to be introduced *after* certain knowledges and skills have been acquired. Critical literacy is about the kind of literate person we ought to try to create. Some of the children in the classroom example above had not yet mastered the skill of decoding print but they were, nevertheless, engaging in critical literacy where the authors' crafting was not merely enjoyed but also disrupted in terms of the versions of reality represented.

Some might want to argue that, having cracked the code, the next priority for literacy should be the different genres – after all these (according to Kress, 1982) have their conventions, formalities and codes – thus limiting opportunities for critical literacy. I think this thinking is misguided. I agree with Rosen (1992) that the different kinds of writing are not so fixed and codified – they are only partially so and to behave as though they are is to accept the messages that power delivers. This is precisely what critical literacy is trying to fight. This is not to suggest that children should not be made aware of different genres – they should, since greater awareness of any genre and how it works confers the freedom to 'break the rules', to reject its hidden agenda and to not be bound by conventions.

Fundamental to the provision for critical literacy in schools is that teachers need to be aware of the social and political aspects of literacy and its implications for practice. (They also need to be aware of the recent psychological research so they can make fully informed decisions regarding their curriculum and pedagogical choices). My own experience as a teacher educator tells me that teachers and teacher educators are frequently naive regarding the sociopolitical nature of pedagogy. This is not surprising when one considers the scale of government intervention in teacher education programmes (at least in England and Wales) and, specifically, its role in defining the literacy curriculum for primary schools. Where staff and curriculum development programmes incorporate principles of critical pedagogy and an emphasis on critical literacy, teachers themselves are 'transformed' as they begin to appreciate the historical and political situatedness of their particular classrooms; they come to realize that, as teachers, they have considerable power; and their practices in classrooms and schools become more collaborative and democratic (Wink, 1997; Hill, Samuels and Beers, 1997; Patterson, Williams and Hutchinson, 1997; Dellinger, 1997).

Critical literacy has its origin, in the broadest sense, in the loss of universal meaning in the world, in the acknowledgement that there are few, if any, universal truths, rather that there are multiple realities and multiple truths – the one certainty being uncertainty. While traditional curriculum is a pedagogy of fixed truths, this new pedagogy is one 'without closure, studiously open to difference' (Kalantzis and Cope, 1993, p. 51). In relation to language as critical literacy, this means there are no absolute, literary truths – there is just language variation with functions appropriate to and relative to cultural experience. Problematizing or unpicking or deconstructing the text or 'reading against the grain' helps explain its cultural and ideological origins, provides more than one 'reading' or 'telling' and affirms multiple realities and ways of being. My main point, however, is that critical literacy ought to have a role in the infant classroom from the beginning and, once basic literacy has been established, its role should increase.

Problematizing texts need not, indeed should not, in my view, become a full-time occupation in any classroom as, on this scale, it could conceivably take the joy out of learning and living, lead to cynicism and make the world seem so foreign and unknowable that learning, even confident living, may seem pointless or impossible. Although not specifically about literacy, Guy Claxton (in press) is worth quoting on the dangers of over-problematizing:

> Uncovering the motive behind the method, the assumption behind the appearance, is skilled, subtle and dangerous work. It makes the world look alien and insubstantial, and can make you seem a stranger to yourself. It takes courage and resilience . . . Compulsive problematisation is as counter-productive as compulsive trivialisation. Sticking an inquisitive nose into everything is as self-defeating as sticking your head in the sand. The cost of reflection is self-consciousness, and while the gaucheness and anxiety that go along with self-consciousness may be acute prices that are worth paying to rid oneself of a bad habit or a pernicious belief, they undermine the ability to function if they become chronic and intense.

One might expect that critical pedagogy, in general, might have the effect of making children insecure about knowledge but in fact there is evidence to the contrary, albeit from second level education. Provided the teacher creates a climate where learners feel secure about taking risks and where knowledge is routinely presented as provisional, there is evidence that children are actually more secure, because they are better prepared for unexpected outcomes (Gilbert, 1993; Langer *et al.*, 1989).

The message from all this for critical literacy is that it should have a place in primary schooling, including the early phase of schooling, and it need not, indeed should not, dominate the pedagogy. My hunch is that it can sit easily with other, less critical and more traditional pedagogies but this is an empirical question meriting further investigation at classroom level.

References

Adams, M. J. (1992) *Beginning to Read*, Cambridge, MA: MIT Press.

Apple, M. W. (1992) The text and cultural politics, *Educational Researcher*, 21(7), 4–12.

Barr, R., Kamil, M. L., Mosenthal, P. and Pearson, P. D. (eds) (1991) *Handbook of Reading Research* (vol. 2), New York: Longman.

Bennett, A. T. (1983) Discourses of power, the dialectics of understanding, the power of literacy, *Journal of Education*, 165(1), 53–74.

Boomer, G. (1989) Literacy: the epic challenge beyond progressivism, *English in Australia*, 89, 4–17.

Christie, F. (1984) Language and schooling, in S. N. Tchudi (ed.), *Language, Schooling and Society* (pp. 21–40), New Jersey: Boynton/Cook Publishers.

Christie, F. (1994) The place of genre in teaching critical social literacy, in A. B. Littlefair (ed.), *Literacy for Life* (pp. 25–46), Cheshire: United Kingdom Reading Association.

Claxton, G. (in press) Learning through the looking glass: salvaging the notion of reflection, in K. Hall and E. Roper (eds), *Beyond Reflection: The Leeds Metropolitan University Education Papers*, Leeds: Leeds Metropolitan University.

Comber, B. (1993) Classroom exploration in critical literacy, *Australian Journal of Language and Literacy*, 16(1), 73–84.

Comber, B. (1994) Critical literacy: an introduction to Australian debates and perspectives, *Journal of Curriculum Studies*, 26(6), 655–68.

Cook-Gumperz, J. (ed.) (1986) *The Social Construction of Literacy*, Cambridge: Cambridge University Press.

Cranny-Francis, A. (1990) *Feminist Fiction: Feminist Uses of Generic Fiction*, Cambridge: Polity Press.

Cranny-Francis, A. (1993) Gender and genre: feminist subversion of genre fiction and its implications for critical literacy, in B. Cope and M. Kalantzis (eds), *Power of Literacy: A Genre Approach to Teaching Writing* (pp. 90–115), London: Falmer Press.

Dellinger, L. (1997) The drama of critical pedagogy: rehearsing the revolution in the literacy classroom, paper presented at the National Reading Conference, 47th Annual Meeting. Phoenix, Arizona, December.

Donald, J. (1983) How illiteracy became a problem (and literacy stopped being one), *Journal of Education*, 165(1), 35–52.

Freire, P. and Macedo, D. (1987) *Reading the Word and the World*, South Hadley, MA: Bergin and Garvey.

Gee, J. P. (1988) The legacies of literacy: From Plato to Freire through Harvey Graff, *Harvard Education Review*, 58(2), 195–212.

Gee, J. P. (1991) What is literacy? in C. Mitchell and K. Weiler (eds), *Rewriting Literacy: Culture and the Discourse of the Other* (pp. 3–11), New York: Bergin and Garvey.

Gilbert, P. (1993) (Sub)versions: using sexist language practices to explore critical literacy, *Australian Journal of Language and Literacy*, 16(4), 323–31.

Gilbert, P. (1994) Authorizing disadvantage: authorship and creativity in the language classroom, in B. Stierer and J. Maybin (eds), *Language, Literacy and Learning in Educational Practice* (pp. 258–76), Buckingham: Open University Press.

Gilmore, P. (1985) 'Gimme room': school resistance, attitude, and access to literacy, *Journal of Education*, 167(1), 111–28.

Giroux, H. A. (1988) Literacy and the pedagogy of voice and political empowerment, *Educational Theory*, 38(1), 61–75.

Giroux, H. A. (1989) *Schooling for Democracy: Critical Pedagogy in the Modern Age*, London: Routledge.

Gough, P. B. (1995) The new literacy: caveat emptor, *Journal of Research in Reading*, 18(2), 79–86.

Graff, H. G. (1987) The legacies of literacy: continuities and contradictions in Western culture and society, *Harvard Educational Review*, 58(3), 280–98.

Hill, M. H., Samuels, B. and Beers, K. (1997), We've learned to teach children – not classes: conflicts create pedagogy through long term staff development, paper presented at the National Reading Conference, 47th Annual Meeting, Phoenix, Arizona, December.

Kalantzis, M. and Cope, B. (1993) Histories of pedagogy, cultures of schooling, in B. Cope and M. Kalantzis (eds), *The Power of Literacy: A Genre Approach to Teaching Writing*, (pp. 38–62), London; Falmer Press.

Kempe, A. (1993) No single meaning: empowering students to construct socially critical readings of the text, *Australian Journal of Language and Literacy*, 16(4), 307–22.

Kintgen, E. R. (1988) Literacy literacy, *Visible Language*, 22(2), 149–68.

Kress, G. (1982) *Learning to Write*, London: Routledge and Kegan Paul.

Langer, E., Hatem, M., Joss, J. and Howell, M. (1989) Conditional teaching and mindful learning: the role of uncertainty in education, *Creativity Research Journal*, 2, 139–50.

Lankshear, C. with Lawler, M. (1987) *Literacy, Schooling and Revolution*, London: Falmer Press.

McLaren, P. L. (1988) Culture or canon? Critical pedagogy and the politics of literacy, *Harvard Educational Review*, 58(2), 213–34.

Morgan, W. (1994) Clothes wear out, learning doesn't: realising past and future in today's critical literacy curriculum, keynote address at the National Conference of the Australian Association for Teachers of English, Perth.

Oakhill, J., Beard, R. and Vincent, D. (eds) (1995) Special issue, The contribution of psychological research, *Journal of Research in Reading*, 18(2).

Patterson, L. A., Williams, N. and Hutchinson, L. (1997) Critical pedagogy: teacher educators' shifting stances, paper presented at the National Reading Conference, 47th Annual Meeting, Phoenix, Arizona, December.

Rosen, H. (1992) The politics of writing, in K. Kimberley, M. Meek and J. Miller (eds), *New Readings: Contributions to an Understanding of Literacy* (pp. 119–30). London: A. and C. Black.

Street, B. V. (1993) The new literacy studies, *Journal of Research in Reading*, 16(2), 81–174.

Wink, J. (1997) *Critical Pedagogy: Notes from the Real World*, New York: Longman.

Index